HEINEMANN MODULAR MATHEMATICS
for
EDEXCEL AS AND A-LEVEL
Pure Mathematics 2

Geoff Mannall Michael Kenwood

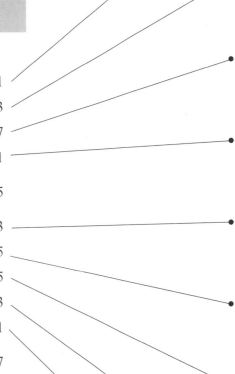

CLASSROOM TEXTBOOK

Heinemann

Edexcel
Success through qualifications

Heinemann Educational Publishers,
a division of Heinemann Publishers (Oxford) Ltd,
Halley Court, Jordan Hill, Oxford, OX2 8EJ

OXFORD JOHANNESBURG BLANTYRE MELBOURNE
AUCKLAND SINGAPORE GABORONE   PORTSMOUTH NH (USA)
CHICAGO

First published 2000

02 01 10 9 8 7 6 5 4 3

ISBN 0 435 51089 4

Cover design by Gecko Limited

Original design by Geoffrey Wadsley; additional design work by Jim Turner

Typeset and illustrated by Tech-Set Limited, Gateshead, Tyne and Wear

Printed in Great Britain by The Bath Press, Bath

Acknowledgements:

The publisher's and authors' thanks are due to Edexcel for permission to
reproduce questions from past examination papers. These are marked with an [E].
    The answers have been provided by the authors and are not the responsibility
of the examining board.

About this book

This book is designed to provide you with the best preparation possible for your Edexcel P2 exam. The series authors are senior examiners and exam moderators themselves and have a good understanding of Edexcel's requirements.

Use this **new edition** to prepare for the new 6-unit specification. Use the first edition (*Heinemann Modular Mathematics for London AS and A-Level*) if you are preparing for the 4-module syllabus.

Finding your way around

To help to find your way around when you are studying and revising use the:

- **edge marks** (shown on the front page) – these help you to get to the right chapter quickly;
- **contents list** – this lists the headings that identify key syllabus ideas covered in the book so you can turn straight to them;
- **index** – if you need to find a topic the **bold** number shows where to find the main entry on a topic.

Remembering key ideas

We have provided clear explanations of the key ideas and techniques you need throughout the book. Key ideas you need to remember are listed in a **summary of key points** at the end of each chapter and marked like this in the chapters:

■ $$\sin^2\theta + \cos^2\theta \equiv 1$$

Exercises and exam questions

In this book questions are carefully graded so they increase in difficulty and gradually bring you up to exam standard.

- **past exam questions** are marked with an [E];
- **review exercises** on pages 85 and 167 help you practise answering questions from several areas of mathematics at once, as in the real exam;
- **exam style practice paper** – this is designed to help you prepare for the exam itself;
- **answers** are included at the end of the book – use them to check your work.

Contents

7 Integration

8 Numerical methods

9 Proof

Processing rational algebraic expressions

1

A rational number is of the form $\dfrac{m}{n}$, where m and n are integers and $n \neq 0$ (see Book P1, page 3).

You have studied how to process rational numbers, or fractions as they are often called, in your GCSE course. The number at the top is called the **numerator** and the number at the bottom is called the **denominator**. In the fraction $\frac{5}{7}$, 5 is the numerator and 7 the denominator. The same is true for an algebraic fraction which is, in fact, a **rational algebraic expression**. For $\dfrac{3x^2}{2x+1}$, the numerator is $3x^2$ and the denominator is $2x + 1$.

Rational expressions in algebra are thus of the form $\dfrac{P(x)}{Q(x)}$, where $P(x)$ and $Q(x)$ are polynomials. Typical examples are $\dfrac{1}{2x-3}$, $\dfrac{x^3+1}{x^2-1}$ and $\dfrac{x^2-2x-3}{2x^2-5x+1}$. In this book, denominators of rational expressions will be either linear or quadratic.

1.1 Simplifying rational algebraic expressions

Cancelling common factors

In simplifying arithmetic fractions you will remember cancelling in the numerator and denominator like this: $\frac{21}{49} = \frac{3}{7}$ by dividing 'top and bottom' by 7.

In algebra, fractions like this: $\dfrac{3x+3}{6x-18}$ can be simplified by first factorising top and bottom to this: $\dfrac{3(x+1)}{6(x-3)}$. Then 3 can be cancelled to leave $\dfrac{x+1}{2(x-3)}$.

Example 1

Simplify $\dfrac{x^2 - 4x - 12}{x^2 - 4}$.

By factorisation: $\dfrac{x^2 - 4x - 12}{x^2 - 4} = \dfrac{(x+2)(x-6)}{(x+2)(x-2)}$

Cancelling out the factor $x + 2$ leaves the simplified expression as

$$\frac{x^2 - 4x - 12}{x^2 - 4} = \frac{x-6}{x-2}$$

Example 2

Simplify $\dfrac{3x^2 - 6x + 3}{12x^2 - 6x - 6}$.

Factorising the numerator and denominator leads to

$$\frac{3x^2 - 6x + 3}{12x^2 - 6x - 6} = \frac{3(x^2 - 2x + 1)}{6(2x^2 - x - 1)} = \frac{3(x-1)^2}{6(x-1)(2x+1)}$$

Cancelling out the numerical factor 3 and the algebraic factor $x - 1$ gives:

$$\frac{3x^2 - 6x + 3}{12x^2 - 6x - 6} = \frac{x-1}{2(2x+1)} \quad \text{as the complete simplification.}$$

Multiplying fractions

To multiply two numerical fractions, you first 'cancel' each factor in either numerator with the same factor, if it exists, in either denominator. Then you multiply the numbers that are left in the numerators to give the numerator in the answer, and you multiply the numbers that are left in the denominators to give the denominator in the answer.

For example:

$$\frac{5}{81} \times \frac{33}{40}$$
$$= \frac{1}{81} \times \frac{33}{8} \qquad \text{(cancel by 5)}$$
$$= \frac{1}{27} \times \frac{11}{8} \qquad \text{(cancel by 3)}$$
$$= \frac{1 \times 11}{27 \times 8}$$
$$= \frac{11}{216}$$

The same methods apply when you multiply algebraic fractions. You first cancel any factor common to both a numerator and a denominator and continue doing this for as many times as you can. You then multiply together the terms remaining in the numerators and multiply together the terms remaining in the denominators.

Example 3

Simplify $\dfrac{14}{x^2-1} \times \dfrac{x-1}{21}$

$$\dfrac{14}{x^2-1} \times \dfrac{x-1}{21} = \dfrac{14}{(x-1)(x+1)} \times \dfrac{x-1}{21} \qquad \text{(factorise } x^2-1)$$

$$= \dfrac{2}{(x-1)(x+1)} \times \dfrac{x-1}{3} \qquad \text{(cancel by 7)}$$

$$= \dfrac{2}{x+1} \times \dfrac{1}{3} \qquad \text{(cancel by } x-1)$$

$$= \dfrac{2 \times 1}{3(x+1)}$$

$$= \dfrac{2}{3(x+1)}$$

Example 4

Simplify $\dfrac{x}{2x^2-x-6} \times \dfrac{x-2}{3x^2}$

$$\dfrac{x}{2x^2-x-6} \times \dfrac{x-2}{3x^2} = \dfrac{x}{(2x+3)(x-2)} \times \dfrac{x-2}{3x^2} \qquad \text{(factorise } 2x^2-x-6)$$

$$= \dfrac{1}{(2x+3)(x-2)} \times \dfrac{x-2}{3x} \qquad \text{(cancel by } x)$$

$$= \dfrac{1}{2x+3} \times \dfrac{1}{3x} \qquad \text{(cancel by } x-2)$$

$$= \dfrac{1 \times 1}{(2x+3)3x}$$

$$= \dfrac{1}{6x^2+9x} = \dfrac{1}{3x(2x+3)}$$

Dividing fractions

As you should know from your GCSE studies, if you are asked to evaluate $\frac{9}{35} \div \frac{27}{25}$ you write $\frac{9}{35} \times \frac{25}{27}$ and then evaluate this. In the same way, to divide one algebraic fraction by another, you take the fraction which comes after the division symbol and turn it upside down. You then change the division symbol into a multiplication symbol and continue as above.

Example 5

Simplify $\dfrac{5x^2}{x^2 - 9} \div \dfrac{3x^3}{2(x + 3)}$.

$$\frac{5x^2}{x^2 - 9} \div \frac{3x^3}{2(x + 3)} = \frac{5x^2}{x^2 - 9} \times \frac{2(x + 3)}{3x^3}$$

$$= \frac{5x^2}{(x - 3)(x + 3)} \times \frac{2(x + 3)}{3x^3} \qquad \text{(factorise } x^2 - 9)$$

$$= \frac{5}{(x - 3)(x + 3)} \times \frac{2(x + 3)}{3x} \qquad \text{(cancel by } x^2)$$

$$= \frac{5}{x - 3} \times \frac{2}{3x} \qquad \text{(cancel by } x + 3)$$

$$= \frac{5 \times 2}{(x - 3)3x}$$

$$= \frac{10}{3x^2 - 9x} = \frac{10}{3x(x - 3)}$$

Example 6

Simplify $\dfrac{15(x - 7)}{6x^2 + 10x - 4} \div \dfrac{10(2x + 3)}{3x^2 + 2x - 1}$.

$$\frac{15(x - 7)}{6x^2 + 10x - 4} \div \frac{10(2x + 3)}{3x^2 + 2x - 1} = \frac{15(x - 7)}{6x^2 + 10x - 4} \times \frac{3x^2 + 2x - 1}{10(2x + 3)}$$

$$= \frac{15(x - 7)}{(2x + 4)(3x - 1)} \times \frac{(3x - 1)(x + 1)}{10(2x + 3)} \qquad \text{(factorise)}$$

$$= \frac{3(x - 7)}{(2x + 4)(3x - 1)} \times \frac{(3x - 1)(x + 1)}{2(2x + 3)} \qquad \text{(cancel by 5)}$$

$$= \frac{3(x - 7)}{2x + 4} \times \frac{x + 1}{2(2x + 3)} \qquad \text{(cancel by } 3x - 1)$$

$$= \frac{3(x - 7)(x + 1)}{2(2x + 4)(2x + 3)}$$

$$= \frac{3x^2 - 18x - 21}{8x^2 + 28x + 24}$$

Adding fractions

Consider the sum $\frac{2}{7} + \frac{3}{5}$. In order to add these fractions you must first write them as **equivalent fractions** that have the same denominator, often called a **common denominator**. In this case a common denominator is 35, because 35 is a multiple of both 7 and 5.

So:
$$\frac{2}{7} + \frac{3}{5} = \frac{2 \times 5}{7 \times 5} + \frac{3 \times 7}{5 \times 7}$$

$$= \frac{10}{35} + \frac{21}{35}$$

$$= \frac{10 + 21}{35}$$

$$= \frac{31}{35}$$

You should know that the common denominator which you use when adding fractions is not *always* the product of the two original denominators. For example, consider the sum $\frac{5}{12} + \frac{7}{18}$. A common denominator of $12 \times 18 = 216$ would work, but it is much simpler to use the **lowest common multiple** (LCM) of 12 and 18.

The lowest common multiple of two integers is the smallest integer that can be divided exactly by each of them.

Since:
$$12 = 2 \times 2 \times 3$$

and:
$$18 = 2 \times 3 \times 3$$

the LCM is $2 \times 2 \times 3 \times 3 = 36$.

So:
$$\frac{5}{12} + \frac{7}{18} = \frac{5 \times 3}{12 \times 3} + \frac{7 \times 2}{18 \times 2}$$

$$= \frac{15}{36} + \frac{14}{36}$$

$$= \frac{29}{36}$$

The same rules apply for the addition of algebraic fractions.

Example 7

Express as a single fraction:

$$\frac{3}{2x+5} + \frac{x-7}{4x^2+10x}$$

$$\frac{3}{2x+5} + \frac{x-7}{4x^2+10x} = \frac{3}{2x+5} + \frac{x-7}{2x(2x+5)}$$

$$= \frac{2x \times 3}{2x(2x+5)} + \frac{x-7}{2x(2x+5)} \qquad \text{(common denominator } 2x(2x+5))$$

$$= \frac{6x}{2x(2x+5)} + \frac{x-7}{2x(2x+5)}$$

$$= \frac{6x+x-7}{2x(2x+5)}$$

$$= \frac{7x-7}{2x(2x+5)}$$

$$= \frac{7(x-1)}{2x(2x+5)}$$

Example 8

Express as a single fraction:

$$\frac{2x+1}{2x^2+14x+20} + \frac{x-3}{3x^2-75}$$

$$\frac{2x+1}{2x^2+14x+20} + \frac{x-3}{3x^2-75} = \frac{2x+1}{2(x+2)(x+5)} + \frac{x-3}{3(x+5)(x-5)}$$

$$= \frac{3(x-5)(2x+1)}{2 \times 3(x+2)(x+5)(x-5)} + \frac{2(x+2)(x-3)}{2 \times 3(x+2)(x+5)(x-5)}$$

$$= \frac{6x^2-27x-15}{6(x+2)(x+5)(x-5)} + \frac{2x^2-2x-12}{6(x+2)(x+5)(x-5)}$$

$$= \frac{6x^2-27x-15+2x^2-2x-12}{6(x+2)(x+5)(x-5)}$$

$$= \frac{8x^2-29x-27}{6(x+2)(x+5)(x-5)}$$

Subtracting fractions

The method used to subtract algebraic fractions is similar to that for adding fractions.

Example 9

Express as a single fraction:

$$\frac{5x - 2}{2(x + 3)^2} - \frac{x - 4}{6(6 - x - x^2)}$$

$$\frac{5x - 2}{2(x + 3)^2} - \frac{x - 4}{6(6 - x - x^2)} = \frac{5x - 2}{2(x + 3)^2} - \frac{x - 4}{2 \times 3(x + 3)(2 - x)}$$

$$= \frac{3(2 - x)(5x - 2)}{2 \times 3(x + 3)^2(2 - x)} - \frac{(x + 3)(x - 4)}{2 \times 3(x + 3)^2(2 - x)}$$

$$= \frac{3(2 - x)(5x - 2) - (x + 3)(x - 4)}{6(x + 3)^2(2 - x)}$$

$$= \frac{-15x^2 + 36x - 12 - x^2 + x + 12}{6(x + 3)^2(2 - x)}$$

$$= \frac{-16x^2 + 37x}{6(x + 3)^2(2 - x)}$$

$$= \frac{x(-16x + 37)}{6(x + 3)^2(2 - x)}$$

Exercise 1A

Express as a single fraction in its lowest terms:

1 $\dfrac{2x - 6}{4x + 12}$

2 $\dfrac{5x + 25}{10x - 20}$

3 $\dfrac{x^2 - 1}{x^2 + 4x + 3}$

4 $\dfrac{2x^2 + 2x - 12}{x^2 - x - 12}$

5 $\dfrac{3x^2}{(2 + x)(3 + 2x)} \times \dfrac{4(3 + 2x)}{9x^5}$

6 $\dfrac{2 - x}{x(x - 4)} \times \dfrac{6x}{(2 - x)(1 + x)}$

7   $\dfrac{1 - x^2}{4x(7 + x)} \times \dfrac{6x^2}{3 + x - 2x^2}$

8   $\dfrac{x^2 + 6x + 9}{3(x + 2)(2x - 1)} \times \dfrac{12x^2 - 42x + 18}{4x^2 - 36}$

9   $\dfrac{x^4 - 25x^2}{2x - 6} \times \dfrac{4x^2 - 20x - 24}{2x^2 + 11x + 5}$

10   $\dfrac{4(x + 7)}{9(x^2 - 25)} \div \dfrac{2(x + 7)(3x - 2)}{15x(x + 5)}$

11   $\dfrac{7x^2(2 - x)}{27(2x - 1)(x + 4)} \div \dfrac{14x(2x - 3)}{9(x + 2)(2x - 1)}$

12   $\dfrac{15x^2 + 30x}{11x^2 - 11x - 22} \div \dfrac{21(3x^2 + 4x - 4)}{44(x^2 - 2x)}$

13   $\dfrac{2(x + 3)^2}{x^2(x - 1)} \div \dfrac{10(x^2 - 9)}{2x^2 + x - 3}$

14   $\dfrac{x^2 + 3x + 2}{x^2 - 3x + 2} \div \dfrac{x^2 + 4x + 3}{2x^2 - 3x + 1}$

15   $\dfrac{1}{4} + \dfrac{1}{x - 2}$ 16 $\dfrac{1}{2x + 1} + \dfrac{2}{x + 3}$

17   $\dfrac{3}{4x - 5} - \dfrac{2}{6 - 2x}$ 18 $\dfrac{5}{4x + 3} + \dfrac{3}{2x - 1} - \dfrac{1}{2}$

19   $\dfrac{6}{2x - 3} - \dfrac{3}{3 - 2x}$ 20 $\dfrac{2}{(x + 3)(x + 1)} + \dfrac{3}{2x - 1}$

21   $\dfrac{x}{(x - 1)(2x + 1)} - \dfrac{2}{x + 4}$

22   $\dfrac{6x}{(5 - 2x)(6 + x)} - \dfrac{7x + 2}{(5 - 2x)(1 - x)}$

23   $\dfrac{2x - 7}{5(x^2 - 4)} + \dfrac{x + 4}{2(x^2 + x - 6)}$

24   $\dfrac{5}{3 - x} + \dfrac{2 + x}{21 - 4x - x^2} - \dfrac{2x - 3}{2x^2 + 13x - 7}$

1.2 Equations containing algebraic fractions

The need to solve equations containing fractions often arises in everyday problems. Here are some further examples.

Example 10

A number when added to its reciprocal makes $\frac{5}{2}$. Find all possible such numbers.

Let x be such a number, then its reciprocal is $\dfrac{1}{x}$.

That is:
$$x + \frac{1}{x} = \tfrac{5}{2}$$

Multiply by $2x$, the common denominator:
$$2x^2 + 2 = 5x$$

$$2x^2 - 5x + 2 = 0$$

Factorising:
$$(2x - 1)(x - 2) = 0$$

So:
$$x = \tfrac{1}{2} \text{ or } 2$$

The possible numbers are $\frac{1}{2}$ and 2.

Example 11

Find the values of x for which

$$\frac{x-2}{x-3} - \frac{x+2}{x+3} = \frac{4}{9}$$

The common denominator is $9(x-3)(x+3)$ so you multiply the equation by this:

$$\frac{9(x-2)\cancel{(x-3)}(x+3)}{\cancel{(x-3)}} - \frac{9(x+2)(x-3)\cancel{(x+3)}}{\cancel{x+3}} = \frac{4 \times \cancel{9}(x-3)(x+3)}{\cancel{9}}$$

$\Rightarrow \qquad 9(x-2)(x+3) - 9(x+2)(x-3) = 4(x-3)(x+3)$

$\Rightarrow \qquad 9(x^2 - 2x + 3x - 6) - 9(x^2 + 2x - 3x - 6) = 4(x^2 - 9)$

$\Rightarrow \qquad 9(x^2 + x - 6) - 9(x^2 - x - 6) = 4(x^2 - 9)$

$\Rightarrow \qquad 9x^2 + 9x - 54 - 9x^2 + 9x + 54 = 4x^2 - 36$

That is: $\qquad 18x = 4x^2 - 36$

$\Rightarrow \qquad 4x^2 - 18x - 36 = 0$

$\Rightarrow \qquad 2x^2 - 9x - 18 = 0$

Factorising: $\qquad (x - 6)(2x + 3) = 0$

$\Rightarrow \qquad x = 6 \text{ or } -\tfrac{3}{2}$

Example 12

Prove that there is no real value of x for which

$$\frac{x-1}{x+3} = \frac{2x-1}{x+7}$$

Multiplying by $(x+3)(x+7)$ gives, after cancelling,

$$(x-1)(x+7) = (x+3)(2x-1)$$
$$x^2 - x + 7x - 7 = 2x^2 + 6x - x - 3$$

That is:
$$0 = x^2 - x + 4$$

Comparing this quadratic equation with $ax^2 + bx + c = 0$ you have $a = 1$, $b = -1$, $c = 4$ so the discriminant is

$$b^2 - 4ac = (-1)^2 - 4(1)(4) = -15 < 0.$$

This equation has no real roots, so there is no real value of x which satisfies the original equation.

Exercise 1B

Solve each of these equations.

1 $x + 2 = \dfrac{3}{x}$

2 $8x + 2 - \dfrac{3}{x} = 0$

3 $\dfrac{1}{x-1} = \dfrac{3}{x+1} - \dfrac{1}{4}$

4 $\dfrac{3}{x+1} + \dfrac{2}{x-5} = 1$

5 $\dfrac{3x-1}{3x} = \dfrac{1}{x+1}$

6 Simplify the expression $\dfrac{7}{(x-4)(x+3)} - \dfrac{4}{(x+3)(x-1)}$ giving your answer as a fraction in its lowest terms.

Hence solve the equation $\dfrac{7}{(x-4)(x+3)} - \dfrac{4}{(x+3)(x-1)} = \dfrac{3}{2}$, giving your answers as surds in their simplest form.

7 The distance from P to Q is $100\,\text{km}$. A car averaged $V\,\text{km}\,\text{h}^{-1}$ from P to Q and $(V+10)\,\text{km}\,\text{h}^{-1}$ on the return journey from Q to P. The difference in journey times was $\frac{5}{6}$ hour. Form an equation and solve it to find V.

8 Some toys, all at the same price, were bought for £40. If the cost of each toy had been £1 more, then two fewer toys could have been bought. Find the number of toys that were bought.

9 Two cities are 200 miles apart. When, because of track re-laying, an inter-city express averages 10 miles per hour less between the cities than normal, the train arrives 40 minutes late. Find the normal average speed of the inter-city express.

10 When 1 is added to the numerator and denominator of the fraction $\dfrac{m}{n}$ the new fraction is $\frac{3}{2}$. When 1 is subtracted from the numerator and denominator of the fraction $\dfrac{m^2}{n^2}$ the new fraction is $\frac{21}{8}$. Find the possible values of m and n.

11 Solve the equation

$$\frac{x-1}{2x-3} = \frac{3x+2}{x+1}$$

giving your answers to 2 decimal places.

12 Prove that the equation

$$\frac{4x+3}{2x-1} + \frac{6x+1}{2x+1} = 3$$

has no real roots.

SUMMARY OF KEY POINTS

1   To multiply algebraic fractions, you first cancel each factor common to both a numerator and a denominator and then multiply together the terms remaining in the numerators and multiply together the terms remaining in the denominators.

2   To divide one algebraic fraction by another, you take the fraction which comes after the division symbol and turn it upside down, change the division symbol into a multiplication symbol and then multiply the resultant fractions.

3   To add or subtract two algebraic fractions you change each fraction to an equivalent fraction with a denominator equal to the lowest common multiple of the two original denominators, and then add or subtract.

4   When solving equations involving fractions, you must first multiply each term in the equation by the common denominator of all the terms. This will eliminate the fractions.

Functions

2

2.1 Mappings and functions

In mathematics you will encounter many situations in which each member of one set of numbers is related to a member of another set of numbers by some well understood rule. For example, the rule $y = 3x + 2$ relates the set of numbers $x = 1, 2, 3$ to the set of numbers $y = 5, 8, 11$.

This section looks at different ways of representing relationships between sets of numbers. Some methods make relationships more visual and easier to remember; they are all intended to help make it easier to record and understand relationships.

Introducing the notation of functions

First think about two sets of numbers X and Y related by a rule. The first set X has members $x_1, x_2, x_3, \ldots$ which produce the members $y_1, y_2, y_3, \ldots$ of the set Y when you apply the rule. One way of recording the relationship is by grouping the members in ordered pairs

$$(x_1, y_1), (x_2, y_2), (x_3, y_3), \ldots$$

Notice that each x value produces just one y value. The rule together with the set X on which it operates is called a **function**. It is usually symbolised by a letter such as f. The set X is called the **domain** of f: here domain means the set of numbers which the function is operating on. The set Y is called the **range** of f: meaning the range of numbers produced by the function.

In symbols we write the function like this:

$$f : x \mapsto y, \quad x \in X, y \in Y$$

This means: 'the function f maps each element x of the set X onto an element y of the set Y'.

$\in$ is shorthand for 'is a member of' and $x \in X$ is shorthand for 'x is a member of the set X'. Sometimes you will work with numbers from the following sets so you need to learn their symbols:

$\mathbb{Z}$ the set of integers	$\mathbb{N}$ the set of natural numbers
$\mathbb{Q}$ the set of rational numbers	$\mathbb{R}$ the set of real numbers

For example, $x \in \mathbb{R}$ is shorthand for 'x is a member of the set of real numbers' or 'x is defined over the real numbers'. The domain of a function is often given in this way.

The function f is sometimes shown as a mapping diagram in which each member of set X is mapped to a member of set Y by an arrow:

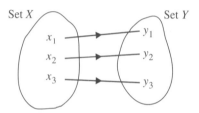

2.2 Graphing a function

More often f is shown as a graph on which the 'points' (x, y) are plotted. The domain is all the x values and the range is all the y values. The x values are sometimes called the **independent variable**. The y values are then called the **dependent variable** – they depend on the x values and on the function.

The equation of the resulting line or curve can be written in the form $y = f(x)$. In this notation $f(x)$ is called the image of x under the function f.

The following examples illustrate the ideas, language and notation of functions.

Example 1
A function f is defined by

$$f : x \mapsto 3x - 1, \quad x \in \mathbb{R}, \ -1 \leqslant x \leqslant 4$$

This means the rule of f is 'multiply each value of x by 3 and take away 1'. This could be shown in a flow chart by

The domain of f is all real values from -1 to 4 inclusive. When $x = -1$, $f(x) = 3 \times (-1) - 1 = -4$ and we write $f(-1) = -4$.

Similarly

$$f(4) = (3 \times 4) - 1 = 11$$

You can find other values the same way, for example: $f(0) = -1$, $f(1) = 2$ and $f(2) = 5$. Here is the graph of f:

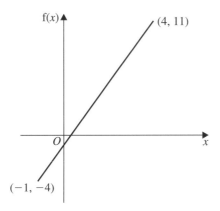

You can see that it is a line segment joining the points $(-1, -4)$ and $(4, 11)$.

The range of f is written as $f(x) \in \mathbb{R}$, $-4 \leqslant f(x) \leqslant 11$.

Example 2
Find the values of $f(-2)$, $f(1)$ and $f(0.3)$ for the function f given by:

$$f : x \mapsto x^3 + 3x, x \in \mathbb{R}$$

Take a value of x, cube it, then add 3 times the value of x taken to obtain the corresponding value of $f(x)$. For example:

$f(-2) = (-2)^3 + 3(-2) = -8 - 6 = -14$

$f(1) = (1)^3 + 3(1) = 1 + 3 = 4$

$f(0.3) = (0.3)^3 + 3(0.3) = 0.027 + 0.9 = 0.927$

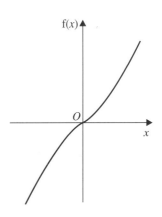

The rule of this function cannot easily be represented by a flow chart but it is worth noting that $f(x) = -f(-x)$ and this is helpful in sketching the graph of f.

The range of f is all real numbers, written as $f(x) \in \mathbb{R}$.

Example 3

Find the range of the function f, defined by

$$f : x \mapsto \frac{1}{x}, x \in \mathbb{R}, x \neq 0$$

We have to exclude zero from the domain of f because $\frac{1}{x}$ is undefined in value at $x = 0$. As you can see from the graph of f, all other real values are contained in the range of f. The range of f is therefore $f(x) \in \mathbb{R}$, $f(x) \neq 0$.

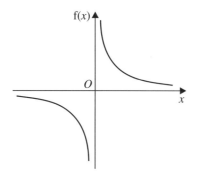

Exercise 2A

In questions 1–5, f is a function whose domain is the set of real numbers. Within the interval given, sketch the graph of f and determine the range of f.

1 $f : x \mapsto 2x - 3, \quad 0 \leqslant x \leqslant 6$

2 $f : x \mapsto 4 - x, \quad -2 \leqslant x \leqslant 2$

3 $f : x \mapsto x^2, \quad -4 \leqslant x \leqslant 4$

4 $f : x \mapsto \frac{1}{x}, \quad 2 \leqslant x \leqslant 10$

5 $f : x \mapsto 2^x, \quad -2 \leqslant x \leqslant 4$

6 Given that $f(x) = \frac{1}{x^2 + 1}$, find the values of

(a) $f(-2)$ (b) $f(-1)$ (c) $f(0)$.

7 Find the range of the function f which is defined by

$$f : x \mapsto \frac{1}{x + 1}, x \in \mathbb{R}, 0 \leqslant x \leqslant 7.$$

In each of the following functions, the rule and the range are given. By sketching the graph, find the domain.

8 $f : x \mapsto 3x + 4,$ range $1 \leqslant y \leqslant 12$

9 $g : x \mapsto 5 - 2x,$ range $-7 \leqslant y \leqslant 11$

2.3 Composite functions

Most functions which you will meet are combinations of two or more basic functions. These are called **composite functions**.

Example 4

Discuss the function f where x is defined over the real numbers by

$$f : x \mapsto 2x - 3$$

The function f is a combination of the two simpler functions g and h which are given by

$g : x \mapsto 2x$ (the 'doubling' function)

$h : x \mapsto x - 3$ (the 'take away 3' function)

The diagram shows how you can combine the functions g and h to obtain the same mapping as given by the function f.

The diagram makes it quite clear that g must be applied *first* and h applied *second* in order to obtain f. We write $h[g(x)]$ when we want g to precede h because the rule of h is applied to the result $g(x)$, which has been obtained already by applying the rule of function g.

$h[g(x)]$ is usually abbreviated to $hg(x)$. *Remember* that hg means '*do g first and then h*'. If the order of applying g and h is reversed, then a different function e is formed.

The function e is given by $e : x \mapsto 2x - 6$.

Example 5

The functions p and q are defined over the real numbers by

$$p : x \mapsto x^2$$

$$q : x \mapsto 5 - 4x$$

Find the values of (a) pq(3)   (b) qp(3)   (c) qq(3).

(a) Note that $q(3) = 5 - 4 \times 3 = 5 - 12 = -7$.
This gives $pq(3) = p[q(3)] = p(-7) = (-7)^2 = 49$

(b) You now have $p(3) = 3^2 = 9$.
This gives $qp(3) = q[p(3)] = q(9) = 5 - 4 \times 9 = -31$

(c) Using $q(3) = -7$ from (a),
$q[q(3)] = q(-7) = 5 - 4(-7) = 5 + 28 = 33$

Exercise 2B

1   The functions f, g and h each have the set of real numbers as
their domain and are defined by

  $f{:}x \mapsto 7 - 2x$

  $g{:}x \mapsto 4x - 1$

  $h{:}x \mapsto 3(x - 1)$

  (a) Find the following composite functions in terms of x.
  (i) fg (ii) gf (iii) fh (iv) hf (v) gh (vi) hg
  (b) Evaluate (i) fg(5) (ii) ff(-2) (iii) fh(0) (iv) hg$(-\frac{1}{2})$
  (v) fgh(3) (vi) ghf(3)
  (c) Find the values of x for which (i) $fg(x) = -15$
  (ii) $gh(x) = 11$ (iii) $hgf(x) = 102$

2   The function g has as its domain all non-zero real numbers
and is given by

$$g(x) = x - \frac{1}{x}$$

  Find the values of (a) g(2)   (b) gg(2)   (c) g$(-\frac{1}{3})$.
  Find also the values of x for which $g(x) = \frac{15}{4}$.

3   Functions g and h whose domains are the set of real numbers
are defined by

$$g : x \mapsto 3 - x \qquad h : x \mapsto x^2 - 1$$

  Find the values of (a) gh(2) (b) hh(2) (c) hg(-3) (d) ggg(0).

4 The composite functions f and g, given by $f(x) = x^3 + 2$ and $g(x) = \dfrac{1}{x} - 3$, could each be formed from two simpler functions. Write down these functions. Assuming that f and g have the set of real numbers as their domain, find the values of fg(2) and gf(2).

5 Given that $f(x) = ax + b$ and $g(x) = bx + a$, and that a and b are constant and unequal, find a relation between a and b for which

$$fg(x) = gf(x)$$

6 The functions f and g are defined over the real numbers and

$$f : x \mapsto 1 + \frac{x}{2} \qquad g : x \mapsto x^2$$

Form the composite functions (a) fg (b) gf (c) ff, expressing each in terms of x in a simplified form.

7 The functions p and q are defined by

$$p : x \mapsto Ax + B \qquad q : x \mapsto Cx + D$$

where A, B, C and D are constants. Given that $pq(x) = qp(x)$, show that

$$D(A - 1) = B(C - 1)$$

8 The functions f and g are defined by

$$f : x \mapsto 2x^2 + 1 \qquad g : x \mapsto 3x - 2$$

Find the functions, fg, gf, ff and gg in terms of x, and sketch their graphs.

2.4 Inverse functions

For any function each member of the domain corresponds to one, and only one, member of the range. Sometimes it is possible to choose a domain and a range so that, if $f : x \mapsto y$ is a function, then $y \mapsto x$ is also a function. We call this function the **inverse function** of f, written

$$f^{-1} : y \mapsto x$$

An inverse function f^{-1} can exist if, and only if, the function f is a one–one mapping. That is, each member of the domain must be paired with one and only one member of the range and each member of the range is paired with only one member of the domain.

Example 6
Discuss the function f given by $f(x) = x^2$.

The function f given by $f(x) = x^2$ with domain the set of real numbers is not one–one. This is clear because, for example, both the numbers 2 and -2 in the domain map to 4 in the range. This type of function is known as a many–one mapping. However, it is worth noting that if you restrict the domain to the set of positive real numbers, you turn the function x^2 into a one–one mapping.

Starting with the one–one function f defined over a suitable domain, you can find the inverse function f^{-1} by following these steps, starting from $y = f(x)$.

1. Interchange x and y to give $x = f(y)$.

2. Express y in terms of x to give $y = f^{-1}(x)$.

3. The inverse function is f^{-1} with domain the same as the range of f.

Example 7
The function f is defined by

$$f : x \mapsto 3x - 1, \qquad x \in \mathbb{R}, \ -1 \leqslant x \leqslant 4$$

Find the inverse function f^{-1} and sketch the graphs of the functions f and f^{-1} on the same axes.

First take $y = 3x - 1$ and change over x and y to obtain

$$x = 3y - 1$$

Rearranging, you get

$$3y = x + 1 \quad \text{and} \quad y = \frac{x+1}{3}$$

That is,

$$f^{-1}(x) = \frac{x+1}{3}$$

Referring to Example 1, where we discussed the same function, you know that the range of f is $-4 \leqslant x \leqslant 11$. This is also the domain of f^{-1}.

Then, $f^{-1} : x \mapsto \dfrac{x+1}{3}, \quad x \in \mathbb{R}, \quad -4 \leqslant x \leqslant 11$.

Finally, draw the graphs of f and f^{-1} on the same axes. Notice that the graphs of f and f^{-1} are reflections of each other in the line $y = x$.

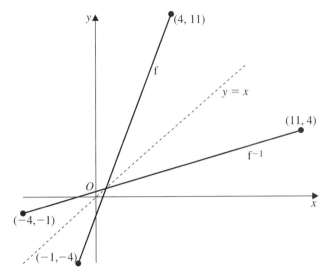

This is true for all one–one functions and their inverse functions because

$$\mathrm{ff}^{-1}(x) = x = \mathrm{f}^{-1}\mathrm{f}(x)$$

Example 8

Sketch the graph of the function f defined by

$$\mathrm{f} : x \mapsto (x - 2)^2, \qquad x \in \mathbb{R}$$

Explain why f cannot have an inverse function. By making an appropriate change to the domain of f define a function g with the same rule as f which has an inverse function g^{-1}. Express g^{-1} in terms of x.

The sketch of a graph should not only indicate the general shape but should also include the coordinates of any points at which the curve meets the coordinate axes, when these can be easily calculated.

The curve with equation $y = (x - 2)^2$ is a parabola of U shape with its vertex, the lowest point, at the point $A(2, 0)$, as shown. This is also the sketch of f. This sketch shows that f is a many–one mapping because, for example, both 0 and 4 in the domain map to 4 in the range. Therefore, the function f cannot possess an inverse function.

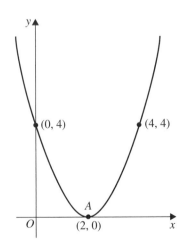

Now consider the function g defined by

$$\mathrm{g} : x \mapsto (x - 2)^2, \qquad x \in \mathbb{R}, x \geqslant 2$$

By restricting the domain of g, compared with that of f, we have made g a one–one function, as shown in the next diagram.

To find the inverse function g^{-1} of g, write

$$y = (x - 2)^2$$

Interchange x and y: $x = (y - 2)^2$

Expressing y in terms of x:

$$y - 2 = \pm\sqrt{x}$$

That is,

$$y = 2 + \sqrt{x}$$

Note that we choose the $+$ sign on the square root so that the graph of g^{-1} is the reflection of the graph of g in the line $y = x$.

The inverse function g^{-1} is therefore given by

$$g^{-1} : x \mapsto 2 + \sqrt{x}, \quad x \in \mathbb{R}, x \geqslant 0$$

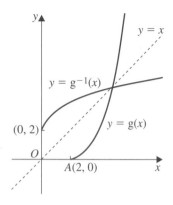

Exercise 2C

In all questions, the domain of each function is the set of real numbers unless specifically stated otherwise. In questions 1–5, sketch the given function f. Find f^{-1}. Sketch on the same diagram the functions f and f^{-1}.

1 $f(x) = 2x$ **2** $f(x) = 2x + 3$ **3** $f(x) = 1 - 2x$

4 $f(x) = x^2, x \leqslant 0$ **5** $f(x) = \dfrac{1}{x}, x > 0$

In questions 6–11 some simple functions are given, where p and q are positive constants. Find the inverse function for each.

6 $f(x) = x + p$ **7** $f(x) = px$ **8** $f(x) = p - x$

9 $f(x) = px + q$ **10** $f(x) = \dfrac{p}{x}, x \neq 0$

11 $f(x) = \dfrac{1}{px + q}, x \neq \dfrac{-q}{p}$

In questions 12–15, find the range of the function whose domain is the set of positive real numbers. Find also the inverse function.

12 $f(x) = \dfrac{1}{x^2}$ **13** $f(x) = \dfrac{1}{x + 1}$

14 $f(x) = (x + 1)^2 - 1$ **15** $f(x) = x^2 + 4x + 5$

16 Find the values of A and B so that

$$(x - A)^2 + B \equiv x^2 - 10x + 29$$

for all values of x.

The function $f : x \mapsto , x^2 - 10x + 29, x \in \mathbb{R}, x \geqslant k$ is one–one. Find the smallest possible positive value of k and the range of f in this case. Find also the inverse function when k takes its smallest possible positive value.

17 Find the inverse function g^{-1} of $g(x) = \dfrac{1}{x-4}$, $x \neq 4$.

18 Given that $f(x) = \dfrac{2x}{x+1}$, $x \in \mathbb{R}$, $x \neq -1$, define the inverse function f^{-1} in a similar form.

19 The function f is defined by
$$f : x \mapsto \frac{5x+1}{x-3}, x \in \mathbb{R}, x \neq 3$$
Find expressions for (a) $ff(x)$ (b) $f^{-1}(x)$.

2.5 Modulus functions

The modulus function $|x|$, $x \in \mathbb{R}$

The **modulus** of any number, positive or negative, is the size of the number without a sign attached.

For example, the modulus of 5, written $|5|$, is 5 and the modulus of -3, written $|-3|$, is 3.

The modulus function, written as $|x|$, is defined as
$$|x| = \begin{cases} x \text{ for all real } x \geqslant 0 \\ -x \text{ for all real } x < 0 \end{cases}$$

Here is the graph of $y = |x|$. It consists of the line $y = x$ for $x \geqslant 0$ and the line $y = -x$ for $x < 0$.

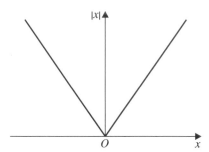

The statement $|x| < p$ means that x is *numerically* less than p; that is $-p < x < p$, where p is a fixed positive number.

The modulus function $|f(x)|$

Remember that $|f(x)|$ is always positive or zero. So $|f(x)| = f(x)$ when $f(x)$ is positive and $|f(x)| = -f(x)$ when $f(x)$ is negative.

If you need to sketch the graph of $y = |f(x)|$, then where $f(x)$ is positive you sketch $f(x)$ and where $f(x)$ is negative you sketch the reflection of $f(x)$ in the x-axis. There is no part of the graph that lies in the region of the xy-plane for which $y < 0$.

Example 9

Sketch the graph of $y = x + 1$ and hence sketch the graph of $y = |x + 1|$.

The graph of $y = x + 1$ has positive gradient, cuts the x-axis at $(-1, 0)$ and cuts the y-axis at $(0, 1)$. It looks like this:

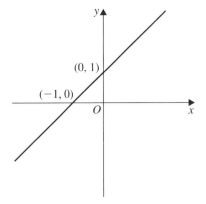

So the sketch of $y = |x + 1|$ looks like this:

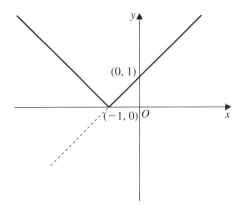

The dotted line shows the y-negative part of the graph of $y = x + 1$ which has been reflected in the x-axis.

Example 10

Sketch the graph of $y = (2 - x)(4 + x)$ and hence sketch the graph of $y = |(2 - x)(4 + x)|$.

The equation $\qquad\qquad y = (2 - x)(4 + x)$

can be written $\qquad\qquad y = 8 - 2x - x^2$

So its graph is a parabola of the 'hill' variety (since the coefficient of x^2 is negative), it cuts the x-axis at $(2, 0)$ and $(-4, 0)$ and it cuts the y-axis at $(0, 8)$. So its graph looks like this:

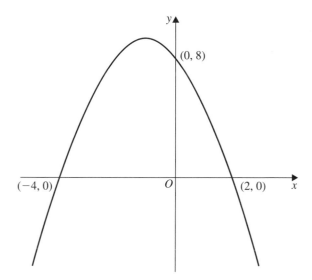

The graph of $y = |8 - 2x - x^2|$ looks like this:

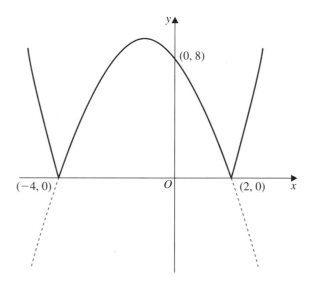

Again, the dotted lines represent the y-negative part of the graph of $y = 8 - 2x - x^2$ which has been reflected in the x-axis.

Example 11

Sketch the graph of $y = \dfrac{1}{x}$ and hence sketch the graph of $y = \left|\dfrac{1}{x}\right|$.

For the equation $y = \dfrac{1}{x}$, when $x = 0$, y is infinite and when $y = 0$, x is infinite. We say that the x- and y-axes are asymptotes.

$\dfrac{\mathrm{d}y}{\mathrm{d}x} = -\dfrac{1}{x^2}$ and since x^2 is always positive or zero, $-\dfrac{1}{x^2}$ is always negative. In particular it is never zero. So the graph of $y = \dfrac{1}{x}$ has no stationary points.

As $x \to \pm\infty$, $y \to 0$ and if $\mathrm{f}(x) = \dfrac{1}{x}$ then $\mathrm{f}(-x) = -\dfrac{1}{x} = -\mathrm{f}(x)$.

The graph looks like this:

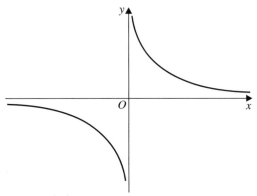

So the graph of $y = \left|\dfrac{1}{x}\right|$ looks like this:

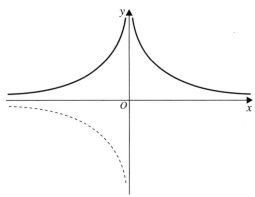

The modulus function f(|x|), x ∈ ℝ

To graph $y = \mathrm{f}(|x|)$ sketch the graph of $y = \mathrm{f}(x)$ for $x \geqslant 0$ and then reflect this in the y-axis to complete the sketch. Here are some examples.

Example 12

Sketch the graph of $y = |x| + 2$.

First sketch $y = x + 2$ for $x \geqslant 0$, like this:

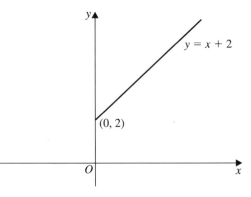

Then to complete the graph of $y = |x| + 2$, reflect in the y-axis like this:

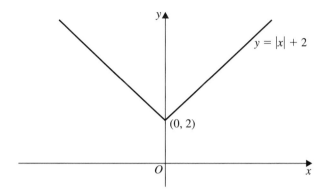

Example 13

Sketch the graph of $y = |x|^2 - 2|x|$.

First sketch $y = x^2 - 2x$ for $x \geqslant 0$ like this:

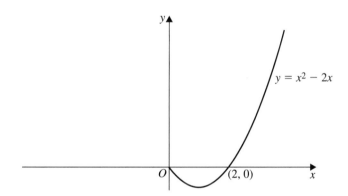

Then add to this graph the reflection in the y-axis like this:

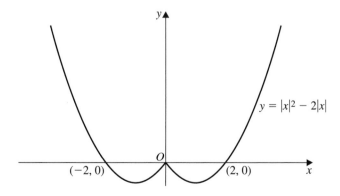

2.6 Sketching simple graphs of the form $y = x^n$

Here are sketch graphs of $y = f(x)$ for some simple standard functions where $f(x) = x^n$, for $n = 1, 2, 3, -1$ and $\frac{1}{2}$.

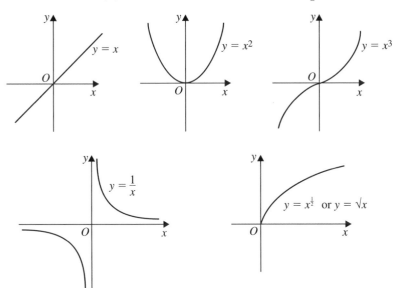

Even and odd functions

An even function has the property $f(x) = f(-x)$. The graph of the function is symmetrical about the line $x = 0$ (the y-axis). If (a, b) is on the graph, so is $(-a, b)$.

$f : x \mapsto x^2$, $x \in \mathbb{R}$ is an even function (see above).

An odd function has the property $f(x) = -f(-x)$, which is more often given as $f(-x) = -f(x)$. If (a, b) is on the graph, so is $(-a, -b)$.

$f : x \mapsto \dfrac{1}{x}$, $x \in \mathbb{R}$, $x \neq 0$, $f : x \mapsto x^3$, $x \in \mathbb{R}$, and $f : x \mapsto x$, $x \in \mathbb{R}$

are odd functions (see above).

2.7 Transforming graphs

Let's look at the effect of a few simple transformations on the graph of $y = f(x)$.

The transformation $y = af(x)$

All points on the x-axis remain unchanged under this transformation.

The general point $[t, f(t)]$ maps to the point $[t, af(t)]$, where t is any point in the domain of f. The following example shows the effect of taking different values of a.

Example 14

Starting with the basic curve $y = x^2$, sketch the curve $y = ax^2$ when $a = 2, \frac{1}{2}, -1, -2$ and $-\frac{1}{2}$.

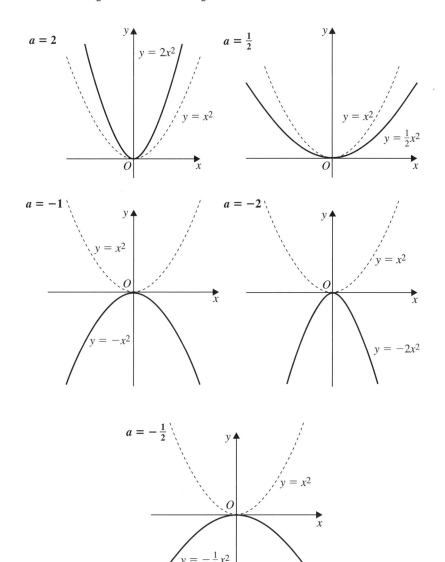

The transformation $y = f(x) + a$

If $a > 0$, the transformation translates the graph a steps in the positive y direction.

If $a < 0$, the transformation translates the graph a steps in the negative y direction.

Example 15

Starting from the basic curve $y = \dfrac{1}{x}$, sketch the curves $y = \dfrac{1}{x} + 3$ and $y = \dfrac{1}{x} - 3$.

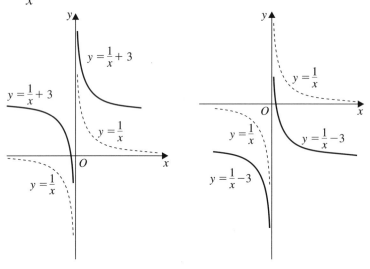

The transformation $y = f(x + a)$

If $a > 0$, the transformation translates the graph a steps to the left, that is, in the negative x direction.

If $a < 0$, the graph is translated a steps to the right, that is, in the positive x direction.

Example 16

Starting from the graph of the function $|x|$, sketch the graph of the functions $|x + 3|$ and $|x - 4|$.

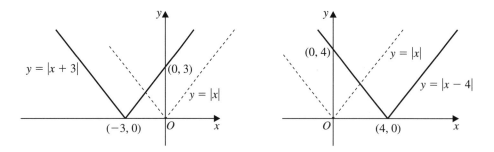

The transformation $y = f(ax)$

Points on the y-axis remain unchanged in this transformation. In general, the point $[t, f(t)]$ maps to the point $[at, f(at)]$, where t is any member of the domain of the function f. The following example shows the effect of taking different values of a.

Example 17

Starting with the basic curve $y = x^3$, sketch the curve $y = (ax)^3$ when $a = 2, \frac{1}{2}, -1, -2$.

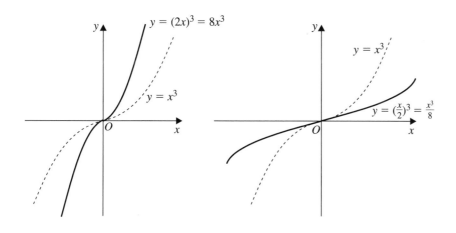

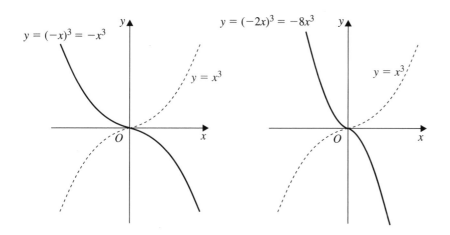

2.8 Solving equations graphically

Equations can be solved using graphs as well as by algebra. The use of a graph is not very efficient if the solutions of an equation are all integers. Under these circumstances it is much quicker to factorise the equation, if you can. However, if the equation has roots which are decimals or if the equation involves functions such as sine, cosine or tangent and may be impossible to factorise, then it may be necessary to draw a graph.

Example 18

Solve the equation $x^3 - 3x + 1 = 0$, giving your answers to one decimal place.

A table of values of $y = x^3 - 3x + 1$ for $-2 \leqslant x \leqslant 2$ is:

x	-2	-1.75	-1.5	-1	-0.5	0	0.25	0.5	1	1.5	1.75	2
y	-1	0.89	2.13	3	2.38	1	0.26	-0.38	-1	-0.13	1.11	3

So the graph looks like this:

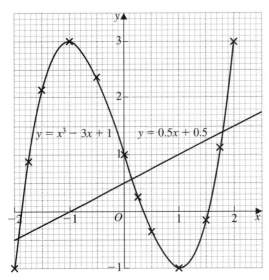

Now the graph is that of $y = x^3 - 3x + 1$. But we wish to solve the equation $x^3 - 3x + 1 = 0$. That is, we need y to be zero. Now $y = 0$ is the equation of the x-axis. So to solve $x^3 - 3x + 1 = 0$, you need to find where the graph of $y = x^3 - 3x + 1$ crosses the x-axis. So you can see that the roots of the equation are approximately -1.9, 0.4 and 1.5.

Using the above graph you could also solve other equations, for example $x^3 - 3.5x + 0.5 = 0$. This equation can be rewritten as:

$$x^3 - 3x - 0.5x + 1 - 0.5 = 0$$

or $$x^3 - 3x + 1 = 0.5x + 0.5$$

That is, it can be rewritten so that the left-hand side of the equation is the left-hand side of the original equation, $x^3 - 3x + 1 = 0$.

If you then draw the graphs of $y = x^3 - 3x + 1$ and $y = 0.5x + 0.5$ (which is the equation of a straight line) then the points where the two graphs intersect give the roots of $x^3 - 3x + 1 = 0.5x + 0.5$. Reading off the x-coordinates of the points of intersection (since the equation to solve is an equation in x) gives the roots of $x^3 - 3.5x + 0.5 = 0$ as $-1.9, 0.1, 1.8$ (to 1 decimal place).

Exercise 2D

In this exercise, take the domain of each function to be the set of real numbers unless informed otherwise.

1 Starting with the graph of the linear function $f(x) = x$, sketch the functions $f(x + 1)$, $f(3x)$, $f(x)$, $f(x) + 1$, $4f(x)$.

2 On the same diagram, for $0 \leqslant x \leqslant 2$, sketch the graphs of the curves with equations $y = x^2$, $y = x^3$, $y = x^4$.

3 Consider the three curves with equations $y = f(x)$, where $f(x) = x^2$, x^3, x^4. For which curve(s) is it true to say that
    (a) $f(x) = f(-x)$
    (b) $f(x) = -f(-x)$ for all values of x?

4 Sketch the graphs of $y = |3x - 2|$ and $y = |x|$. Determine the coordinates of the points of intersection of the two graphs.

5 Given that $f(x) = \dfrac{1}{x}$, $x > 0$, sketch on the same axes the graphs of $y = f(x)$, $y = f(3x)$, $y = 3f(x)$, $y = f(x + 3)$.

6 Given that $f(x) = (x + 2)^2$, sketch on the same axes the graph of $y = f(x)$ with the graph of
    (a) $y = f(x) - 2$ (b) $y = f(x - 2)$
    (c) $y = -2f(x)$ (d) $y = f(2x)$.

7 The functions g and h are defined for all real x by
    $$g : x \mapsto 2 + \frac{x}{3}$$
    $$h : x \mapsto 3(x - 2)$$
    (a) Show that $g^{-1} = h$.
    (b) Sketch the graphs of $y = gg(x)$ and $y = hh(x)$.
    (c) Sketch the graphs of $y = g(x + 2)$ and $y = h(x - 6)$.

8 Given that $f(x) = x^2$, sketch in separate diagrams the graphs of
    (a) $y = -f(x)$ (b) $y = f(2 - x)$ (c) $y = 2 - f(x)$
    (d) $y = f(2x)$ (e) $y = 2f(x)$.

9 Sketch the graphs of $y = |5x - 4|$ and $y = |2x + 3|$. Hence deduce the coordinates of their points of intersection.

10 Sketch the graph of $y = |x^2 + x|$. Hence solve the equation $|x^2 + x| = 6$.

11 Given that $f(x) = x^2 - 4x$, $x \in \mathbb{R}$, sketch, in separate diagrams, the graphs of
(a) $y = |f(x)|$ (b) $y = f(|x|)$.
Hence solve the equations
(c) $|f(x)| = 4$ (d) $f(|x|) = -3$.

12 Solve the equations
(a) $|3x + 5| = |5x|$
(b) $|6x - 7| = |2x + 5|$
(c) $|x^2 - 4| = 3|x|$

13 Sketch the graphs of $y = |x|$ and $y = |x^2 - 2|$. Hence, or otherwise, find the values of x for which
$$|x^2 - 2| = |x|$$

14 For $-2\pi \leqslant x \leqslant 2\pi$ sketch, on separate diagrams, the graphs of
(a) $y = |f(x)|$ (b) $y = f(|x|)$
where $f(x) = \sin x$.

15 Draw the graph of $y = \dfrac{210}{x} - 40$ for values of x from 1 to 7.

Use a scale of 2 cm to 1 unit on the x-axis and a scale of 1 cm to 10 units on the y-axis.
Using the same axes and scales draw appropriate straight lines to find a value of x which satisfies the equation

(a) $\dfrac{210}{x} = 84$ (b) $\dfrac{210}{x} - 20x = 40$ [E]

16 (a) Draw the graph of $y = 5 - (x - 1)^2$ for values of x from -2 to $+4$, taking 2 cm to represent 1 unit on both axes.
(b) Using the same scales and axes, draw the graph of $y = \frac{1}{2}x - 2$.
(c) Obtain, in the form $ax^2 + bx + c = 0$, where a, b and c are integers, the equation which is satisfied by the x-coordinates of the points of intersection of these two graphs.
(d) Use your graphs to estimate the two solutions of this equation.   [E]

17 Draw the graph of $y = x^3 - x - 3$ for values of x from -2 to $+2$, using 2 cm to represent 1 unit on the x-axis and 1 cm to represent 1 unit on the y-axis.

(a) Use your graph to estimate a root of the cubic equation $x^3 - x - 3 = 0$.

(b) Using the same axes and scales, draw the graph of $y = 2x - 4$ and hence find estimates for the roots of the equation $x^3 - 3x + 1 = 0$. [E]

18 Draw the graph of $y = \frac{1}{10}(x^3 + 2x^2 + 7)$ for values of x from -4 to $+3$, using 2 cm to represent 1 unit on each axis.

(a) Use your graph to estimate a root of the equation $x^3 + 2x^2 + 2 = 0$.

(b) By drawing a suitable straight line, find estimates for the three roots of the equation $x^3 + 2x^2 - 10x - 13 = 0$. [E]

19 Draw the graph of $y = \frac{1}{10}(x^3 - 2x^2 + 11)$ for values of x from -4 to $+3$, using 2 cm to represent 1 unit on each axis.

(a) Use your graph to estimate a root of the equation $x^3 - 2x^2 + 11 = 0$.

(b) By drawing a suitable straight line, find estimates for two of the three roots of the equation $x^3 - 2x^2 - 10x + 1 = 0$. [E]

SUMMARY OF KEY POINTS

1 A function is a mapping between two variables, usually called x, the independent variable, and y, the dependent variable. The function is given by f and written as $\text{f} : x \mapsto y$. The set of values taken by x, the independent variable, is called the domain and the resulting set of values arising for y is called the range.

2 When defining a function, it is necessary to state both the rule for getting from each x to the corresponding y and the set of values assigned for x (the domain).

3 In forming composite functions gf, apply f first, followed by g. Remember that, in general $\text{fg}(x) \neq \text{gf}(x)$.

4 For a one–one function f, the inverse function f^{-1} exists, and $\text{ff}^{-1}(x) = \text{f}^{-1}\text{f}(x) = x$.

5 The graph of $y = \text{f}^{-1}(x)$ is a reflection of the graph of $y = \text{f}(x)$ in the line $y = x$.

6 $|x| = x$ for $x \geqslant 0$ and $|x| = -x$ for $x < 0$.

7 To sketch the graph of $y = |\text{f}(x)|$, where $\text{f}(x)$ is positive or zero, sketch $y = \text{f}(x)$ and where $\text{f}(x)$ is negative sketch the reflection of $\text{f}(x)$ in the x-axis.

8   To sketch the graph of $y = f(|x|)$, sketch the graph of $y = f(x)$ for $x \geqslant 0$ and then reflect this in the y-axis to complete the sketch.

9   For an even function f, $f(x) = f(-x)$.
    For an odd function f, $f(-x) = -f(x)$.

10 Transformations:
    $y = af(x)$: points on x-axis remain unchanged and $[t, f(t)] \mapsto [t, af(t)]$.
    $y = f(x) + a$: translates in y^+ direction for $a > 0$ and in y^- direction for $a < 0$.
    $y = f(x + a)$: translates in x^- direction for $a > 0$, and in x^+ direction for $a < 0$.
    $y = f(ax)$: all points on y-axis remain unchanged and $[t, f(t)] \mapsto [at, f(at)]$.

11 To solve the equation $f(x) = g(x)$ graphically, draw the graphs of $y = f(x)$ and $y = g(x)$ and find the x-coordinates of the points of intersection of the two graphs.

Sequences and series

3

3.1 Sequences and recurrence relations

As you saw in Book P1, section 4.1, a sequence $u_1, u_2, u_3 \ldots, u_n \ldots$ can be defined by using a rule or formula for the nth term in terms of n.

■ **A sequence can be defined also by one or more of the first few terms, together with a general relationship between, say, the $(n-1)$th and the nth terms of the series, often given as**

$$u_n = f(u_{n-1})$$

This is called a recurrence relation.

Example 1
A sequence is defined by the recurrence relation

$$u_n = 4u_{n-1}$$

where $u_1 = \frac{1}{4}$. Determine the second, third and tenth terms of the sequence.

For $n = 2$, $u_2 = 4u_1 = 4\left(\frac{1}{4}\right) = 1$

For $n = 3$, $u_3 = 4u_2 = 4(1) = 4$

Now $u_n = 4u_{n-1} = 4(4u_{n-2}) = 4^2 u_{n-2} = 4^3\, 4u_{n-3} = 4^4 u_{n-4}$, etc.

So it is clear that

$$u_n = 4u_{n-1} = 4^2 u_{n-2} = 4^3 u_{n-3} = \ldots = 4^{n-1} u_1$$

So $\qquad u_{10} = 4^9 u_1 = 4^9\left(\frac{1}{4}\right) = 4^8 = 65\,536$

Example 2
Investigate the sequences obtained for the following recurrence relation when (a) $u_1 = 5$ (b) $u_1 = 1$:

$$u_n = \tfrac{1}{2}u_{n-1} + 1, n > 1$$

(a) Starting with $u_1 = 5$ and using the recurrence relation gives:
$u_2 = 3.5$, $u_3 = 2.75$, $u_4 = 2.375$, $u_5 = 2.1875$ and $u_6 = 2.093\,75$.

These terms form a decreasing sequence of numbers that appear to be getting successively nearer to 2. Continuing the process

$u_{10} = 2.005\,859\,4$, which does not prove the hypothesis but confirms that it is along the right lines.

Taking $u_1 = 2 + s$, where s is a positive number, gives:

$$u_2 = 2 + \frac{s}{2}, u_3 = 2 + \frac{s}{4} \ldots \text{and } u_n = 2 + \frac{s}{2^{n-1}}$$

The terms $\frac{s}{2}, \frac{s}{4}, \frac{s}{8}, \ldots$ are halving with each step and it is clear that this is a decreasing sequence in which the value of the nth term approaches the value 2 as n approaches infinity.

(b)   Starting with $u_1 = 1$ and using the recurrence relation gives $u_2 = 1.5$, $u_3 = 1.75$, $u_4 = 1.875$, $u_5 = 1.9375$, $u_6 = 1.968\,75$.

This is an increasing sequence of numbers which are getting successively nearer to 2. This can be proved by a method similar to that given in (a).

In each case, the sequence **converges** to the value 2.

Exercise 3A

In questions 1–5, find the first four terms of the sequence and then investigate further to decide whether or not the sequence is convergent. For any convergent series, find the limiting value.

1   $u_n = 2u_{n-1} - 4$, $u_1 = 3$, $n > 1$
2   $u_n = 2u_{n-1} + 4$, $u_1 = 3$, $n \geqslant 1$
3   $u_n = \frac{1}{2}(u_{n-1} + 2)$, $u_1 = 0$, $n \geqslant 1$
4   $u_n = \frac{1}{3}u_{n-1} + 1$, $u_1 = 3$, $n \geqslant 1$
5   $u_n = \frac{1}{5}(u_{n-1} - 1)$, $u_1 = 2$, $n \geqslant 1$
6   A sequence is given by the recurrence relation:

$$u_n = 1 + \frac{1}{u_{n-1} + 1}, u_1 = 1, n \geqslant 1$$

Work out the 2nd, 3rd and 4th terms of the sequence and find the limiting value of the sequence.

7   In a sequence of increasing numbers, the differences between consecutive terms are 1, 2, 1, 2, 1... The 1st, 2nd and 3rd terms are 5, 6, and 8.
Find the 20th, 40th and 100th terms of the sequence. Explain the reasoning in your method.

8   For the sequence $u_1, u_2, u_3, \ldots u_n, \ldots$ the terms are related by $u_n = 2u_{n-2}$ where $n \geqslant 1$, $u_1 = 2$ and $u_2 = 5$.
Find the values of u_7, u_{11} and u_{14}.

9 The sequence given by $t_1, t_2, t_3, \ldots t_n, \ldots$ has $t_n = kt_{n-1}$, $n \geqslant 1$ and k is given below. Given that $t_1 = 1$, investigate the sequence generated when:

(a) $k = 2$ (b) $k = \frac{1}{2}$ (c) $k = (-1)^n$ (d) $k = (-\frac{1}{2})^n$

Which, if any, of these sequences are convergent?

10 The sequence $u_1, u_2, u_3, \ldots u_n, \ldots$ is defined by the relation $u_n = 2u_{n-1} + 6$, $n \geqslant 1$. Given that $u_n = u_1$ for all positive integers n, find the value of u_1.

11 A sequence of numbers v_n, where $n = 1, 2, 3, \ldots$ is given by the recurrence relation

$$v_n = \sqrt{(v_{n-1})}, \ v_1 = 100$$

Show that this sequence converges, and find the limiting value.

Discuss also the convergence of this sequence when $v_1 = \frac{1}{100}$ and find the limiting value.

12 The 1st and 2nd terms of a sequence are 1 and 3. Each successive term is the product of the immediately preceding two terms. For example, the 3rd term is 3 and the 4th is 9. Write down a recurrence relation for the sequence and find the 10th and 13th terms.

3.2 Binomial series for a positive, integral index

Binomial expressions

From the algebra covered in Book P1, you will be quite familiar with terms like y^0, $3y^1$, $4p^2$, $-5z^3$, etc., where each term is called a **monomial**. That is, it is an expression consisting of a single term.

Expressions like $1 + x$, $2 - 3x$, $a + bx$ are called **binomial** because they each consist of just two terms joined by a $+$ or a $-$ sign. As you will have read in Book P1, expressions with many terms, such as $3 - 4x + x^2 + x^3$ or $x^4 - x^2 - 2x - 5$, are called **polynomials**.

Often you will find that in the course of your work you need to expand expressions such as $(1 + x)^3$ or $(2 - 3x)^5$, or more generally $(a + b)^n$, where n is a positive integer. We start by considering some simple examples, where binomial expressions are squared and cubed.

Example 3
Expand (a) $(1 + x)^2$ (b) $(1 + x)^3$.

(a) Removing the brackets gives

$$(1 + x)^2 = 1(1 + x) + x(1 + x)$$
$$= 1 + x + x + x^2$$
$$= 1 + 2x + x^2$$

(b) Using the result found in (a):

$$(1 + x)^3 = (1 + x)(1 + x)^2$$
$$= (1 + x)(1 + 2x + x^2)$$
$$= 1(1 + 2x + x^2) + x(1 + 2x + x^2)$$
$$= 1 + 2x + x^2 + x + 2x^2 + x^3$$

Hence: $$(1 + x)^3 = 1 + 3x + 3x^2 + x^3$$

Example 4
Expand (a) $(1 - x)^2$ (b) $(1 - x)^3$.

These expansions could be done by multiplying out the brackets as in example 3. It is quicker, however, to take the results from example 3 and replace x by $-x$. Then you have:

(a) $(1 - x)^2 = 1 + 2(-x) + (-x)^2 = 1 - 2x + x^2$

(b) $(1 - x)^3 = 1 + 3(-x) + 3(-x)^2 + (-x)^3$
$$= 1 - 3x + 3x^2 - x^3$$

Example 5
Expand $(1 - 2x)^3$.

This expansion can be done by putting $-2x$ in the place of x in the expansion of $(1 + x)^3$. Then you get:

$$(1 - 2x)^3 = 1 + 3(-2x) + 3(-2x)^2 + (-2x)^3$$
$$= 1 - 6x + 12x^2 - 8x^3$$

Simple binomial expansions such as $(1 + x)^2$ and $(1 + x)^3$ are obtained by multiplying out brackets. Then other similar binomial expressions may be expanded by using these results, as shown in examples 4 and 5. Although these illustrations are really simple, the methods used are of great importance and you will see them used again both in this chapter and in other contexts.

Exercise 3B

1 By using the expansion of $(1 + x)^2$, expand each of the following:
   (a) $(1 + 3x)^2$ (b) $(1 - 5x)^2$ (c) $(1 - x^2)^2$
   (d) $(1 + 2x^3)^2$ (e) $[1 - (x - 2)^2]^2$

2 Use the expansion of $(1 + x)^3$ to expand:
   (a) $(1 + 2y)^3$ (b) $(1 - x^3)^3$ (c) $(1 + 3x^{-1})^3$

3 By considering the products $(1 + x)(1 + x)^3$ and $(1 + x)(1 + x)^4$ find the expansion of (a) $(1 + x)^4$ (b) $(1 + x)^5$

4 Using the results you obtained in question 3, or otherwise, work out (a) $(1 - 3x)^4$ (b) $(1 + 2x)^5$.

Pascal's triangular array

From your work in this chapter, you can build up these expansions:

$$(1 + x)^1 = 1 + x$$

$$(1 + x)^2 = 1 + 2x + x^2$$

$$(1 + x)^3 = 1 + 3x + 3x^2 + x^3$$

Also: $$(1 + x)^0 = 1$$

You can summarise this by writing down only the coefficients, in this way:

Expansion	Coefficients in ascending powers of x					
$(1 + x)^0$				1		
$(1 + x)^1$			1		1	
$(1 + x)^2$		1		2		1
$(1 + x)^3$	1		3		3		1
$(1 + x)^4$	1	4		6		4	1
$(1 + x)^5$	1	5	10		10	5	1

. . . . and so on . . . .

This continuing triangular array is known as **Pascal's triangle** and it provides you with a means of determining *any* coefficient in the expansion of $(1 + x)^n$ for integral n up to, say, $n = 20$ (or more if you have the time!) but a better method is available for larger n as you will see later in this chapter.

Each entry E in the array, except the 'ones' at each end, is the sum of the two entries on either side of E in the previous line. For reference, call line $(1+x)^0$ line 0, $(1+x)^1$ line 1, $(1+x)^2$ line 2, etc. Each new line of the array is formed from the previous line in this way. For example, the 10 in line 5 comes from adding the 6 and 4 in line 4.

Example 6

Expand $(1+x)^7$ in ascending powers of x. Hence find the first four terms of the expansion of $(1+4x)^7$ in ascending powers of x.

Line 7 of Pascal's triangle is 1 7 21 35 35 21 7 1 and hence the expansion of $(1+x)^7$ in ascending powers of x is

$$1 + 7x + 21x^2 + 35x^3 + 35x^4 + 21x^5 + 7x^6 + x^7$$

If you replace x by $4x$, you find that the first four terms of the expansion of $(1+4x)^7$ are:

$$1 + 7(4x) + 21(4x)^2 + 35(4x)^3$$
$$= 1 + 28x + 336x^2 + 2240x^3$$

Example 7

Determine the first four terms of the expansion of $(1-x)^{13}$ in ascending powers of x. Show that the estimate B of 0.999^{13} obtained by using these four terms of the series is $0.987\,077\,714$.

By considering the next term in your series show that B is *not correct* to 9 decimal places.

The first four entries in line 13 of Pascal's triangle are:

$$1, \quad 13, \quad 78, \quad 286$$

and hence the first four terms in the expansion of $(1-x)^{13}$ are

$$1 - 13x + 78x^2 - 286x^3$$

Put $x = 0.001$ in this expansion:

$$(1 - 0.001)^{13} = 0.999^{13} \approx 1 - 0.013 + 0.000\,078 - 0.000\,000\,286$$
$$= 0.987\,077\,714, \text{ as required}$$

The fifth Pascal triangle number in line 13 is 715 and the fifth term in the expansion of $(1+x)^{13}$ is $715x^4$. When $x = 0.001$, this term is $0.000\,000\,000\,715$ and so $0.999^{13} \approx 0.987\,077\,714\,715$. So 0.999^{13} is $0.987\,077\,715$ (9 d.p.) and estimate B is *not* correct to 9 decimal places.

The expansion of $(a+b)^n$, where n is a positive integer using Pascal's triangle

If you multiply directly and remove the brackets, you can easily establish that:

$$(a+b)^2 = a^2 + 2ab + b^2$$
$$(a+b)^3 = a^3 + 3a^2b + 3ab^2 + b^3$$
$$(a+b)^4 = a^4 + 4a^3b + 6a^2b^2 + 4ab^3 + b^4$$
$$(a+b)^5 = a^5 + 5a^4b + 10a^3b^2 + 10a^2b^3 + 5ab^4 + b^5$$

Using Pascal's triangular array and continuing this process, you can produce expansions for $(a+b)^n$ where $n = 6, 7, \ldots$.

Example 8

Expand in descending powers of x: (a) $(2x+3)^4$ (b) $(x - x^{-1})^3$.

(a) Write $a = 2x$ and $b = 3$ in the expansion of $(a+b)^4$. This gives:

$$(2x+3)^4 = (2x)^4 + 4(2x)^3(3) + 6(2x)^2(3)^2 + 4(2x)(3)^3 + (3)^4$$
$$= 16x^4 + 96x^3 + 216x^2 + 216x + 81$$

(b) Write $a = x$ and $b = -x^{-1}$ in the expansion of $(a+b)^3$. This gives:

$$(x - x^{-1})^3 = x^3 + 3x^2(-x^{-1}) + 3x(-x^{-1})^2 + (-x^{-1})^3$$
$$= x^3 - 3x + 3x^{-1} - x^{-3}$$

Exercise 3C

1   Expand $(1 + 5x)^3$.
    Use your expansion to simplify $(1 + 5x)^3 + (1 - 5x)^3$.

2   Expand $(1 - \frac{1}{2}x)^n$, for $n = 2, 3, 4$.

3   Expand $(2 - 3x)^3$ and $(3 + 2x)^3$.
    Hence express $3(2 - 3x)^3 - 2(3 + 2x)^3$ in terms of x.

4   Find, in ascending powers of x, the first four terms in the expansions of (a) $(1 - 2x)^6$ (b) $(2 - x)^7$.

5   Find, in descending powers of y, the first three non-zero terms in the expansion of $(1 - 4y)^9 - (1 + 4y)^9$.

6   Use the binomial series of $(1 - 2x)^8$ to evaluate 0.98^8 to 7 decimal places.

7   Use the first four terms in the binomial expansion of $(1 + 4x)^{12}$ in ascending powers of x to determine an approximation for
    (a) 1.004^{12} (b) 0.996^{12}
    justifying in each case the accuracy of your approximation.

8 Simplify $(4 - 3x)^3 - (3 + 4x)^3$.

9 Find and simplify the first three terms of the expansion of $(5x - 2)^4$ in descending powers of x.

10 The first three terms in the expansion of $(A + x)^m$ in ascending powers of x are $64 + 192x + Bx^2$. Find the values of m, A and B.

11 Simplify:
(a) $(1 + \sqrt{3})^4 + (1 - \sqrt{3})^4$
(b) $(\sqrt{2} + \sqrt{3})^4 + (\sqrt{2} - \sqrt{3})^4$

12 Find the expansion of $(z - \frac{1}{z})^9$ in descending powers of z.

13 Find the coefficients of the terms indicated in the following expansions:
(a) $(1 - 2x)^{14}$; x^2 term   (b) $(2 + 3x)^5$; x^3 term
(c) $(1 - 2x^3)^5$; x^9 term   (d) $(3 - 4x)^7$; x^6 term

14 Find the term that is independent of x in the expansion of

$$(3x - \tfrac{1}{3x})^6$$

15 Evaluate

$$\int_0^1 (2x^2 + 1)^3 \, dx$$

3.3 Expanding $(a + b)^n$ generally for positive integral n

As you have already observed the first few lines of Pascal's triangular array are:

line

0				1				
1			1		1			
2		1		2		1		
3	1		3		3		1	
4	1	4		6		4		1

.. . . and so on . . . .

The question you may have asked, and, in fact, you *should* have asked is 'What are the entries in the nth line?'. By observation, you can see that the nth line will have $(n + 1)$ numbers, of which the first is 1 and the second is n. The third number is

$$\frac{n(n - 1)}{1 \times 2}$$

and the fourth is

$$\frac{n(n-1)(n-2)}{1 \times 2 \times 3}$$

For example in line 4 you have

$$1, 4, \frac{4 \times 3}{1 \times 2}, \frac{4 \times 3 \times 2}{1 \times 2 \times 3}, \frac{4 \times 3 \times 2 \times 1}{1 \times 2 \times 3 \times 4}$$

That is 1, 4, 6, 4, 1.

Test the formula for yourself for different values of n. The general term in the expansion of $(1+x)^n$ is taken to be the x^r term, where r is any positive integer less than or equal to n.

The coefficient of x^r in the expansion of $(1+x)^n$ is

$$\frac{n(n-1)(n-2) \times \ldots (n-r+1)}{1 \times 2 \times 3 \times \ldots \times r}$$

The number $1 \times 2 \times 3 \times \ldots \times r$, that is the number obtained when all the integers from 1 to r inclusive are multiplied together, is written in shorthand form as $r!$ and called '**factorial r**'.

If this notation is used, then you find that the coefficient of x^r is:

$$\frac{n(n-1)(n-2) \ldots (n-r+1)}{r!}$$

$$= \frac{n(n-1)(n-2) \ldots (n-r+1)(n-r)(n-r-1) \ldots 2 \times 1}{r!\,(n-r)(n-r-1) \ldots 2 \times 1}$$

$$= \frac{n!}{r!(n-r)!}$$

This is the form in which you should learn and memorise this coefficient. You will not be expected to prove or derive this formula for the coefficient of the x^r term in the expansion of $(1+x)^n$ but you must be able to apply it soundly.

Notation

You will find that the coefficient

$$\frac{n!}{r!(n-r)!}$$

is often written as

$$\binom{n}{r} \quad or \quad {}^nC_r$$

There will probably be a button on your calculator marked ${}^nC_r$. Also 'factorial 0', 0!, is defined to be 1.

■ **You should remember that** $\binom{\boldsymbol{n}}{\boldsymbol{r}} = {}^{\boldsymbol{n}}\boldsymbol{C_r} = \dfrac{\boldsymbol{n!}}{\boldsymbol{r!(n-r)!}}$

So you now have these formulae:

- $(1 + x)^n = 1 + \binom{n}{1}x + \binom{n}{2}x^2 + \ldots + \binom{n}{r}x^r + \ldots + x^n$

- $(a + b)^n = a^n + \binom{n}{1}a^{n-1}b + \binom{n}{2}a^{n-2}b^2 + \ldots + \binom{n}{r}a^{n-r}b^r + \ldots + b^n$

which you should memorise and learn how to apply.

Example 9

Evaluate the following coefficients:

(a) $\binom{5}{3}$ (b) $\binom{9}{5}$

Using the formula, you have:

(a) $\binom{5}{3} = \dfrac{5!}{3!(5-3)!} = \dfrac{120}{6 \times 2} = 10$

(b) $\binom{9}{5} = \dfrac{9!}{5!(9-5)!} = \dfrac{362\,880}{120 \times 24} = 126$

Example 10

Find the first 4 terms in ascending powers of x of the expansion of $(3 - 2x)^9$.

Applying the formula for $(a + b)^n$ where $a = 3$, $b = -2x$, $n = 9$:

$(3 - 2x)^9 = 3^9 + \binom{9}{1}(3^8)(-2x) + \binom{9}{2}(3^7)(-2x)^2 + \binom{9}{3}(3^6)(-2x)^3 + \ldots$

$\qquad = 19\,683 - 118\,098x + 314\,928x^2 - 489\,888x^3 + \ldots$

Example 11

Determine the first four terms in the expansion of $(1 + x)^{21}$ in ascending powers of x. Hence find the coefficient of x^3 in the expansion of $(2 - 3x)(1 + x)^{21}$.

Using the binomial expansion:

$$(1 + x)^{21} = 1 + \binom{21}{1}x + \binom{21}{2}x^2 + \binom{21}{3}x^3 + \ldots$$
$$= 1 + 21x + 210x^2 + 1330x^3 + \ldots$$

Now:

$$(2 - 3x)(1 + x)^{21} = (2 - 3x)(1 + 21x + 210x^2 + 1330x^3 + \ldots)$$

The coefficient of $x^3 = 2(1330) - 3(210) = 2030$

Example 12

In the expansion of $(1 + x)^n$ in ascending powers of x, the coefficients of x^2 and x^3 are equal. Find the value of n.

The coefficient of x^2 is

$$\binom{n}{2} = \frac{n!}{2!(n-2)!}$$

The coefficient of x^3 is

$$\binom{n}{3} = \frac{n!}{3!(n-3)!}$$

Since these are equal: $\qquad \dfrac{n!}{2!(n-2)!} = \dfrac{n!}{3!(n-3)!}$

That is: $\qquad\qquad\qquad 2!(n-2)! = 3!(n-3)!$

$$\frac{(n-2)!}{(n-3)!} = \frac{3!}{2!}$$

$$n - 2 = 3$$

So: $\qquad\qquad\qquad\qquad n = 5$

Example 13

Find the coefficient of x^{16} in the expansion of $(2x - x^2)^{10}$.

Extract the factor x^{10} like this:

$$(2x - x^2)^{10} = [x(2-x)]^{10} = x^{10}(2-x)^{10}$$

You now need to find the coefficient of x^6 in the expansion of $(2-x)^{10}$ in order to find the coefficient of x^{16} in the expansion of $x^{10}(2-x)^{10}$.

That is: $\qquad \binom{10}{6}2^4(-x)^6 = 210 \times 16x^6 = 3360x^6$

So the required coefficient is 3360.

Exercise 3D

1 Find the first three terms in the expansion of $(1-x)^{23}$ in ascending powers of x.

2 Given that $(1+x)^{15} = 1 + Ax + Bx^2 + Cx^3 + \dots$, find A, B and C.

3 Find, in descending powers of x, the first three terms in the expansion of $(5x-3)^7$.

4 Simplify $(3+2x)^4 + (3-2x)^4$.

5 Obtain, in ascending powers of y, the first four terms in the expansion of (a) $(1-5y)^8$ (b) $(1-4y)(1-5y)^8$.

6 Obtain, in ascending powers of x, the first four terms in the expansion of $(1+x)^{10}$.

Find an approximation of $(0.998)^{10}$ from your expansion to the best degree of accuracy possible, justifying your decision.

7 Expand and simplify the first three terms, in descending powers of x, in the expansion of $(x + 2x^{-1})^{10} - (x - 2x^{-1})^{10}$.

8 Given that $(\sqrt{3} - 2)^6 = a\sqrt{3} + b$, find the values of a and b.

9 Show that

$$\frac{\sqrt{2} - 1}{\sqrt{2} + 1} = 3 - 2\sqrt{2}$$

and that

$$\frac{\sqrt{2} + 1}{\sqrt{2} - 1} = 3 + 2\sqrt{2}$$

Hence find the exact value of

$$\left(\frac{\sqrt{2} - 1}{\sqrt{2} + 1}\right)^5 + \left(\frac{\sqrt{2} + 1}{\sqrt{2} - 1}\right)^5$$

10 $P(x) \equiv \left(x^2 - \dfrac{3}{x}\right)^n$

Find the term that is independent of x in the expansion of $P(x)$,
(a) when $n = 3$ (b) when $n = 12$.

11 Use the binomial expansion to find the value of
(a) $(1.001)^{12}$, correct to 8 decimal places
(b) $(9.999)^{15}$, correct to 10 significant figures.

12 The coefficients of the x and x^2 terms in the expansion of $(1 + kx)^n$ are 44 and 924 respectively. Find the values of the constants k and n and the coefficient of the x^3 term in the expansion.

13 Expand $(1 + ax)^7$ in ascending powers of x up to and including the term in x^3.
In the expansion of $(b + x)(1 + ax)^7$ in ascending powers of x, the first and second terms are 5 and $71x$ respectively. Find
(a) the values of the constants a and b
(b) the x^2 and x^3 terms in this expansion.

14 The coefficients of x, x^2 and x^3 in the expansion of $(1 + x)^n$ are the first three terms of an arithmetic series. Show that $n = 7$.

15 The first three terms in the expansion of $(1 + kx)^n$ are 1, $14x$ and $84x^2$ respectively. Find the values of the constants k and n and the coefficients of the x^3 and x^4 terms.

16 Find the coefficient of x^{12} in the expansion of $(x - y)^{18}$.
Evaluate this term when $x = 6$ and $y = 3^{-1}$.

17 Find the expansion of $(1 + y)^6$.
By writing $y = x + x^2$, find the first four terms, in ascending powers of x, of the expansion of $(1 + x + x^2)^6$.
By putting $x = 0.01$ in your four terms, find an approximation for $(1.0101)^6$.

18 Part of the expansion of $(a + bx)^5$ is $32 + 40x + 20x^2$. Find the values of the constants a and b and the remaining terms of the expansion.

19 Find the first four terms, in descending powers of x, of the expansion of $(x^2 + 1)^{40}$.

20 The first three terms of the expansion of $(1 + kx)^n$ in ascending powers of x are 1, $\frac{17}{4}x$ and $\frac{17}{2}x^2$.
Find the values of the constants k and n and the terms in x^3 and x^4.

SUMMARY OF KEY POINTS

1 A sequence defined by one or more of the first few terms, together with a general relationship between two or more terms of the sequence is called a recurrence relation.

2 Binomial expressions consist of two terms, for example $a + bx$.

3 Pascal's triangular array of binomial coefficients is:

$$
\begin{array}{ccccccccc}
 & & & & 1 & & & & (1+x)^0 \\
 & & & 1 & & 1 & & & (1+x)^1 \\
 & & 1 & & 2 & & 1 & & (1+x)^2 \\
 & 1 & & 3 & & 3 & & 1 & (1+x)^3 \\
1 & & 4 & & 6 & & 4 & & 1 \quad (1+x)^4
\end{array}
$$

. . . . etc . . . .

4 Factorial n, written $n!$, is
$1 \times 2 \times 3 \times 4 \times \ldots \times (n - 1) \times n$.

5 $\dbinom{n}{r} = {}^nC_r = \dfrac{n!}{r!(n-r)!}$

6 $(1+x)^n = 1 + \dbinom{n}{1}x + \dbinom{n}{2}x^2 + \ldots + \dbinom{n}{r}x^r + \ldots + x^n$

7 $(a+b)^n = a^n + \dbinom{n}{1}a^{n-1}b + \dbinom{n}{2}a^{n-2}b^2 + \ldots + \dbinom{n}{r}a^{n-r}b^r + \ldots$
$\qquad \ldots + b^n$

Trigonometry

4

In Book P1 you learned some of the basics of trigonometry. This chapter will extend your knowledge. Three more trigonometric ratios are introduced, with their graphs. The inverse trigonometric functions are defined, with their graphs. The addition and sum and product formulae are derived. Finally, identities that relate the various trigonometric ratios to each other are formulated by using Pythagoras' theorem together with the identities for double and half angles. These enable you to solve other sorts of trigonometric equations, in addition to those that you learned to solve in Book P1.

4.1 Secant, cosecant and cotangent

There are six trigonometric ratios in total. You have already met the ratios sine, cosine and tangent. The three others are **secant**, **cosecant** and **cotangent**. These are defined as follows:

- **secant x (written sec x)** $= \dfrac{1}{\cos x}$

- **cosecant x (written cosec x)** $= \dfrac{1}{\sin x}$

- **cotangent x (written cot x)** $= \dfrac{1}{\tan x}$

So:

$$\sec 137° = \frac{1}{\cos 137°} = -\frac{1}{\cos 43°}$$
$$= -\frac{1}{0.731\,35}$$
$$= -1.367 \text{ (3 d.p.)}$$

$$\operatorname{cosec} 231° = \frac{1}{\sin 231°} = -\frac{1}{\sin 51°}$$
$$= -\frac{1}{0.777\,14}$$
$$= -1.287 \text{ (3 d.p.)}$$

$$\cot 253° = \frac{1}{\tan 253°} = +\frac{1}{\tan 73°}$$
$$= +\frac{1}{3.27085}$$
$$= +0.306 \text{ (3 d.p.)}$$

Drawing the graphs of sec *x*, cosec *x* and cot *x*

Graphing sec *x*

Here is a table of values for the function $y = \sec x$ when $0 \leqslant x \leqslant 360°$. Each value of y is given to two decimal places, where appropriate.

x	0	30°	45°	60°	90°	120°	135°	150°	180°	210°	225°	240°	270°	300°	315°	330°	360°
y	1	1.15	1.41	2	$\pm\infty$	-2	-1.41	-1.15	-1	-1.15	-1.41	-2	$\pm\infty$	2	1.41	1.15	1

If you plot these figures on a graph, it looks like this:

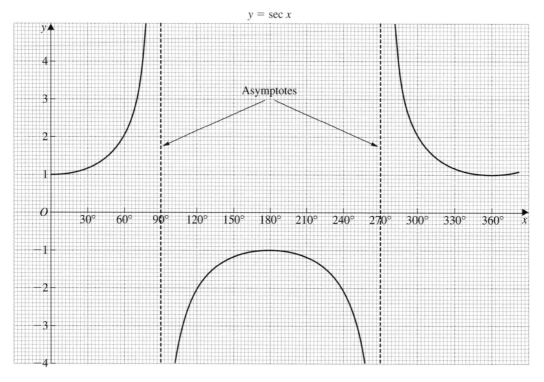

$y = \sec x$

The curve will repeat itself again and again for values of x above 360° and below 0. The function has a local minimum of 1 and a local maximum of -1. The minimum occurs at 0, 360°, 720°, 1080°, etc; in other words, at $\pm 360n°$, where n is an integer. The maximum occurs at 180°, 540°, 900°, etc.; in other words, at $180° \pm 360n°$.

The curve does not meet the x-axis. It has asymptotes at $90°, 270°, 450°$, etc.; in other words, at $90° \pm 180n°$. It has a period of $360°$.

Graphing cosec *x*

Here is a table of values for the function $y = \text{cosec } x$ when $0 \leqslant x \leqslant 360°$. Again each value is given to 2 decimal places, where appropriate.

x	0	30°	45°	60°	90°	120°	135°	150°	180°	210°	225°	240°	270°	300°	315°	330°	360°
y	$\pm\infty$	2	1.41	1.15	1	1.15	1.41	2	$\pm\infty$	−2	−1.41	−1.15	−1	−1.15	−1.41	−2	$\pm\infty$

The curve looks like this:

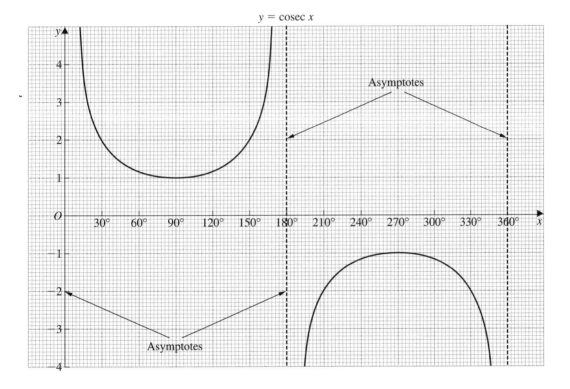

$y = \text{cosec } x$

Again the main feature of the curve is that it is periodic. It has a period of $360°$. Its local minimum is again 1 and its local maximum -1. But this time the minimum occurs at $90°, 450°, 810°$, and so on; in other words, at $90° \pm 360n°$. The maximum value occurs at $270°, 630°, 990°$, and so on; in other words, at $270° \pm 360n°$.

Again, the graph does not meet the x-axis. It has asymptotes at $0, 180°, 360°$, etc.; that is, at $\pm 180n°$.

Graphing cot x

Here is a table of values for $y = \cot x$ when $0 \leqslant x \leqslant 360°$.

x	0	30°	45°	60°	90°	120°	135°	150°	180°	210°	225°	240°	270°	300°	315°	330°	360°
y	$\pm\infty$	1.73	1	0.58	0	−0.58	−1	−1.73	$\pm\infty$	1.73	1	0.58	0	−0.58	−1	−1.73	$\pm\infty$

The curve looks like this:

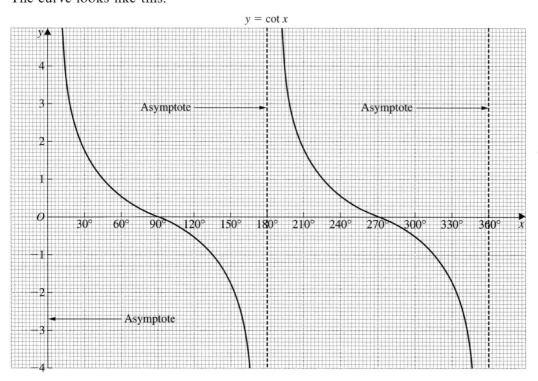

$y = \cot x$

Again, the curve is periodic with period 180°. It cuts the x-axis at 90°, 270°, 450°, and so on; in other words, at $90° \pm 180n°$. It has asymptotes at 0, 180°, 360°, and so on; that is, at $\pm 180n°$.

You must memorise the main features of the curves $y = \sec x$, $y = \operatorname{cosec} x$ and $y = \cot x$ – their shape, their maximum and minimum values and where they occur, the points at which $y = \cot x$ cuts the x-axis, and the position of the asymptotes. For an advanced course in mathematics you must be able to sketch these three curves from memory.

You must be able to evaluate these functions using both degrees and radians, as necessary.

Example 1

Find, to 4 significant figures, the value of

(a) $\cot 127°$

(b) $\operatorname{cosec} 200°$

(c) $\sec 349°$

(a) $\cot 127° = \dfrac{1}{\tan 127°} = -\dfrac{1}{\tan 53°} = -0.7536$ (4 s.f.)

(b) $\operatorname{cosec} 200° = \dfrac{1}{\sin 200°} = -\dfrac{1}{\sin 20°} = -2.924$ (4 s.f.)

(c) $\sec 349° = \dfrac{1}{\cos 349°} = \dfrac{1}{\cos 11°} = 1.019$ (4 s.f.)

Example 2
Find, in degrees to $0.1°$, the values of x for which $0 \leqslant x \leqslant 180°$ and

(a) $\sec x = -2.2$
(b) $\operatorname{cosec} x = 2.2$
(c) $\cot x = -0.3$

(a) $\cos x = -\dfrac{1}{2.2} \Rightarrow x = 117.0°$

(b) $\sin x = \dfrac{1}{2.2} \Rightarrow x = 27.0°$ or $153.0°$

(c) $\tan x = -\dfrac{1}{0.3} \Rightarrow x = 106.7°$

Example 3
Find, in surd form, the exact values of

(a) $\sec 30°$
(b) $\operatorname{cosec} (-300°)$

(a) $\sec 30° = \dfrac{1}{\cos 30°} = \dfrac{1}{\frac{\sqrt{3}}{2}} = \dfrac{2}{\sqrt{3}} = \tfrac{2}{3}\sqrt{3}$

(b) $-300°$ is in the first quadrant. So:

$\operatorname{cosec} (-300°) = \dfrac{1}{\sin (-300°)} = \dfrac{1}{\sin 60°} = \dfrac{1}{\frac{\sqrt{3}}{2}} = \tfrac{2}{3}\sqrt{3}$

4.2 Inverse trigonometric functions

You know from chapter 2 that only one–one functions can have an inverse function. The functions $\sin x$, $\cos x$ and $\tan x$ for $x \in \mathbb{R}$ are many–one functions, as you saw in section 4.2

If, however, the domain of each of these functions is suitably restricted, then it is possible to make the function one–one and to define an inverse function. This is how it is done for the function $\sin x$.

You know that $\sin x$ for the domain $-\frac{\pi}{2} \leqslant x \leqslant \frac{\pi}{2}$ takes all real values in the range $-1 \leqslant \sin x \leqslant 1$ and that it is a one–one function. The graph of the curve $y = \sin x$, $-\frac{\pi}{2} \leqslant x \leqslant \frac{\pi}{2}$, looks like this, where x is in radians:

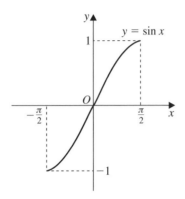

The inverse function of $\sin x$, $-\frac{\pi}{2} \leqslant x \leqslant \frac{\pi}{2}$, is called **arcsin x**. Its domain is $-1 \leqslant x \leqslant 1$ and its range is $-\frac{\pi}{2} \leqslant \arcsin x \leqslant \frac{\pi}{2}$. The graph of $y = \arcsin x$, $-1 \leqslant x \leqslant 1$ looks like this:

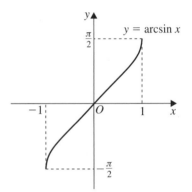

The curves $y = \sin x$ and $y = \arcsin x$ are reflections of each other in the line $y = x$.

The inverse functions of $\cos x$ and $\tan x$ are given by
arccos x with domain $-1 \leqslant x \leqslant 1$ and range $0 \leqslant \arccos x \leqslant \pi$
arctan x with domain $x \in \mathbb{R}$ and range $-\frac{\pi}{2} < x < \frac{\pi}{2}$

The graphs of the functions and the inverse functions look like this:

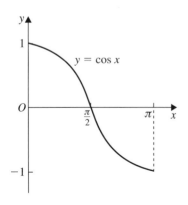

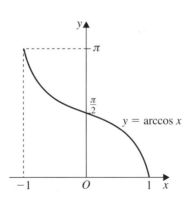

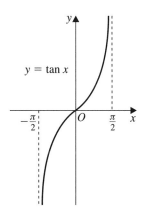

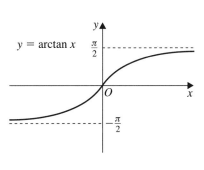

Note: In solutions you may sometimes need to use degrees but more usually for work of this level radians are used; furthermore, radians must be used if derivatives or integrals are being considered.

Example 4

Write down, in radians, the values of (a) $\arcsin\left(-\frac{1}{2}\right)$
(b) $\arccos\left(-\frac{1}{2}\right)$ (c) $\arctan\frac{1}{2}$.

(a) $\arcsin\left(-\frac{1}{2}\right) = -\frac{\pi}{6}$ (or -0.524 radians from your calculator)

(b) $\arccos\left(-\frac{1}{2}\right) = \frac{2\pi}{3}$ (or 2.094 radians from your calculator)

(c) $\arctan\frac{1}{2} = 0.464$ radians (from your calculator)

4.3 Identities

In this triangle

$$\frac{y}{r} = \sin\theta \quad \text{and} \quad \frac{x}{r} = \cos\theta$$

Now
$$\frac{\sin\theta}{\cos\theta} = \frac{y}{r} \div \frac{x}{r} = \frac{y}{r} \times \frac{r}{x} = \frac{y}{x} = \tan\theta$$

Also:
$$\frac{\cos\theta}{\sin\theta} = \frac{x}{r} \div \frac{y}{r} = \frac{x}{r} \times \frac{r}{y} = \frac{x}{y} = \cot\theta$$

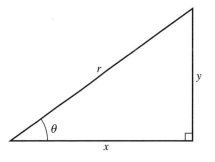

■ **Remember:** $\cot\theta \equiv \dfrac{1}{\tan\theta}, \tan\theta \equiv \dfrac{\sin\theta}{\cos\theta}$ **and** $\cot\theta \equiv \dfrac{\cos\theta}{\sin\theta}$

In this triangle you have
$$x^2 + y^2 = r^2 \qquad \text{(Pythagoras' theorem)}$$
Dividing by r^2 gives
$$\frac{x^2}{r^2} + \frac{y^2}{r^2} = \frac{r^2}{r^2}$$

or:
$$\frac{x^2}{r^2} + \frac{y^2}{r^2} = 1$$

That is:
$$\left(\frac{x}{r}\right)^2 + \left(\frac{y}{r}\right)^2 = 1$$

Using the facts that $\frac{y}{r} = \sin\theta$ and $\frac{x}{r} = \cos\theta$ gives:

$$\cos^2\theta + \sin^2\theta \equiv 1$$

or, more usually:

■ $$\mathbf{\sin^2\theta + \cos^2\theta \equiv 1}$$

which you have seen already in Book P1 (section 2.6).

Divide both sides by $\cos^2\theta$:

$$\frac{\sin^2\theta}{\cos^2\theta} + \frac{\cos^2\theta}{\cos^2\theta} \equiv \frac{1}{\cos^2\theta}$$

$$\left(\frac{\sin\theta}{\cos\theta}\right)^2 + 1 \equiv \left(\frac{1}{\cos\theta}\right)^2$$

That is:
$$\tan^2\theta + 1 \equiv \sec^2\theta$$

or, more usually:

■ $$\mathbf{\sec^2\theta \equiv 1 + \tan^2\theta}$$

Again, starting from $\sin^2\theta + \cos^2\theta \equiv 1$, divide both sides by $\sin^2\theta$:

$$\frac{\sin^2\theta}{\sin^2\theta} + \frac{\cos^2\theta}{\sin^2\theta} \equiv \frac{1}{\sin^2\theta}$$

$$1 + \left(\frac{\cos\theta}{\sin\theta}\right)^2 \equiv \left(\frac{1}{\sin\theta}\right)^2$$

That is:
$$1 + \cot^2\theta \equiv \mathrm{cosec}^2\theta$$

or, more usually:

■ $$\mathbf{\mathrm{cosec}^2\theta \equiv 1 + \cot^2\theta}$$

Although these three identities have been proved for θ acute, they are, in fact, true for all values of θ. You will not be asked to prove them, but you must learn them and use them confidently. They are very useful in the study of Advanced level mathematics. It is therefore *very* important that you remember them. You will be expected to use them in proving other simple identities, in the solution of equations and in calculus.

The general strategy when you are asked to prove an identity is to take the left-hand side (LHS) of the identity and try to rearrange it to obtain the right-hand side (RHS) of the identity, or vice versa if this looks as though it may prove more fruitful.

Example 5

Prove that

$$\tan^2 \theta - \cot^2 \theta \equiv (\sec \theta - \csc \theta)(\sec \theta + \csc \theta)$$

$$\begin{aligned}
\text{LHS} &= \tan^2 \theta - \cot^2 \theta \\
&= (\sec^2 \theta - 1) - (\csc^2 \theta - 1) \\
&= \sec^2 \theta - 1 - \csc^2 \theta + 1 \\
&= \sec^2 \theta - \csc^2 \theta \\
&= (\sec \theta - \csc \theta)(\sec \theta + \csc \theta) \\
&= \text{RHS}
\end{aligned}$$

Example 6

Prove that

$$2 - \tan^2 A \equiv 2\sec^2 A - 3\tan^2 A$$

$$\begin{aligned}
\text{RHS} &= 2\sec^2 A - 3\tan^2 A \\
&= 2(1 + \tan^2 A) - 3\tan^2 A \\
&= 2 + 2\tan^2 A - 3\tan^2 A \\
&= 2 - \tan^2 A \\
&= \text{LHS}
\end{aligned}$$

Exercise 4A

1 Find, to 4 significant figures, the value of:
   (a) $\cot 39°$ (b) $\sec 47°$ (c) $\csc 63°$
   (d) $\sec 23°$ (e) $\cot 149°$ (f) $\csc 323°$
   (g) $\sec 253°$ (h) $\csc 129°$ (i) $\cot 300°$
   (j) $\csc 283°$

2 Find, to 4 significant figures, the value of:
   (a) $\cot 1.6^c$ (b) $\sec 3.4^c$ (c) $\csc 2.3^c$
   (d) $\cot 4.8^c$ (e) $\csc 5^c$ (f) $\sec 6^c$
   (g) $\cot 3.8^c$ (h) $\cot 5.7^c$ (i) $\sec 6.83^c$
   (j) $\csc 8.23^c$

3 Find the values of x, in degrees to $0.1°$, for $0 < x \leqslant 360°$ where:
   (a) $\sec x = 1.813$ (b) $\csc x = -2.164$
   (c) $\cot x = -1.23$ (d) $\sec x = -1.114$
   (e) $\sec x = -1.132$ (f) $\cot x = 0.147$
   (g) $\sec x = 1.614$ (h) $\csc x = 1.816$
   (i) $\cot x = 1.213$ (j) $\csc x = 1.142$

4 Find the values of x, in radians to 3 decimal places, for
$0 < x \leqslant 2\pi$ where:

(a) $\sec x = 1.624$ (b) $\operatorname{cosec} x = -1.624$

(c) $\cot x = 0.718$ (d) $\sec x = -1.934$

(e) $\operatorname{cosec} x = 2.016$ (f) $\cot x = -1.913$

(g) $\sec x = 1.323$ (h) $\operatorname{cosec} x = -1.762$

(i) $\cot x = -0.323$ (j) $\sec x = -2.053$

5 Find, in radians in terms of π, the value of:

(a) $\arcsin 1$ (b) $\arcsin(-\frac{\sqrt{3}}{2})$ (c) $\arccos \frac{\sqrt{3}}{2}$

(d) $\arccos 0$ (e) $\arctan(-\sqrt{3})$ (f) $\arctan(2 + \sqrt{3})$

6 Giving your answer in radians to 2 decimal places, find the
value of:

(a) $\arcsin 0.75$ (b) $\arctan 7$ (c) $\arccos(-0.735)$

(d) $\arcsin(-0.993)$ (e) $\arccos(-0.111)$ (f) $\arctan(-0.352)$

7 Given that $y = \operatorname{cosec} x$, $-\frac{\pi}{2} \leqslant x \leqslant \frac{\pi}{2}$, $x \neq 0$, sketch the graphs
of the curves $y = \operatorname{cosec} x$ and $y = \operatorname{arccosec} x$, where $\operatorname{arccosec} x$
is the inverse function of $\operatorname{cosec} x$, $-\frac{\pi}{2} \leqslant x \leqslant \frac{\pi}{2}$, $x \neq 0$.

8 Given that $y = \cot x$, $-\frac{\pi}{2} < x < \frac{\pi}{2}$, $x \neq 0$, sketch the graphs of
the curves $y = \cot x$ and $y = \operatorname{arccot} x$, where $\operatorname{arccot} x$ is the
inverse function of $\cot x$, $-\frac{\pi}{2} < x < \frac{\pi}{2}$, $x \neq 0$.

9 Given that $y = \sec x$, $0 \leqslant x \leqslant \pi$, $x \neq \frac{\pi}{2}$, sketch the graphs of
the curves $y = \sec x$ and $y = \operatorname{arcsec} x$, where $\operatorname{arcsec} x$ is the
inverse function of $\sec x$, $0 \leqslant x \leqslant \pi$, $x \neq \frac{\pi}{2}$.

10 Find the smallest positive value of x for which

(a) $\tan 2x = \sqrt{3}$

(b) $\sin(2x - 3) = \frac{1}{2}$

(c) $\sin x = \cos(\arctan 1)$

Prove the identities:

11 $\cos^2 \theta + 3\sin^2 \theta \equiv 3 - 2\cos^2 \theta$

12 $\operatorname{cosec} \theta - \sin \theta \equiv \cos \theta \cot \theta$

13 $\cot^2 \theta + \cos^2 \theta \equiv (\operatorname{cosec} \theta - \sin \theta)(\operatorname{cosec} \theta + \sin \theta)$

14 $\sec^2 \theta - \sin^2 \theta \equiv \tan^2 \theta + \cos^2 \theta$

15 $\sec^4 \theta - \tan^4 \theta \equiv 2\sec^2 \theta - 1$

16 $(\cos\theta + \sec\theta)^2 \equiv \tan^2\theta + \cos^2\theta + 3$

17 $\cos^4\theta - \sin^4\theta \equiv \cos^2\theta - \sin^2\theta$

18 $\text{cosec}^2\theta(\tan^2\theta - \sin^2\theta) \equiv \tan^2\theta$

19 $\left(\dfrac{1+\sin\theta}{\cos\theta}\right)^2 + \left(\dfrac{1-\sin\theta}{\cos\theta}\right)^2 \equiv 2 + 4\tan^2\theta$

20 $(\tan\theta + \sec\theta)(\cot\theta + \text{cosec}\,\theta) \equiv (1+\sec\theta)(1+\text{cosec}\,\theta)$

21 Given that $p\sin\theta = 4$ and $p\cos\theta = 4\sqrt{3}$, $p > 0$, find p and the smallest positive value of θ.

22 Given that $q\,\text{cosec}\,\alpha = 17$ and $q\cot\alpha = 8$, $q > 0$, find q and the smallest positive value of α.

23 If $3\tan u = c$ and $4\sec u = d$, find a relation between c and d.

24 If $24\sin\beta = m$ and $7\cos\beta = m$, $m > 0$, find m and the possible values of β in the interval $0 \leqslant \beta \leqslant 360°$.

4.4 The addition formulae $\sin(A \pm B)$, $\cos(A \pm B)$, $\tan(A \pm B)$ and simple applications

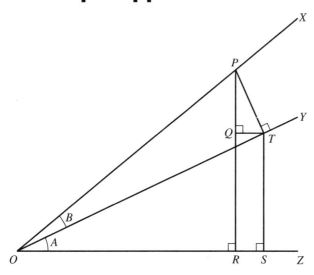

In the diagram the angles $TOR = A$ and $POT = B$ are each acute and the angle $POR = (A + B)$ is also acute. PT is perpendicular to OY, PR is perpendicular to OZ, TS is perpendicular to OZ and QT is perpendicular to PR.

Since QT is parallel to OS,

$$\angle QTO = \angle TOS = A$$

Since $\angle PTO = 90°$, $\angle PTQ = 90° - A$. Since PQT is a triangle,

$$\angle PQT + \angle PTQ + \angle QPT = 180°$$

That is:

$$90° + (90° - A) + \angle QPT = 180°$$

$$180° - A + \angle QPT = 180°$$

$$\angle QPT = A$$

Now:

$$\sin(A + B) = \frac{PR}{OP}$$

$$= \frac{PQ + QR}{OP}$$

$$= \frac{PQ + TS}{OP}$$

$$= \frac{PQ}{OP} + \frac{TS}{OP}$$

$$= \left(\frac{PQ}{PT} \times \frac{PT}{OP}\right) + \left(\frac{TS}{OT} \times \frac{OT}{OP}\right)$$

$$= \cos A \sin B + \sin A \cos B$$

■ So: $\quad \sin(A + B) \equiv \sin A \cos B + \cos A \sin B$

Similarly:

$$\cos(A + B) = \frac{OR}{OP}$$

$$= \frac{OS - RS}{OP}$$

$$= \frac{OS - QT}{OP}$$

$$= \frac{OS}{OP} - \frac{QT}{OP}$$

$$= \left(\frac{OS}{OT} \times \frac{OT}{OP}\right) - \left(\frac{QT}{PT} \times \frac{PT}{OP}\right)$$

■ $\quad \cos(A + B) \equiv \cos A \cos B - \sin A \sin B$

We have shown that

$$\sin(A + B) \equiv \sin A \cos B + \cos A \sin B$$

and

$$\cos(A + B) \equiv \cos A \cos B - \sin A \sin B$$

for A and B acute. However, these identities are, in fact, true for *all* values of A and B.

So replacing B by $-B$ in the identity for $\sin(A + B)$ gives

$$\sin(A - B) \equiv \sin A \cos(-B) + \cos A \sin(-B)$$

or:

- $$\sin(A - B) \equiv \sin A \cos B - \cos A \sin B$$

and replacing B by $-B$ in the identity for $\cos(A + B)$ gives

$$\cos(A - B) \equiv \cos A \cos(-B) - \sin A \sin(-B)$$
$$= \cos A \cos B - \sin A(-\sin B)$$

- $$\cos(A - B) \equiv \cos A \cos B + \sin A \sin B$$

Now

$$\tan(A + B) \equiv \frac{\sin(A + B)}{\cos(A + B)}$$

$$= \frac{\sin A \cos B + \cos A \sin B}{\cos A \cos B - \sin A \sin B}$$

$$= \frac{\dfrac{\sin A \cos B}{\cos A \cos B} + \dfrac{\cos A \sin B}{\cos A \cos B}}{\dfrac{\cos A \cos B}{\cos A \cos B} - \dfrac{\sin A \sin B}{\cos A \cos B}}$$

- $$\tan(A + B) \equiv \frac{\tan A + \tan B}{1 - \tan A \tan B}$$

Replace B by $-B$:

$$\tan(A - B) \equiv \frac{\tan A + \tan(-B)}{1 - \tan A \tan(-B)}$$

$$= \frac{\tan A - \tan B}{1 - \tan A(-\tan B)}$$

- $$\tan(A - B) \equiv \frac{\tan A - \tan B}{1 + \tan A \tan B}$$

Example 7

Evaluate $\tan 75°$ without the use of a calculator.

$$\tan 75° \equiv \tan(45° + 30°)$$

$$= \frac{\tan 45° + \tan 30°}{1 - \tan 45° \tan 30°}$$

$$= \frac{1 + \dfrac{1}{\sqrt{3}}}{1 - \left(1 \times \dfrac{1}{\sqrt{3}}\right)}$$

$$= \frac{\sqrt{3} + 1}{\sqrt{3} - 1}$$

Example 8

Given that angles A and B are acute and $\sin A = \frac{4}{5}$ and $\cos B = \frac{7}{25}$, find, without the use of a calculator, the value of

(a) $\cos(A + B)$ (b) $\tan(A - B)$.

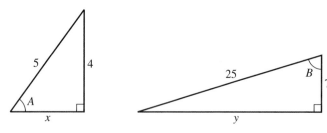

Using Pythagoras' theorem:

$$x^2 + 16 = 25 \qquad\qquad y^2 + 49 = 625$$
$$x^2 = 9 \qquad\qquad\qquad y^2 = 576$$
$$x = 3 \qquad\qquad\qquad\quad y = 24$$

(a)
$$\cos(A + B) \equiv \cos A \cos B - \sin A \sin B$$
$$= \left(\tfrac{3}{5} \times \tfrac{7}{25}\right) - \left(\tfrac{4}{5} \times \tfrac{24}{25}\right)$$
$$= \tfrac{21}{125} - \tfrac{96}{125}$$
$$= -\tfrac{75}{125} = -\tfrac{3}{5}$$

(b)
$$\tan(A - B) \equiv \frac{\tan A - \tan B}{1 + \tan A \tan B}$$
$$= \frac{\frac{4}{3} - \frac{24}{7}}{1 + \left(\frac{4}{3} \times \frac{24^{8}}{7}\right)}$$
$$= \frac{\frac{28}{21} - \frac{72}{21}}{1 + \frac{32}{7}}$$
$$= \frac{-\frac{44}{21}}{\frac{39}{7}}$$
$$= -\tfrac{44}{{}_{3}\cancel{21}} \times \tfrac{\cancel{7}}{39}$$
$$= -\tfrac{44}{117}$$

Example 9

Find the exact value of

$$\sin 157^\circ \cos 97^\circ - \cos 157^\circ \sin 97^\circ$$

$$\sin 157^\circ \cos 97^\circ - \cos 157^\circ \sin 97^\circ = \sin(157^\circ - 97^\circ)$$

$$= \sin 60^\circ = \frac{\sqrt{3}}{2}$$

Example 10

Given that $\sin A = \frac{12}{13}$ and $90° < A < 180°$, and $\tan B = \frac{4}{3}$ and $180° < B < 270°$, find the value of:
(a) $\sin(A + B)$ (b) $\cos(A - B)$.

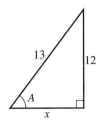
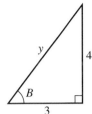

If A and B were acute, then by Pythagoras' theorem:

$$x^2 + 12^2 = 13^2 \qquad\qquad y^2 = 4^2 + 3^2$$
$$x^2 + 144 = 169 \qquad\qquad y^2 = 16 + 9$$
$$x^2 = 25 \qquad\qquad y^2 = 25$$
$$x = 5 \qquad\qquad y = 5$$

If A were acute then $\sin A$ would be $\frac{12}{13}$ and $\cos A$ would be $\frac{5}{13}$. But since $90° < A < 180°$

$$\sin A = \frac{12}{13} \quad \text{and} \quad \cos A = -\frac{5}{13}$$

Similarly, if B were acute then $\sin B$ would be $\frac{4}{5}$ and $\cos B$ would be $\frac{3}{5}$. However, $180° < B < 270°$. So

$$\sin B = -\frac{4}{5} \quad \text{and} \quad \cos B = -\frac{3}{5}$$

(a) $\qquad \sin(A + B) \equiv \sin A \cos B + \cos A \sin B$

$$= \tfrac{12}{13}\left(-\tfrac{3}{5}\right) + \left(-\tfrac{5}{13}\right)\left(-\tfrac{4}{5}\right)$$
$$= -\tfrac{36}{65} + \tfrac{20}{65}$$
$$= -\tfrac{16}{65}$$

(b) $\qquad \cos(A - B) \equiv \cos A \cos B + \sin A \sin B$

$$= \left(-\tfrac{5}{13}\right)\left(-\tfrac{3}{5}\right) + \left(\tfrac{12}{13}\right)\left(-\tfrac{4}{5}\right)$$
$$= \tfrac{15}{65} - \tfrac{48}{65}$$
$$= -\tfrac{33}{65}$$

Exercise 4B

1 Find, without using a calculator, the exact value of:
   (a) $\sin 75°$ (b) $\cos 75°$
   (c) $\tan 105°$ (d) $\sin 15°$
   (e) $\cos 105°$ (f) $\tan 15°$
   (g) $\sin 165°$ (h) $\cos 165°$

2 Find, without using a calculator, the exact value of:

(a) $\sin 40° \cos 50° + \cos 40° \sin 50°$

(b) $\cos 70° \cos 10° + \sin 70° \sin 10°$

(c) $\dfrac{\tan 80° + \tan 40°}{1 - \tan 80° \tan 40°}$

(d) $\cos 20° \cos 40° - \sin 20° \sin 40°$

(e) $\sin 50° \cos 20° - \cos 50° \sin 20°$

(f) $\dfrac{\tan 47° - \tan 17°}{1 + \tan 47° \tan 17°}$

3 Simplify:

(a) $\sin \theta \cos 3\theta + \cos \theta \sin 3\theta$

(b) $\cos 5\theta \cos 2\theta + \sin 5\theta \sin 2\theta$

(c) $\dfrac{\tan 4\theta - \tan 2\theta}{1 + \tan 4\theta \tan 2\theta}$

(d) $3 \sin 7\theta \cos 2\theta - 3 \cos 7\theta \sin 2\theta$

(e) $4 \sin 6\theta \sin 4\theta + 4 \cos 6\theta \cos 4\theta$

(f) $2 \sin \theta \sin 4\theta + 2 \cos \theta \cos 4\theta$

4 If A and B are acute angles such that $\sin A = \frac{3}{5}$ and $\sin B = \frac{12}{13}$, find the exact value of:

(a) $\sin (A + B)$ (b) $\cos (A - B)$

(c) $\tan (A + B)$ (d) $\cot (A - B)$

5 If $\sin A = \frac{3}{5}$ and $\cos B = \frac{5}{13}$ where A is obtuse and B is acute, find the exact value of:

(a) $\sin (A - B)$ (b) $\sec (A + B)$

(c) $\tan (A - B)$ (d) $\cot (A + B)$

6 If $\cos A = \frac{5}{13}$ and $\sin B = \frac{24}{25}$ where A is acute and B is obtuse, find the exact value of:

(a) $\sin (A + B)$ (b) $\operatorname{cosec} (A - B)$

(c) $\cos (A - B)$ (d) $\sec (A + B)$

(e) $\tan (A - B)$ (f) $\cot (A + B)$

7 Find, without using calculus, (i) the greatest, (ii) the least value that the following can take, and state the value of θ, $0 < \theta \leqslant 360°$, for which these values occur.

(a) $\sin \theta \cos 70° + \cos \theta \sin 70°$

(b) $\sin \theta \cos 20° - \cos \theta \sin 20°$

(c) $\sin 25° \cos \theta + \cos 25° \sin \theta$

8 Find, without using calculus, the least value of the following and the value of θ, $0 < \theta \leqslant 360°$, for which this value occurs.

(a) $\cos 50° \cos \theta + \sin 50° \sin \theta$

(b) $\sin \theta \sin 43° + \cos \theta \cos 43°$

(c) $3 \cos \theta \cos 105° - 3 \sin \theta \sin 105°$

4.5 Double angle formulae

In section 4.4 you were introduced to the identity

$$\sin (A + B) \equiv \sin A \cos B + \cos A \sin B$$

Now let $B = A$; then:

$$\sin (A + A) \equiv \sin A \cos A + \cos A \sin A$$

That is:
$$\sin 2A \equiv \sin A \cos A + \sin A \cos A$$

or:

■ $$\sin 2A \equiv 2 \sin A \cos A$$

Similarly:

$$\cos (A + B) \equiv \cos A \cos B - \sin A \sin B$$

Again, let $B = A$:

$$\cos (A + A) \equiv \cos A \cos A - \sin A \sin A$$

That is:

■ $$\cos 2A \equiv \cos^2 A - \sin^2 A$$

Now $$\sin^2 A + \cos^2 A \equiv 1$$

or $$\cos^2 A \equiv 1 - \sin^2 A$$

So: $$\cos 2A \equiv (1 - \sin^2 A) - \sin^2 A$$

■ $$\cos 2A \equiv 1 - 2 \sin^2 A$$

Also, since $\sin^2 A + \cos^2 A \equiv 1$,

$$\sin^2 A \equiv 1 - \cos^2 A$$

So if $\cos 2A \equiv \cos^2 A - \sin^2 A$, then

$$\cos 2A \equiv \cos^2 A - (1 - \cos^2 A)$$
$$\equiv \cos^2 A - 1 + \cos^2 A$$

or:

■ $$\cos 2A \equiv 2 \cos^2 A - 1$$

Finally, you learned in section 4.4 that

$$\tan (A + B) \equiv \frac{\tan A + \tan B}{1 - \tan A \tan B}$$

Let $B = A$; then:

$$\tan (A + A) \equiv \frac{\tan A + \tan A}{1 - \tan A \tan A}$$

So:

$$\blacksquare \qquad \tan 2A \equiv \frac{2 \tan A}{1 - \tan^2 A}$$

These five results are known as the **double angle formulae**, because they allow you to convert from double angles $(2A)$ to single angles (A). Once again, you must learn these.

Half angle formulae

From the double angle formulae you can find the half angle formulae.

$$\cos 2A \equiv 1 - 2 \sin^2 A$$

So: $\qquad\qquad 2 \sin^2 A \equiv 1 - \cos 2A$

or: $\qquad\qquad \sin^2 A \equiv \tfrac{1}{2}(1 - \cos 2A)$

Let $A = \tfrac{1}{2}\theta$. Then:

$$\blacksquare \qquad \sin^2 \tfrac{1}{2}\theta \equiv \tfrac{1}{2}(1 - \cos \theta)$$

Also: $\qquad\qquad \cos 2A \equiv 2 \cos^2 A - 1$

So: $\qquad\qquad 2 \cos^2 A \equiv \cos 2A + 1$

or: $\qquad\qquad \cos^2 A \equiv \tfrac{1}{2}(\cos 2A + 1)$

Again, let $A = \tfrac{1}{2}\theta$. Then:

$$\blacksquare \qquad \cos^2 \tfrac{1}{2}\theta \equiv \tfrac{1}{2}(1 + \cos \theta)$$

So, given the value of $\cos \theta$, you can now find the value of $\sin \tfrac{1}{2}\theta$ and $\cos \tfrac{1}{2}\theta$. This will be particularly useful in integration and in the solution of equations.

Example 11

Evaluate exactly $2 \sin 15° \cos 15°$.

Since $2 \sin A \cos A \equiv \sin 2A$,

then: $\qquad 2 \sin 15° \cos 15° \equiv \sin(2 \times 15°)$

$$= \sin 30°$$

$$= \tfrac{1}{2}$$

Example 12

Given that θ is acute and $\sin\theta = \frac{5}{13}$, find the exact value of $\sin 2\theta$.

By Pythagoras' theorem:

$$x^2 + 5^2 = 13^2$$

$$x^2 + 25 = 169$$

$$x^2 = 169 - 25 = 144$$

$$x = 12$$

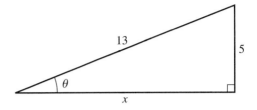

So:

$$\cos\theta = \frac{12}{13}$$

$$\sin 2\theta \equiv 2\sin\theta\cos\theta$$

$$= 2 \times \tfrac{5}{13} \times \tfrac{12}{13}$$

$$= \tfrac{120}{169}$$

Example 13

Prove the identity: $\cot A - \tan A \equiv 2\cot 2A$

$$\text{RHS} \equiv 2\cot 2A$$

$$= \frac{2}{\tan 2A}$$

$$= 2\left(\frac{1 - \tan^2 A}{2\tan A}\right)$$

$$= 2\left(\frac{1}{2\tan A} - \frac{\tan^2 A}{2\tan A}\right)$$

$$= \frac{\not{2}}{\not{2}\tan A} - \frac{\not{2}\tan^2 A}{\not{2}\tan A}$$

$$= \frac{1}{\tan A} - \tan A$$

$$= \cot A - \tan A$$

$$= \text{LHS}$$

Example 14

Eliminate θ from $x = \cos 2\theta - 1$, $y = 2\sin\theta$.

$$x = \cos 2\theta - 1$$

$$= (1 - 2\sin^2\theta) - 1$$

$$x = -2\sin^2\theta$$

Now $y = 2\sin\theta$

$$\frac{y}{2} = \sin\theta$$

$$\left(\frac{y}{2}\right)^2 = \sin^2\theta$$

So:

$$x = -2\left(\frac{y}{2}\right)^2$$

$$= \frac{-2y^2}{4}$$

$$4x + 2y^2 = 0$$

or:

$$2x + y^2 = 0$$

Exercise 4C

1 Find, without using a calculator, the exact value of:

(a) $2\sin 75° \cos 75°$ (b) $\cos^2 22\frac{1}{2}° - \sin^2 22\frac{1}{2}°$

(c) $\dfrac{2\tan 67\frac{1}{2}°}{1 - \tan^2 67\frac{1}{2}°}$ (d) $1 - 2\sin^2 15°$

(e) $2\cos^2 105°$ (f) $\sec 112\frac{1}{2}° \operatorname{cosec} 112\frac{1}{2}°$

(g) $\dfrac{1 - \tan^2 15°}{\tan 15°}$ (h) $\sin^2 75°$

2 If $\cos\theta = \frac{3}{5}$ and θ is acute, find the exact value of:

(a) $\sin 2\theta$ (b) $\cos 2\theta$ (c) $\tan 2\theta$

3 If $\tan\theta = \frac{12}{5}$ and θ is acute, find the exact value of:

(a) $\sin 2\theta$ (b) $\cos 2\theta$ (c) $\tan 2\theta$

4 Given that $\sin\theta = \frac{7}{25}$ and that θ is obtuse, find the exact value of:

(a) $\sin 2\theta$ (b) $\sec 2\theta$ (c) $\cot 2\theta$

5 Given that $\tan\theta = -\frac{3}{4}$ and that θ is obtuse, find the exact value of:

(a) $\sec 2\theta$ (b) $\operatorname{cosec} 2\theta$ (c) $\tan 2\theta$

6 Given that $\sin 2\theta = 1$ and that θ is acute, find the exact value of:

(a) $\sin\theta$ (b) $\cos\theta$ (c) $\tan\theta$

7 Find the possible values of $\tan\frac{1}{2}\theta$ when $\tan\theta = \frac{3}{4}$.

8 Find the possible values of $\tan\frac{1}{2}\theta$ when $\tan\theta = \frac{7}{24}$.

9 Obtain an expression for $\sin 3\theta$ in terms of $\sin\theta$ and hence find the value of $\sin 3\theta$ if $\sin\theta = \frac{1}{8}$.

10 Obtain an expression for $\cos 3\theta$ in terms of $\cos \theta$ and hence find the value of $\cos 3\theta$ if $\cos \theta = \frac{1}{4}$.

11 Eliminate θ from the following pairs of equations:

(a) $x = \sin 2\theta + 2$, $\quad y = \cos \theta$

(b) $x = 1 + \cos \theta$, $\quad y = 3 \cos 2\theta$

(c) $x = \tan 2\theta$, $\quad y = \tan \theta$

(d) $x = 3 + \cos 2\theta$, $\quad y = \sec \theta$

(e) $x = \operatorname{cosec} \theta$, $\quad y = 1 - \cos 2\theta$

Prove the following identities:

12 $\dfrac{\cos 2A}{\cos A - \sin A} \equiv \cos A + \sin A$

13 $2 \operatorname{cosec} 2\theta \equiv \sec \theta \operatorname{cosec} \theta$

14 $\cot \theta - \tan \theta \equiv 2 \cot 2\theta$

15 $\tan 2\theta \sec \theta \equiv 2 \sin \theta \sec 2\theta$

16 $\sin 2\theta \equiv \dfrac{2 \tan \theta}{1 + \tan^2 \theta}$

17 $\dfrac{1}{\cos \theta - \sin \theta} - \dfrac{1}{\cos \theta + \sin \theta} \equiv 2 \sin \theta \sec 2\theta$

18 $\dfrac{\sin 2\theta}{1 - \cos 2\theta} \equiv \cot \theta$

19 $\tan 3\theta \equiv \dfrac{3 \tan \theta - \tan^3 \theta}{1 - 3 \tan^2 \theta}$

20 $\dfrac{\sin 2\theta + \sin \theta}{\cos 2\theta + \cos \theta + 1} \equiv \tan \theta$

4.6 Sum and product formulae

Starting from the identities for $\sin (A + B)$ and $\sin (A - B)$ you have:

$$\sin (A + B) \equiv \sin A \cos B + \cos A \sin B$$
$$\sin (A - B) \equiv \sin A \cos B - \cos A \sin B$$

If you add these identities you get

■ $\qquad$ **2 sin A cos $B \equiv$ sin $(A + B)$ + sin $(A - B)$**

If you subtract the second from the first you get

■ $\qquad$ **2 cos A sin $B \equiv$ sin $(A + B)$ − sin $(A - B)$**

Similarly by considering the identities for $\cos(A+B)$ and $\cos(A-B)$ you obtain:

- $$2\cos A \cos B \equiv \cos(A+B) + \cos(A-B)$$
- $$2\sin A \sin B \equiv \cos(A-B) - \cos(A+B)$$

These identities change *products* of sines and/or cosines into *sums*.

Example 15

Express as a sum:

(a) $2\cos 80° \cos 40°$ (b) $\sin 3x \cos x$.

(a) Using the identity

$$2\cos A \cos B \equiv \cos(A+B) + \cos(A-B)$$

with $A = 80°$ and $B = 40°$ you have

$$2\cos 80° \cos 40° = \cos(80° + 40°) + \cos(80° - 40°)$$
$$= \cos 120° + \cos 40°$$

(b) Using the identity

$$2\sin A \cos B \equiv \sin(A+B) + \sin(A-B)$$

with $A = 3x$ and $B = x$ you have

$$2\sin 3x \cos x = \sin(3x + x) + \sin(3x - x)$$

That is: $\sin 3x \cos x = \frac{1}{2}[\sin 4x + \sin 2x]$

If you now write $A + B = P$ and $A - B = Q$, by adding

$$(A+B) + (A-B) = 2A = P + Q \text{ or } A = \frac{P+Q}{2},$$

and by subtracting

$$(A+B) - (A-B) = 2B = P - Q \text{ or } B = \frac{P-Q}{2}$$

The four formulae which change products of sines and/or cosines into sums can be changed around to give:

- $$\sin P + \sin Q \equiv 2\sin\frac{P+Q}{2}\cos\frac{P-Q}{2}$$

- $$\sin P - \sin Q \equiv 2\cos\frac{P+Q}{2}\sin\frac{P-Q}{2}$$

- $$\cos P + \cos Q \equiv 2\cos\frac{P+Q}{2}\cos\frac{P-Q}{2}$$

- $$\cos Q - \cos P \equiv 2\sin\frac{P+Q}{2}\sin\frac{P-Q}{2}$$

You should remember that all eight formulae can be very quickly obtained from the basic identities for $\sin(A \pm B)$ and $\cos(A \pm B)$.

Example 16

Express as a product:

(a) $\sin 72° - \sin 48°$ (b) $\cos 48° - \cos 72°$.

(a) Use the identity

$$\sin P - \sin Q \equiv 2\cos\frac{P+Q}{2}\sin\frac{P-Q}{2}$$

with $P = 72°$ and $Q = 48°$, to obtain

$$\sin 72° - \sin 48° = 2\cos\frac{72° + 48°}{2}\sin\frac{72° - 48°}{2}$$
$$= 2\cos 60°\sin 12°$$

(b) Use the identity

$$\cos Q - \cos P \equiv 2\sin\frac{P+Q}{2}\sin\frac{P-Q}{2}$$

with $P = 72°$, $Q = 48°$ to obtain

$$\cos 48° - \cos 72° = 2\sin\frac{72° + 48°}{2}\sin\frac{72° - 48°}{2}$$
$$= 2\sin 60°\sin 12°$$

4.7 Solving trigonometric equations

In chapter 2, section 2.7 of Book P1 you were shown how to solve trigonometric equations such as:

$$\sin 2x = \tfrac{1}{2} \quad \text{for} \quad 0 < x \leqslant 2\pi$$

and : $\quad \tan(3x - 40°) = 0.61 \quad \text{for} \quad 0 < x \leqslant 360°$

Now that you know a number of trigonometric identities, you can solve some further trigonometric equations. In all such equations, the strategy is to reduce the equation to one trigonometric ratio only, using the identities proved in this chapter.

Example 17

Solve the equation

$$6\cos^2\theta + \sin\theta - 5 = 0 \quad \text{for} \quad 0 < \theta \leqslant 360°$$

$$6\cos^2\theta + \sin\theta - 5 = 0$$
$$6(1 - \sin^2\theta) + \sin\theta - 5 = 0$$
$$6 - 6\sin^2\theta + \sin\theta - 5 = 0$$
$$-6\sin^2\theta + \sin\theta + 1 = 0$$

or: $\qquad\qquad 6\sin^2\theta - \sin\theta - 1 = 0$

$$(3\sin\theta + 1)(2\sin\theta - 1) = 0$$

So either $3 \sin \theta + 1 = 0$ or $2 \sin \theta - 1 = 0$

that is: $\qquad\qquad \sin \theta = -\frac{1}{3} \quad$ or $\quad \sin \theta = \frac{1}{2}$

Thus: $\qquad\qquad \theta = 199.5°, \, 340.5°$ or $\theta = 30°, \, 150°$

So $\theta = 30°, \, 150°, \, 199.5°, \, 340.5°$.

Example 18

Solve the equation

$$\cos \theta \cos 30° - \sin \theta \sin 30° = \tfrac{1}{2}$$

for $-180° < \theta < 180°$.

$$\cos \theta \cos 30° - \sin \theta \sin 30° = \tfrac{1}{2}$$

$\Rightarrow \qquad\qquad \cos(\theta + 30°) = \tfrac{1}{2}$

That is: $\qquad\qquad \theta + 30° = -60°, \, 60°$

So: $\qquad\qquad\qquad \theta = -90°$ or $30°$

Example 19

Solve the equation

$$\sec^2 \theta = 3 - \tan \theta$$

for $0 \leqslant \theta < 360°$.

Since $\sec^2 \theta \equiv 1 + \tan^2 \theta$,

$$\sec^2 \theta = 3 - \tan \theta$$

$\Rightarrow \qquad\qquad 1 + \tan^2 \theta = 3 - \tan \theta$

$$\tan^2 \theta + \tan \theta - 2 = 0$$

$$(\tan \theta - 1)(\tan \theta + 2) = 0$$

$$\tan \theta = 1 \quad \text{or} \quad \tan \theta = -2$$

$$\theta = 45°, \, 225° \quad \text{or} \quad \theta = 116.6°, \, 296.6°$$

So: $\qquad\qquad \theta = 45°, \, 116.6°, \, 225°, \, 296.6°$

Example 20

Solve the equation

$$\cos(\theta + 60°) = \sin \theta$$

for $0 < \theta \leqslant 360°$.

$$\cos(\theta + 60°) = \sin \theta$$

$\Rightarrow \qquad\qquad \cos \theta \cos 60° - \sin \theta \sin 60° = \sin \theta$

So: $\qquad\qquad (\cos \theta \times \tfrac{1}{2}) - (\sin \theta \times \tfrac{\sqrt{3}}{2}) = \sin \theta$

That is:
$$\cos\theta - \sqrt{3}\sin\theta = 2\sin\theta$$
$$\cos\theta = 2\sin\theta + \sqrt{3}\sin\theta$$
$$\cos\theta = (2+\sqrt{3})\sin\theta$$
$$\frac{1}{2+\sqrt{3}} = \frac{\sin\theta}{\cos\theta}$$
$$\tan\theta = \frac{1}{2+\sqrt{3}}$$

So:
$$\theta = 15° \text{ or } 195°$$

Example 21
Solve $\cos 2\theta = \tan 2\theta$ for $0 \leqslant \theta \leqslant \pi$.

Since $\tan 2\theta = \dfrac{\sin 2\theta}{\cos 2\theta}$,
$$\cos 2\theta = \tan 2\theta$$
$$\Rightarrow \qquad \cos 2\theta = \frac{\sin 2\theta}{\cos 2\theta}$$
$$\cos^2 2\theta = \sin 2\theta$$
$$1 - \sin^2 2\theta = \sin 2\theta$$
$$\sin^2 2\theta + \sin 2\theta - 1 = 0$$
$$\sin 2\theta = \frac{-1 \pm \sqrt{(1+4)}}{2}$$
$$= \frac{-1 \pm \sqrt{5}}{2}$$
$$= 0.618\,03 \text{ or } -1.618\,03$$

Reject $\sin 2\theta = -1.618\,03$ ($\sin x$ has a minimum value of -1)
$$2\theta = 0.666\,23 \text{ or } 2.475\,35$$
$$\theta = 0.333\,11 \text{ or } 1.237\,67$$

So:
$$\theta = 0.333^c \text{ or } 1.238^c \text{ (3 d.p.)}$$

Example 22
Solve $\cos 3x + \cos x = 0$ for $0 \leqslant x \leqslant \pi$.

Using the formula
$$\cos P + \cos Q = 2\cos\frac{P+Q}{2}\cos\frac{P-Q}{2}$$

you have
$$\cos 3x + \cos x = 2\cos\frac{3x+x}{2}\cos\frac{3x-x}{2}$$
$$= 2\cos 2x \cos x$$

The equation to solve now is

$$2\cos 2x \cos x = 0$$

Either $\cos 2x = 0 \Rightarrow 2x = \frac{\pi}{2}, \frac{3\pi}{2} \Rightarrow x = \frac{\pi}{4}, \frac{3\pi}{4}$

or $\cos x = 0 \Rightarrow x = \frac{\pi}{2}$.

The complete solution is $x = \frac{\pi}{4}, \frac{\pi}{2}, \frac{3\pi}{4}$.

Exercise 4D

In questions 1–5 write each of the following as a product of factors of sines and cosines

1 $\sin 40° + \sin 76°$ **2** $\sin 40° - \sin 16°$

3 $\cos 100° + \cos 56°$ **4** $\cos 72° - \cos 58°$

5 $\cos 8.5° - \cos 50.7°$

In questions 6–10 write each of the following as a sum or difference of sines and/or cosines.

6 $2\cos 47° \sin 13°$ **7** $2\sin 47° \sin 13°$

8 $\sin 128° \cos 69°$ **9** $\cos 250° \cos 130°$

10 $\sin 30°(\cos 60° \cos 20° + \sin 60° \sin 20°)$

Solve these equations for $0 \leqslant \theta \leqslant 360°$, giving θ to 1 decimal place where appropriate:

11 $\sin\theta \cos 15° + \cos\theta \sin 15° = 0.4$

12 $\cos\theta \cos 33° - \sin\theta \sin 33° = -0.2$

13 $\dfrac{\tan 47° - \tan\theta}{1 + \tan 47° \tan\theta} = 1.5$ **14** $\cos(\theta - 45°) = \frac{1}{\sqrt{3}}\cos\theta$

15 $\sin(\theta + 30°) = 2\cos\theta$ **16** $2\cos(\theta - 60°) = \sin\theta$

17 $\sin(\theta + 15°) = 3\cos(\theta - 15°)$ **18** $2\sin\theta \cos\theta = 1 - 2\sin^2\theta$

19 $\sin 2\theta + \sin\theta - \tan\theta = 0$ **20** $\sin 2\theta + \sin\theta = 0$

21 $\cos 2\theta = 2\sin\theta$ **22** $\tan 2\theta + \tan\theta = 0$

23 $3\cos^2\theta - 2\sin\theta - 2 = 0$ **24** $3\sec^2\theta + 1 = 8\tan\theta$

25 $2 + \cos\theta \sin\theta = 8\sin^2\theta$ **26** $\sin 2\theta = \cos\theta$

27 $3\cos 2\theta - 7\cos\theta - 2 = 0$ **28** $\sec^2\theta = 4\tan\theta$

29 $2\sin 2\theta = \tan\theta$ **30** $\sin 2\theta - \tan\theta = 0$

31 $\operatorname{cosec}^2\theta = 3\cot\theta - 1$ **32** $3\cos 2\theta + 2\sin^2\theta + 1 = 2\sin\theta$

33 $(\sin\theta + \cos\theta)^2 = \frac{1}{2}$ **34** $2\tan\theta + \sin 2\theta \sec\theta = 1 + \sec\theta$

35 $\sin(2\theta - 30°) = \cos(2\theta + 30°)$

36 $\cot\theta + 3\cot 2\theta - 1 = 0$ **37** $\tan(3\theta - 20°) = \sqrt{2} - 1$

38 $3\tan\theta + 4\sin\theta = 0$ **39** $\sin 4\theta \sin\theta = 0$

40 $\cos 2\theta \cos 4\theta = 0$ **41** $\sin 5\theta \cos 3\theta = 0$

42 $\sin 3\theta + \sin\theta = 0$ **43** $\cos\theta - \cos 2\theta + \cos 3\theta = 0$

4.8 Alternative forms of
a cos θ + *b* sin θ

The form of the curve with equation $y = \cos x$ is well known to you and is shown below for real values of x.

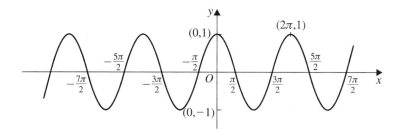

Note that the domain of the function $\cos x$ is $x \in \mathbb{R}$, that the range is $[-1, 1]$ and that it is a many–one mapping.

Section 2.7 described simple transformations of graphs. Any curve with equation $y = R\cos(x + \alpha)$, where R is a positive constant and α is constant looks like this:

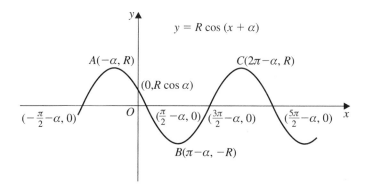

This curve is similar to that of $y = \cos x$ but it is enlarged by a factor R parallel to the y-axis and translated by α in the direction of the negative x-axis. The curve meets the y-axis at $(0, R\cos\alpha)$ and the x-axis at the points $\cdots(-\frac{\pi}{2} - \alpha, 0)$, $(\frac{\pi}{2} - \alpha, 0)$, $(\frac{3\pi}{2} - \alpha, 0)$, $\cdots$. The stationary points $\cdots A(-\alpha, R)$, $C(2\pi - \alpha, R)$, $\cdots$ are maximum points, and $\cdots B(\pi - \alpha, -R)$, $\cdots$ are minimum points.

Now:

$$y = R\cos(x + \alpha)$$
$$\equiv R\cos x \cos\alpha - R\sin x \sin\alpha$$

and this expression for y is of the form $a\cos x + b\sin x$, where a and b are constants.

Notice that $a = R\cos\alpha$ and $b = -R\sin\alpha$.

In a similar way $a\cos\theta + b\sin\theta$ can be expressed in the form $R\sin(\theta + \beta)$, where R is a positive constant and β is a constant.

That is: $\qquad a\cos\theta + b\sin\theta \equiv R\sin(\theta + \beta)$

because $\qquad a\cos\theta + b\sin\theta \equiv R\sin\theta\cos\beta + R\cos\theta\sin\beta$

and you can see that $a = R\sin\beta$ and $b = R\cos\beta$. When expressing $a\cos\theta + b\sin\theta$ in these forms, the values of the constants α and β are usually chosen to be the smallest value, either positive or negative, that is possible.

Example 23

Express each of the following in the form $R\cos(x \pm \alpha)$, where $R > 0$ and $|\alpha|$ is as numerically small as possible:

(a) $8\cos x - 6\sin x$ $\qquad$ (b) $-8\cos x + 6\sin x$

(a) You have $\qquad R\cos(x + \alpha) \equiv 8\cos x - 6\sin x$

That is: $\qquad R\cos x\cos\alpha - R\sin x\sin\alpha \equiv 8\cos x - 6\sin x$

Hence $R\cos\alpha = 8$ and $R\sin\alpha = 6$

By squaring and adding:

$$R^2(\cos^2\alpha + \sin^2\alpha) = 8^2 + 6^2 = 100 \Rightarrow R = 10$$

$$\tan\alpha = \frac{R\sin\alpha}{R\cos\alpha} = \frac{6}{8} \Rightarrow \alpha = 36.9°$$

So: $\qquad 8\cos x - 6\sin x \equiv 10\cos(x + 36.9°)$

(b) You have: $\quad R\cos(x + \alpha) \equiv -8\cos x + 6\sin x$

So: $\qquad R\cos x\cos\alpha - R\sin x\sin\alpha \equiv -8\cos x + 6\sin x$

and remember $R > 0$.

$$R\cos\alpha = -8 \text{ and } R\sin\alpha = -6$$

$$R^2(\cos^2\alpha + \sin^2\alpha) = (-8)^2 + (-6)^2 = 100$$

$\Rightarrow$ $$R = 10$$

$$\cos\alpha = -\tfrac{8}{10} \text{ and } \sin\alpha = -\tfrac{6}{10}$$

that is, α lies in the *third* quadrant, i.e.

$$-180° < \alpha < -90°, \text{ so } \alpha = -143.1°$$

So: $\qquad -8\cos x + 6\sin x \equiv 10\cos(x - 143.1°)$

Example 24

Express each of the following in the form $R\sin(x \pm \alpha)$ where $R > 0$ and $|\alpha|$ is as small as possible:

(a) $8\cos x - 6\sin x$ $\qquad$ (b) $-8\cos x + 6\sin x$

(a) You have $\quad R\sin(x+\alpha) \equiv 8\cos x - 6\sin x$

So: $\qquad R\sin x\cos\alpha + R\cos x\sin\alpha \equiv 8\cos x - 6\sin x$

Hence: $\qquad R\cos\alpha = -6$ and $R\sin\alpha = 8$

$$R^2(\cos^2\alpha + \sin^2\alpha) = (-6)^2 + 8^2 = 100 \Rightarrow R^2 = 100$$

R is positive $\Rightarrow R = 10$

Hence: $\qquad \cos\alpha = -\frac{6}{10}$ and $\sin\alpha = \frac{8}{10}$

That is, α lies in the second quadrant $(90° < \alpha < 180°)$, and $\alpha = 126.9°$.

$$8\cos x - 6\sin x \equiv 10\sin(x + 126.9°)$$

(b) You have $\quad R\sin(x - \alpha) \equiv 6\sin x - 8\cos x$

That is: $\quad R\sin x\cos\alpha - R\cos x\sin\alpha \equiv 6\sin x - 8\cos x$

Hence: $\qquad R\cos\alpha = 6$ and $R\sin\alpha = 8$

As before, $R^2(\cos^2\alpha + \sin^2\alpha) = 6^2 + 8^2 \Rightarrow R = 10$

$$\cos\alpha = \frac{6}{10} \text{ and } \sin\alpha = \frac{8}{10}$$

As both $\cos\alpha$ and $\sin\alpha$ are positive, α is in the first quadrant $(0° < \alpha < 90°) \Rightarrow \alpha = 53.1°$.

$$6\sin x - 8\cos x = 10\sin(x - 53.1°)$$

The advantages of taking $a\cos\theta + b\sin\theta$ in the form $R\cos(\theta + \alpha)$ or in the form $R\sin(\theta + \beta)$ are many. In particular, you can write down maximum and minimum values of the expression immediately, and solve equations of the form $a\cos\theta + b\sin\theta = c$ economically without further processing, by using a calculator. The shape of the curve $y = a\cos x + b\sin x$ can be determined at once. Further advantages will be apparent when you study complex numbers later in a course of pure mathematics.

Example 25

Express $3\cos x + 4\sin x$ in the form $R\cos(x - \alpha)$, where $R > 0$ and α is acute. Hence find the maximum value of $3\cos x + 4\sin x$ and the smallest positive value of x for which this occurs.

You have: $\qquad R\cos(x - \alpha) \equiv 3\cos x + 4\sin x$

That is: $\quad R\cos x\cos\alpha + R\sin x\sin\alpha \equiv 3\cos x + 4\sin x$

$\Rightarrow \qquad\qquad R\cos\alpha = 3, \ R\sin\alpha = 4$

Squaring and adding gives

$$R^2(\cos^2\alpha + \sin^2\alpha) = 3^2 + 4^2 = 25$$

$$R^2 = 25 \Rightarrow R = 5$$

$$\tan \alpha = \frac{R \sin \alpha}{R \cos \alpha} = \tfrac{4}{3} \Rightarrow \alpha = 53.1° \text{ (or 0.93 radians)}$$

That is: $3 \cos x + 4 \sin x \equiv 5 \cos (x - 53.1°)$

Since $-1 \leqslant \cos x \leqslant 1$, you have:

$$-5 \leqslant 5 \cos (x - 53.1°) \leqslant 5$$

The maximum value of $3 \cos x + 4 \sin x$ is 5 and the smallest value of x for which this occurs is $53.1°$ (because when $x = 53.1°$ then $x - 53.1° = 0$).

Example 26

Express $12 \sin x - 5 \cos x$ in the form $R \sin (x - \alpha)$, where $R > 0$ and α lies in $(0, \frac{\pi}{2})$. Hence solve the equation

$$12 \sin x - 5 \cos x = 7, \qquad 0 \leqslant x < 2\pi$$

You have: $R \sin (x - \alpha) \equiv 12 \sin x - 5 \cos x$

$\Rightarrow \qquad R \sin x \cos \alpha - R \cos x \sin \alpha \equiv 12 \sin x - 5 \cos x$

$\Rightarrow \qquad R \cos \alpha = 12 \text{ and } R \sin \alpha = 5$

Squaring and adding:

$$R^2 (\cos^2 \alpha + \sin^2 \alpha) = 144 + 25 = 169$$

$$R^2 = 169 \Rightarrow R = 13$$

$$\tan \alpha = \frac{R \sin \alpha}{R \cos \alpha} = \tfrac{5}{12} \Rightarrow \alpha = 0.3948 \text{ radians}$$

Hence: $12 \sin x - 5 \cos x \equiv 13 \sin (x - 0.3948)$

The equation $12 \sin x - 5 \cos x = 7$ can now be rewritten as

$$13 \sin (x - 0.3948) = 7$$

That is: $\sin (x - 0.3948) = \tfrac{7}{13}$

Hence: $x - 0.3948 = 0.5686 \text{ or } \pi - 0.5686$

$\Rightarrow \qquad x = 0.963 \text{ or } 2.968 \text{ radians (to 3 decimal places)}$

Sometimes an equation will need processing before you can express it in a form like $R \cos (x + \alpha)$.

Example 27

Solve, for $0 \leqslant \theta \leqslant 360°$, the equation

$$4 \cos \theta + 3 \sin \theta = 3.5 \sec \theta$$

Multiply by $\cos\theta$ to give

$$4\cos^2\theta + 3\cos\theta\sin\theta = 3.5$$

Remember that $\cos 2\theta \equiv 2\cos^2\theta - 1$, so $4\cos^2\theta \equiv 2 + 2\cos 2\theta$ and $\sin 2\theta \equiv 2\sin\theta\cos\theta$, so $3\sin\theta\cos\theta \equiv \frac{3}{2}\sin 2\theta$.

So the equation can be written as

$$2 + 2\cos 2\theta + \tfrac{3}{2}\sin 2\theta = 3.5$$

That is: $\qquad\qquad 4\cos 2\theta + 3\sin 2\theta = 3$

Now you can express $4\cos 2\theta + 3\sin 2\theta$ in the form $R\cos(2\theta - \alpha)$.

$$R\cos 2\theta\cos\alpha + R\sin 2\theta\sin\alpha \equiv 4\cos 2\theta + 3\sin 2\theta$$

So: $\qquad\qquad R\cos\alpha = 4, \quad R\sin\alpha = 3$

Hence $R = 5$ and $\tan\alpha = \frac{3}{4} \Rightarrow \alpha = 36.87°$. The equation can now be written as

$$5\cos(2\theta - 36.87°) = 3$$

$\Rightarrow \qquad\qquad \cos(2\theta - 36.87°) = \tfrac{3}{5}$

$2\theta - 36.87° = 53.13°$ or $306.87°$ or $360° + 53.13°$ or $360° + 306.87°$

$2\theta = 90°$ or $343.74°$ or $450°$ or $703.74°$

$\theta = 45°$ or $171.9°$ or $225°$ or $351.9°$ (1 d.p.)

Exercise 4E

In questions 1–5, $R > 0$ and α is the smallest positive angle possible. Express each in the form required, stating the value of R and the value of α, to the nearest tenth of a degree.

1 $\quad 8\cos x - 15\sin x, R\cos(x + \alpha)$
2 $\quad 5\sin x + 12\cos x, R\sin(x + \alpha)$
3 $\quad 3\sin x - \cos x, R\sin(x - \alpha)$
4 $\quad 6\cos x + 8\sin x, R\cos(x - \alpha)$
5 $\quad \cos x - \sin x, R\cos(x + \alpha)$

In questions 6–10, use the results of your work in questions 1–5 to find for each function the greatest and least values, stating the smallest positive value of x for which these occur.

6 $\quad 8\cos x - 15\sin x$ $\qquad$ **7** $\quad 5\sin x + 12\cos x$
8 $\quad 3\sin x - \cos x$ $\qquad$ **9** $\quad 6\cos x + 8\sin x$
10 $\quad \cos x - \sin x$

In questions 11–15 find the values of x in degrees to 1 d.p. in the interval $[0, 360°]$ for which:

11 $4 \sin x - 3 \cos x = 2.5$ **12** $5 \cos x + 12 \sin x = 6$

13 $\cos x + \sin x = \frac{1}{2}$ **14** $5 \cos 2x + 2 \sin 2x = 3$

15 $15 \cos 3x - 8 \sin 3x = 17$

In questions 16–20, find the values of x in radians to 2 d.p. in the interval $[0, 2\pi]$.

16 $\cos x - \sin x = 1$

17 $4 \cos x + 3 \sin x = 3$

18 $8 \cos x + 15 \sin x = -11$

19 $6 \sin 2x - \cos 2x = 3$

20 $20 \sin \dfrac{x}{2} - 21 \cos \dfrac{x}{2} = 14.5$

21 Solve the equation $7 \cos x - 24 \sin x = 12.5$, giving all solutions in degrees to 1 decimal place between 0 and $360°$. Find also the least value of $7 \cos x - 24 \sin x$ and state the smallest positive value of x for which this occurs.

22 Given that $3 \sin x - \cos x \equiv R \sin(x - \alpha)$, $R > 0$ and $0 < \alpha < 90°$, find R and α.
Hence solve the equation

$$3 \sin x - \cos x = 2$$

giving all solutions in the interval $[0, 720°]$.

23 Find, to the nearest tenth of a degree, all solutions in the interval $[-360°, 360°]$ of the equation

$$3 \cos x + 4 \sin x = \frac{5\sqrt{3}}{2}$$

24 Express $2 \cos 4x + 3 \sin 4x$ in the form $R \cos(4x - \alpha)$, where $R > 0$ and α lies in the interval $\left[0, \dfrac{\pi}{2}\right]$.
Hence find:
(a) the minimum value of

$$\frac{1}{2 \cos 4x + 3 \sin 4x}$$

and the smallest positive value of x when this occurs.
(b) the values of x, in radians to 2 decimal places, for which $2 \cos 4x + 3 \sin 4x = 2$ in the interval $[0, 2\pi]$.

25 Express $4 \sin x + 3 \cos x$ in the form $R \sin (x + \alpha)$ where $R > 0$ and α lies in the interval $\left[0, \dfrac{\pi}{2}\right]$.

(a) Find the greatest and the least values of

$$\frac{1}{4 \sin x + 3 \cos x + 12}$$

(b) Determine, in radians to 2 decimal places, the values of x in the interval $[0, 2\pi]$ for which

$$(4 \sin x + 3 \cos x)^2 = \tfrac{1}{2}$$

SUMMARY OF KEY POINTS

1 $\sec x = \dfrac{1}{\cos x}$

   $\operatorname{cosec} x = \dfrac{1}{\sin x}$

   $\cot x = \dfrac{1}{\tan x}$

2 The inverse function of $\sin x$ is $\arcsin x$ and has domain $-1 \leqslant x \leqslant 1$ and range $-\dfrac{\pi}{2} \leqslant \arcsin x \leqslant \dfrac{\pi}{2}$.

3 The inverse function of $\cos x$ is $\arccos x$ and has domain $-1 \leqslant x \leqslant 1$ and range $0 \leqslant \arccos x \leqslant \pi$.

4 The inverse function of $\tan x$ is $\arctan x$ and has domain $x \in \mathbb{R}$ and range $-\dfrac{\pi}{2} < x < \dfrac{\pi}{2}$.

5 Pythagoras' theorem can be written
   $$\sin^2 \theta + \cos^2 \theta \equiv 1$$
   or $$\sec^2 \theta \equiv 1 + \tan^2 \theta$$
   or $$\operatorname{cosec}^2 \theta \equiv 1 + \cot^2 \theta$$

6 The compound angle formulae are
   $$\sin (A + B) \equiv \sin A \cos B + \cos A \sin B$$
   $$\sin (A - B) \equiv \sin A \cos B - \cos A \sin B$$
   $$\cos (A + B) \equiv \cos A \cos B - \sin A \sin B$$
   $$\cos (A - B) \equiv \cos A \cos B + \sin A \sin B$$

   $$\tan (A + B) \equiv \frac{\tan A + \tan B}{1 - \tan A \tan B}$$

   $$\tan (A - B) \equiv \frac{\tan A - \tan B}{1 + \tan A \tan B}$$

7 The double angle formulae are

$\sin 2A \equiv 2 \sin A \cos A$

$\cos 2A \equiv \cos^2 A - \sin^2 A \equiv 2 \cos^2 A - 1 \equiv 1 - 2 \sin^2 A$

$\tan 2A \equiv \dfrac{2 \tan A}{1 - \tan^2 A}$

8 The half angle formulae are

$\sin^2 \frac{1}{2}\theta \equiv \frac{1}{2}(1 - \cos \theta)$

$\cos^2 \frac{1}{2}\theta \equiv \frac{1}{2}(1 + \cos \theta)$

9 The sum $\rightarrow$ product formulae are

$\sin P + \sin Q \equiv 2 \sin \dfrac{P+Q}{2} \cos \dfrac{P-Q}{2}$

$\sin P - \sin Q \equiv 2 \cos \dfrac{P+Q}{2} \sin \dfrac{P-Q}{2}$

$\cos P + \cos Q \equiv 2 \cos \dfrac{P+Q}{2} \cos \dfrac{P-Q}{2}$

$\cos Q - \cos P \equiv 2 \sin \dfrac{P+Q}{2} \sin \dfrac{P-Q}{2}$

10 The product $\rightarrow$ sum formulae are

$2 \sin A \cos B \equiv \sin (A + B) + \sin (A - B)$

$2 \cos A \sin B \equiv \sin (A + B) - \sin (A - B)$

$2 \cos A \cos B \equiv \cos (A + B) + \cos (A - B)$

$2 \sin A \sin B \equiv \cos (A - B) - \sin (A + B)$

11 $a \cos \theta + b \sin \theta \equiv R \cos (\theta + \alpha)$

where $a = R \cos \alpha$ and $b = -R \sin \alpha$.

Also: $R = \sqrt{(a^2 + b^2)}$ and $\tan \alpha = -\dfrac{b}{a}$

12 $a \cos \theta + b \sin \theta \equiv R \sin (\theta + \beta)$

where $a = R \sin \beta$ and $b = R \cos \beta$.

Also: $R = \sqrt{(a^2 + b^2)}$ and $\tan \beta = \dfrac{a}{b}$

Review exercise 1

1 Express $\dfrac{2}{2x-1} - \dfrac{1}{2x+1} - \dfrac{2}{4x^2-1}$ as a single algebraic

   fraction in its lowest terms.

2 The functions f and g are defined by

   $$f : x \mapsto x^2$$
   $$g : x \mapsto \tfrac{1}{2}x + 1$$

   for all real values of x in the domain $0 \leqslant x \leqslant 3$.
   (a) Find $f^{-1}(x)$ and $g^{-1}(x)$ in terms of x.
   (b) Sketch, in the same diagram, the graphs of f, g, f^{-1} and g^{-1}.

3 (a) Use the binomial theorem to expand $(3 + 10x)^4$, giving
   each coefficient as an integer.
   (b) Use your expansion, with an appropriate value of x, to
   find the exact value of $(1003)^4$, stating the value of x which
   you have used.   [E]

4 (a) Solve, for $0 \leqslant x < 360$, the equation

   $$2 \cos (x + 50)^\circ = \sin (x + 40)^\circ$$

   giving your answers to one decimal place.
   (b) Solve, for $0 \leqslant x < 2\pi$, the equation

   $$\cos 2x = 2 \sin^2 x$$

   giving your answer in terms of π.

5 Express $\dfrac{7x - 15}{2(x - 2)(x - 1)} - \dfrac{7}{2x}$

   as a single fraction in its lowest terms.   [E]

6 The functions f and g are defined by

$$f : x \mapsto 2x + 1, \quad x \in \mathbb{R}$$

$$g : x \mapsto \frac{1}{x}, \quad x \in \mathbb{R}, \, x \neq 0$$

(a) Calculate the value of gf(2).

(b) Find $g^{-1}(x)$ in terms of x.

(c) Calculate the values of x for which $fg(x) = x$. [E]

7 Given that $(1.01)^{30} = 1.3478$ to 5 significant figures, show that the magnitude of the error in using the first three terms of the binomial expansion of $(1 + x)^{30}$ to estimate the value of $(1.01)^{30}$ is less than 0.01. Find also the numerical value of the coefficient of x^5 and x^{25} in this expansion. [E]

8 (a) Given that α is acute and $\tan \alpha = \frac{3}{4}$, prove that

$$3 \sin(\theta + \alpha) + 4 \cos(\theta + \alpha) \equiv 5 \cos \theta$$

(b) Given that $\sin x = 0.6$ and $\cos x = -0.8$, evaluate $\cos(x + 270°)$ and $\cos(x + 540°)$. [E]

9 Express $\dfrac{1}{x^2 - x} + \dfrac{1}{x}$ as a single fraction in its lowest terms.

10 (i) Given that $x + \dfrac{1}{x} = 3$,

(a) expand $\left(x + \dfrac{1}{x} \right)^3$ and use your expression to show that

$$x^3 + \frac{1}{x^3} = 18$$

(b) expand $\left(x + \dfrac{1}{x} \right)^5$

Use your expansion and the previous result to find the value of

$$x^5 + \frac{1}{x^5}$$

(ii) Given that $(1 + 3x)^{15} \equiv 1 + Ax + Bx^2 + Cx^3 + \dots$, find the values of the constants A, B and C. [E]

11 The functions f and g are defined by

$$f : x \mapsto 5x - 1, \quad x \in \mathbb{R}$$

$$g : x \mapsto \frac{2x}{x + 3}, \quad x \in \mathbb{R}, \, x \neq -3$$

(a) Evaluate $f^{-1}(4)$ and fg(3).

(b) Express $g^{-1}(x)$ in terms of x.

12 Find the values of x in $(0, 360°)$ for which

$$7\cos x + \sin x = 5$$

giving each answer to one decimal place.

13 Solve for t the equation

$$\frac{t-3}{t+1} = 2 - \frac{3}{t}$$

14 The functions f, g are defined by

$$\text{f} : x \mapsto 6x - 1, \quad x \in \mathbb{R}$$

$$\text{g} : x \mapsto \frac{4}{x-1}, \quad x \in \mathbb{R}, x \neq 1.$$

Find in its simplest form
(a) the inverse function f^{-1}
(b) the composite function fg.
(c) Determine the values of x which satisfy $\text{f}(x) = \text{g}(x)$. [E]

15 In the binomial expansion, in ascending powers of x, of $(1 - ax)^6$, where a is a real constant, the fourth term is $-540x^3$. Find the value of a.

16 Prove that

$$(\cos X + \cos Y)^2 + (\sin X + \sin Y)^2 \equiv 4\cos^2\left(\frac{X-Y}{2}\right)$$

Without using a calculator, prove that $\cos 15° = \dfrac{\sqrt{2} + \sqrt{6}}{4}$
and that $\cos 15° \cos 75° = \frac{1}{4}$. [E]

17 Two functions f and g are defined by

$$\text{f} : x \mapsto \frac{25}{3x-2}, \quad x \in \mathbb{R}, 1 < x \leqslant 9$$

$$\text{g} : x \mapsto x^2, \quad x \in \mathbb{R}, 1 < x \leqslant 3$$

Find
(a) the range of f
(b) the inverse function f^{-1}, stating its domain
(c) the composite function fg, stating its domain
(d) the solutions of the equation $\text{fg}(x) = \dfrac{2}{x-1}$. [E]

18 Expand $(1 + ax)^8$ in ascending powers of x up to and including the term in x^2.

The coefficients of x and x^2 in the expansion of

$$(1 + bx)(1 + ax)^8$$

are 0 and -36 respectively.

Find the values of a and b, given that $a > 0$ and $b < 0$.   [E]

19 (a) The curve with equation

$$y = 2 + k \sin x$$

passes through the point with coordinates $\left(\dfrac{\pi}{2}, -2\right)$.

Find the value of k and the greatest value of y.

(b) Find, to the nearest tenth of a degree, the angles θ between $0°$ and $360°$ for which

$$2 \sec^2 \theta = 8 - \tan \theta$$ [E]

20 The function f is given by

$$f : x \mapsto 7 - 12x - 4x^2, \ x \in \mathbb{R}$$

(a) Find the values of the positive constants A, B and C for which
$$A - (Bx + C)^2 \equiv 7 - 12x - 4x^2$$

(b) Using the values found in (a), or otherwise, find

(i) the range of f

(ii) the set of values of x for which $f(x) < 0$.   [E]

21 Express in its simplest form

$$\frac{5x - 3}{2x^2 - x - 15} + \frac{2x - 5}{3x^2 - 7x - 6}$$ [E]

22 Express $7 \cos x - \sin x$ in the form $R \cos(x + \alpha)$, where $R > 0$ and $0 < \alpha < \dfrac{\pi}{2}$.

Hence determine the values of x in the interval $0 \leqslant x \leqslant 2\pi$ for which

$$7 \cos x - \sin x = \sqrt{2}$$

giving your answers in radians to 2 decimal places.   [E]

23 The functions f and g are defined by

$$f : x \mapsto x^2 + 3, \ x \in \mathbb{R}$$
$$g : x \mapsto 2x + 1, \ x \in \mathbb{R}$$

(a) Find, in a similar form, the function fg.

(b) Find the range of the function fg.

(c) Solve the equation

$$f(x) = 12g^{-1}(x)$$ [E]

24 (a) Expand $(2+x)^4$ and $(2-x)^4$ in ascending powers of x.

(b) Use your expansions to show that the equation

$$(2+x)^4 - (2-x)^4 = 80$$

simplifies to the cubic equation $x^3 + 4x - 5 = 0$.

(c) Show that 1 is a root of $x^3 + 4x - 5 = 0$.

(d) Show that there are no further real roots of this cubic equation. [E]

25 (a) Solve the equation $\sin 2x = \cos^2 x$, for $0° \leqslant x \leqslant 360°$, giving your answer in degrees to one decimal place where appropriate.

(b) Solve the equation $\cos 2x = 2\sin^2 x$ giving the solutions in $(0, 2\pi)$ in radians, as multiples of π. [E]

26 Given that

$$(1 + kx)^8 = 1 + 12x + px^2 + qx^3 + \dots, \text{ for all } x \in \mathbb{R},$$

(a) find the value of k, the value of p and the value of q.

(b) Using your values of k, p and q find the numerical coefficient of the x^3 term in the expansion of

$$(1 - x)(1 + kx)^8$$ [E]

27 Find the first three terms in the expansion in ascending powers of x of $(1 - 2x)^7$.

Given that x is so small that x^3 and higher powers of x may be neglected, show that

$$(1 - x)(1 - 2x)^7 \equiv 1 + ax + bx^2$$

where a and b are constants to be found. [E]

28 Given that $f(x) = 3x - 2$ and $g(x) = x^2$,

(a) find $f(1)$ and $g(-3)$.

(b) Express $f^{-1}(x)$ and $ff(x)$ in terms of x.

(c) Solve, for x, the equation $f(x) = 10$.

(d) Express $gf(x)$ in terms of x, simplifying your answer.

(e) Solve, for x, the equation $gf(x) - g(x) = 25$, giving your answers to 2 decimal places. [E]

29 Find, in degrees, the value of the acute angle α, for which

$$\cos\theta - (\sqrt{3})\sin\theta \equiv 2\cos(\theta + \alpha)$$

for all values of θ.

Solve the equation

$$\cos x - (\sqrt{3})\sin x = \sqrt{2}, \ 0° \leqslant x \leqslant 360° \qquad \text{[E]}$$

30 (a) Express $\dfrac{3}{2(x+1)} - \dfrac{3x-1}{2(x-1)(x-2)}$ as a single fraction,

simplifying the numerator as much as possible.

(b) Find, without using tables, the numerical value of

(i) $144^{\frac{1}{2}}$ (ii) 3^{-3} (iii) $3^{\frac{3}{4}}.3^{-\frac{1}{2}}.3^{-\frac{1}{4}}$

(c) Find the value of $\left(x + \dfrac{1}{x}\right)^2 + \left(x - \dfrac{1}{x}\right)^2$ when $x = \sqrt{5}$.

31 In the binomial expansion of $(1 + px)^6$ in ascending powers of x, the coefficient of x^2 is 135. Given that p is a positive integer,

(a) find the value of p

(b) evaluate the coefficient of x^3 in the expansion.

32 (a) Solve, in radians, the equation

$$\sin\left(x + \frac{\pi}{6}\right) = 2\cos x$$

giving all solutions in the range $0 \leqslant x < 2\pi$.

(b) (i) Use the formula

$$\tan(A - B) = \frac{\tan A - \tan B}{1 + \tan A \tan B}$$

to show that

$$\tan\left(\theta - \frac{\pi}{4}\right) = \frac{\tan\theta - 1}{\tan\theta + 1}$$

(ii) Hence, or otherwise, solve, in radians to 3 significant figures, the equation

$$\tan\left(\theta - \frac{\pi}{4}\right) = 6\tan\theta$$

giving all solutions in the range $-\pi < \theta < \pi$.   [E]

33 (a) Show that $7\cos x - 4\sin x$ may be expressed in the form $R\cos(x + \alpha)$, where R is $\sqrt{65}$ and $\tan\alpha = \frac{4}{7}$.

(b) Find, in radians to 2 decimal places, the smallest positive value of x for which $7\cos x - 4\sin x$ takes its maximum value.

(c) Find, in radians to 2 decimal places, the two smallest positive values of x for which

$$7 \cos x - 4 \sin x = 4.88 \qquad \text{[E]}$$

34 A sequence of terms $\{u_n\}$ is defined, for $n \geqslant 1$, by the recurrence relation

$$u_{n+2} = 2k u_{n+1} + 15 u_n$$

where k is a constant. Given that $u_1 = 1$ and $u_2 = -2$,

(a) find an expression, in terms of k, for u_3.

(b) Hence find an expression, in terms of k, for u_4.

Given also that $u_4 = -38$,

(c) find the possible values of k. \qquad [E]

35 The expansion of $(1 - 4x^2)(1 + ax)^8$ in ascending powers of x is

$$1 + Ax + 108x^2 + \ldots$$

Find the possible values of A and of a.

36 A sequence of numbers u_1, u_2, u_3, ... is generated by the relation $u_n = 2 \sin\left(\dfrac{n\pi}{3}\right)$.

Find u_1, u_2, u_3, u_4, u_5 and u_6 and name the type of sequence which has been generated by this relation.

37 Express $3 \cos x + 2 \sin x$ in the form $R \cos(x - \alpha)$, where R is positive and α is an acute angle. Find, to $0.1°$, the values of x between 0 and $360°$ which satisfy the equation

$$3 \cos x + 2 \sin x = 2.75$$

38 Sketch the graph of $y = |3x + 2|$.

Hence, or otherwise, find the complete set of values of x for which

$$|3x + 2| < 4x \qquad \text{[E]}$$

39 The function f is defined by

$$\text{f} : x \mapsto x^2 - 4x, \ |x| \leqslant 1, \ x \in \mathbb{R}$$

(a) Show that f is a one-one function and find its inverse in the form $\text{f}^{-1} : x \mapsto \text{f}^{-1}(x)$.

(b) Given also that the function g is given by $\text{g} : x \mapsto 3x + 2$, $x \in \mathbb{R}$, find, in surd form, the value of x for which

$$\text{f}^{-1}(x) = \text{g}(x)$$

40 Expand $\left(1 - \frac{1}{2}x\right)^{21}$ in ascending powers of x up to and including the term in x^3, simplifying each coefficient.

41 By expressing $5\cos\theta + 12\sin\theta$ in the form $R\sin(\theta + \alpha)$, find the greatest and least values of

$$(5\cos\theta + 12\sin\theta)^3$$

42 Write down the binomial expansion for $(1 + y)^{10}$ in ascending powers of y as far as the term containing y^3. Use this series to obtain

(a) the expression of $(1 + x - x^2)^{10}$ in ascending powers of x as far as the term containing x^3

(b) the value of $(0.99)^{10}$ correct to 5 decimal places. [E]

43 The sequence u_1, u_2, u_3, ... is generated from the relation

$$u_{n+1} = \frac{n+1}{n}u_n \text{ and } u_1 = 2.$$

(a) Find the values of u_2, u_3 and u_4.

(b) Prove that $u_n = nu_1 = 2n$.

(c) Find $\displaystyle\sum_{r=1}^{2N} u_r$.

44 Solve for x the equation

$$\frac{1}{x-1} - \frac{1}{x+1} = \frac{5}{4x+8}$$

given that $x < 0$.

45 (a) *Without the use of a calculator*, find the values of

(i) $\sin 40° \cos 10° - \cos 40° \sin 10°$

(ii) $\dfrac{1}{\sqrt{2}}\cos 15° - \dfrac{1}{\sqrt{2}}\sin 15°$

(iii) $\dfrac{1 - \tan 15°}{1 + \tan 15°}$

(b) Find, to one decimal place, the values of x, $0 \leqslant x \leqslant 360$, which satisfy the equation

$$2\sin x° = \cos(x° - 60°)$$ [E]

46 A sequence of terms $u_1, u_2, u_3 \ldots, u_n, \ldots$ is built up using odd integers in this way:

$u_1 = (1)$
$u_2 = (3, 5)$
$u_3 = (7, 9, 11)$
$u_4 = (13, 15, 17, 19)$
and so on $\ldots$

Find, in terms of n, only the first and last odd numbers in u_n.

47 Find, in radians in terms of π, the values of x in the interval $-\pi \leqslant x \leqslant \pi$ for which
(a) $3 \sin x + \cos 2x = 2$
(b) $\sin 3x + \sin x = \sin 2x$.

48 Starting with expansions for $\sin(A + B)$ and $\cos(A + B)$, prove that
$$\sin 3\theta \equiv 3 \sin \theta - 4 \sin^3 \theta$$

Hence solve for $0 \leqslant x \leqslant 360$,
$$\sin 3x° = \sin^2 x°$$

49 Find, in radians to two decimal places, those values of θ for which
$$\cos \theta + \tfrac{1}{2} \sin \frac{\theta}{2} = 0 \quad \text{and} \quad -2\pi \leqslant \theta \leqslant 2\pi$$

50 (a) Find the term independent of x in the expansion of
$$\left(\frac{1}{3x} - \frac{3x^2}{2} \right)^9.$$
(b) Find the value of n for which the coefficients of x, x^2 and x^3 in the expansion of $(1 + x)^n$ where $n \geqslant 3$ form three consecutive terms of an arithmetic series.

51 Find the values of x for which
$$\frac{1}{x} - \frac{x}{x - 2} = \frac{7}{4x + 1}$$

52 (a) Using the identities

$$\sin(A + B) \equiv \sin A \cos B + \cos A \sin B$$

and $\cos(A + B) \equiv \cos A \cos B - \sin A \sin B$

show that $\sin 2A \equiv 2 \sin A \cos A$

and $\cos 2A \equiv 2 \cos^2 A - 1$

(b) Solve, for $0 \leqslant x \leqslant 2\pi$, giving your answers in radians, the equations

(i) $\sin 2x \sin x = \cos x$

(ii) $\sin\left(x + \dfrac{\pi}{3}\right) + \sin\left(x - \dfrac{\pi}{3}\right) = 1$

(c) In $\triangle ABC$, $AB = 3$ cm, $AC = 5$ cm, $\angle ABC = 2\theta°$ and $\angle ACB = \theta°$. Calculate, to 3 significant figures, the value of θ. [E]

53 Given that

$$f(x) \equiv (x - \alpha)(x + \beta), \ \alpha > \beta > 0$$

sketch on separate diagrams the curves with equations

(a) $y = f(x)$ (b) $y = -f(x + \alpha)$

On each sketch,

(c) write the coordinates of any points at which the curve meets the coordinate axes

(d) show with a dotted line the axis of symmetry of the curve and state its equation. [E]

54 In the binomial expansion of $\left(1 + \dfrac{x}{k}\right)^n$, where k is a constant and n is a positive integer, the coefficients of x and x^2 are equal.

(a) Show that $2k = n - 1$.

For the case when $n = 7$

(b) deduce the value of k.

(c) Hence find the first three terms in the expansion in ascending powers of x. [E]

55 Given that $y = \left(x + \dfrac{1}{x}\right)^3 + \left(x - \dfrac{1}{x}\right)^3$, where $x \in \mathbb{R}$, $x \neq 0$,

(a) prove that $y = 2x^3 + 6x^{-1}$

(b) find the values of y for which $\dfrac{dy}{dx} = 0$. [E]

56 Using the formula $\cos(A + B) \equiv \cos A \cos B - \sin A \sin B$

(a) show that

$$\cos(A - B) - \cos(A + B) \equiv 2 \sin A \sin B$$

(b) Hence show that

$$\cos 2x - \cos 4x \equiv 2\sin 3x \sin x$$

(c) Find all solutions in the range $0 \leqslant x \leqslant \pi$ of the equation

$$\cos 2x - \cos 4x = \sin x$$

giving all your solutions in multiples of π radians. **[E]**

57

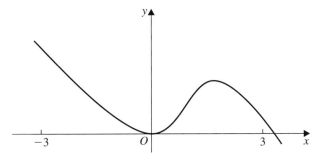

The figure shows a sketch of the curve with equation
$y = \mathrm{f}(x)$.
In separate diagrams show, for $-3 \leqslant x \leqslant 3$, sketches of the
curves with equation

(a) $y = \mathrm{f}(-x)$ (b) $y = -\mathrm{f}(x)$ (c) $y = \mathrm{f}(|x|)$

Mark on each sketch the x-coordinate of any point, or points,
where a curve touches or crosses the x-axis. **[E]**

58 In the binomial expansion of $(1 + kx)^n$, where k is a constant
and n is a positive integer, the coefficients of x and x^2 are equal.
(a) Show that $k(n - 1) = 2$.
Given that $nk = 2\frac{1}{3}$, find
(b) the value of k
(c) the value of n. **[E]**

59 The diagram shows the graph of the quadratic function f
whose domain is the set of real numbers. The graph meets the
x-axis at $(1, 0)$ and $(3, 0)$ and the stationary point is $(2, -1)$.
(a) State the range of f and find the equation of the graph in
the form $y = \mathrm{f}(x)$.
(b) On separate axes, sketch the graphs of
(i) $y = \mathrm{f}(x + 2)$,
(ii) $y = \mathrm{f}(2x)$.
(c) On each graph write in the coordinates of the points at
which the graph meets the coordinate axes and write in the
coordinates of the stationary point. **[E]**

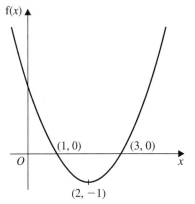

60 Find in terms of π the values of x for which

$$\sin x + \sin 3x + \sin 5x = 0$$

and $0 \leqslant x \leqslant \pi$.

61 A function f is defined by

$$f : x \mapsto 1 - \frac{1}{x}, \quad x \in \mathbb{R}, x \neq 0, x \neq 1.$$

Find (a) $ff(x)$
(b) $fff(x)$
(c) $f^{-1}(x)$.   [E]

62 (a) On the same axes, sketch the graphs of $y = 2 - x$ and $y = 2|x + 1|$.
(b) Hence, or otherwise, find the values of x for which $2 - x = 2|x + 1|$.   [E]

63 The coefficient of x^3 in the expansion of $\left(3x + \dfrac{k}{3x}\right)^7$ is 63.

Find the possible values of the constant k.   [E]

64 (a) Sketch, on a single diagram, the graphs of $y = a^2 - x^2$ and $y = |x + a|$, where a is a constant and $a > 1$.
(b) Write down the coordinates of the points where the graph of $y = a^2 - x^2$ cuts the coordinate axes.
Given that the two graphs intersect at $x = 4$,
(c) calculate the value of a.   [E]

65 The curve with equation $y = f(x)$ meets the coordinate axes at the points $(-1, 0)$, $(4, 0)$ and $(0, 3)$, as shown in the diagram. Using a separate diagram for each, sketch the curve with equation
(a) $y = f(x - 1)$
(b) $2y = -f(x)$.
On each sketch, write in the coordinates of the points at which the curve meets the coordinate axes.   [E]

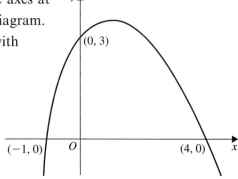

66 The function f is an odd function defined on the interval $[-2, 2]$. Given that

$$f(x) = -x, \qquad 0 \leqslant x < 1$$
$$f(x) = x - 2, \quad 1 \leqslant x \leqslant 2$$

(a) sketch the graph of f for $-2 \leqslant x \leqslant 2$

(b) find the values of x for which $f(x) = -\frac{1}{2}$. **[E]**

67 Find all the values of θ in the interval $-180° \leqslant \theta \leqslant 180°$ for which
$$\text{cosec}^2\,\theta = 1 + 2\sec^2\theta$$

giving your answers to one decimal place.

68 For all values of θ, prove that
$$8\sin^4\theta \equiv 3 - 4\cos 2\theta + \cos 4\theta$$

Hence find, in radians in terms of π, the values of x in $(-\pi, \pi)$ for which
$$\cos 4x - 4\cos 2x + 1 = 0$$

69 Functions f and g are defined by

$$\text{f}: \quad x \mapsto \frac{4}{x-2}, \quad x \in \mathbb{R}, x \neq 2$$
$$\text{g}: \quad x \mapsto x + 2, \quad x \in \mathbb{R}$$

(a) Prove that $\text{gf}: x \mapsto \dfrac{2x}{x-2}, \quad x \in \mathbb{R}, x \neq 2.$

(b) Find $(\text{gf})^{-1}$ in the form
$$(\text{gf})^{-1}: x \mapsto \ldots. \qquad \textbf{[E]}$$

70 Find the values of x in the interval $(0, 360)$ for which $\tan^2 x° + 2\sec x° = 5$, giving your answers to one decimal place.

71 A sequence of numbers is generated from the recurrence relation $u_n = -u_{n-1}$, $n \geqslant 2$. Given that $u_1 = \sqrt{2}$ show that a formula for u_n could be $u_n = \sec\left(\dfrac{4n-3}{4}\pi\right)$.

Name the type of sequence which is being generated.

72 The function g is defined by

$$\text{g}: x \mapsto \frac{1}{1+x}, \text{ where } x \in \mathbb{R}, x \neq -1$$

Given that $g(x) = g[g(x)]$, show that $x^2 + x - 1 = 0$. Hence find, to 2 decimal places, the values of x for which $g(x) = g[g(x)]$. **[E]**

73 Find the values of x for which
$$\frac{1}{x^2 - 4} + \frac{3}{x + 2} = \frac{4}{5}$$

74 Assuming that $\sin 3A \equiv 3 \sin A - 4 \sin^3 A$ and by writing $B = \frac{\pi}{2} - A$, or otherwise, prove that
$$\cos 3B \equiv 4 \cos^3 B - 3 \cos B$$
Prove also that $\tan 3B \equiv \dfrac{3 \tan B - \tan^3 B}{1 - 3 \tan^2 B}$, where $|\tan B| \neq \dfrac{1}{\sqrt{3}}$

75 Functions f and g are defined by
$$\text{f} : x \mapsto 4 - x, \quad x \in \mathbb{R}$$
$$\text{g} : x \mapsto 3x^2, \quad x \in \mathbb{R}$$

(a) Find the range of g.

(b) Solve $\text{gf}(x) = 48$.

(c) Sketch the graph of $y = |\text{f}(x)|$ and hence find the values of x for which $|\text{f}(x)| = 2$.

76 The functions f and g are defined for all real values of x by
$$\text{f} : x \mapsto x^2$$
$$\text{g} : x \mapsto 4 - 9x$$

(a) Express the composite function gf in terms of x.

(b) Sketch the curve with equation $y = \text{gf}(x)$ and show on your sketch the coordinates of the points at which your curve intersects the x-axis.

(c) Determine the range of the function gf.

(d) Find the value of x for which $\text{g}(x) = \text{g}^{-1}(x)$, where g^{-1} is the inverse function of g. [E]

77 Find the values of x between $0°$ and $720°$ for which
$$2 \sin x - \cos x = 2$$
giving your answers, where necessary, to one decimal place.

78 Assuming the identities for $\sin (A + B)$ and $\sin (A - B)$, prove that
$$\sin^2 (A + B) - \sin^2 (A - B) \equiv 4 \sin A \sin B \cos A \cos B$$
Hence prove that
$$\sin^2 8x - \sin^2 6x \equiv \sin 2x \sin 14x$$

79 Expand $(x + y)^6$, simplifying each term. Hence find the value of $(4.01)^6$, giving your answer to the nearest integer. [E]

80 Simplify $\dfrac{x+1}{2x-1} - \dfrac{x-1}{2x+1} + \dfrac{3}{4x^2-1}$ giving your answer as a

single fraction in its lowest terms.

81 Show that $2x-1$ is a factor of $4x^3 - 7x + 3$.

Find those values of t, to 2 decimal places, for which

$$4\sec^3 t - 7\sec t + 3 = 0, \quad 0 \leqslant t \leqslant 2\pi$$

82 Prove that

$$2\sin A \cos B \equiv \sin(A+B) + \sin(A-B)$$

Solve the equation, for $0 \leqslant x \leqslant 360$,

$$10\sin(2x° + 42°)\cos(2x° - 42°) = 1$$

83 (a) Find the binomial expansion of $(1 + kx)^{11}$ in ascending
powers of x up to and including the term in x^3, where k is a
negative constant.

Given that the coefficient of the term in x^2 is $\frac{55}{9}$, find

(b) the value of k, and hence

(c) the coefficient of x^3.

84 Find the values of x for which

$$\frac{3}{x+1} = \frac{19}{4x-1} - \frac{2}{x-1}$$

85 Find, to 2 decimal places, those values of x for which

$$3\cos 2x + 7\cos x = 0 \text{ and } 0 \leqslant x \leqslant 2\pi$$

86 Given that $\sec A = -\frac{17}{15}$ where $\dfrac{\pi}{2} < A < \pi$ find, without using

a calculator, the exact values of

(a) $\operatorname{cosec} A$ (b) $\sin 2A$ (c) $\tan 2A$

87 Simplify completely:

$$\dfrac{y - 7 + \dfrac{10}{y}}{\dfrac{y}{2} - \dfrac{3}{2} - \dfrac{5}{y}}$$

88 Find the values of x in radians in the interval $(0, 2\pi)$ for which

$$8 \sec^2 x = 2 \tan x + 9$$

giving each answer to 2 decimal places.

89 By using the identities for $\cos(A + B)$ and $\cos(A - B)$, prove that

(a) $1 + \cos 2x = 2 \cos^2 x$

(b) $2(\cos^2 P + \cos^2 Q + \cos^2 R) - 3 \equiv \cos(P - Q)\cos(P + Q)$
$+ \cos(Q - R)\cos(Q + R) + \cos(R - P)\cos(R + P)$

90 The functions f and g are defined, for $x \in \mathbb{R}$, by

$$\text{f} : x \mapsto \frac{1}{x + 2}, \quad x \neq -2$$

$$\text{g} : x \mapsto \frac{x - 4}{x + 2}, \quad x \neq -2$$

Define, in a similar manner, the functions

(a) fg   (b) g^{-1}

91 (a)

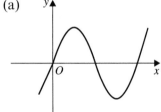

(b)

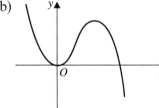

(c)

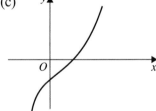

(d)

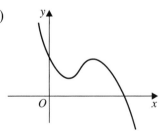

Sketch graphs of four cubic functions are shown. The functions f_1, f_2, f_3 and f_4 are given for $x \in \mathbb{R}$ by

$\text{f}_1 : x \mapsto (x^2 + 1)(2 - x)$, $\text{f}_2 : x \mapsto x(x - 1)(x - 2)$,

$\text{f}_3 : x \mapsto (x^2 + 1)(x - 1)$, $\text{f}_4 : x \mapsto x^2(1 - x)$

Match up the functions with the sketch graphs and write the coordinates of the points where a curve meets the coordinate axes.

92 In the binomial expansion of $\left(1 + \dfrac{x}{n}\right)^n$ in ascending powers of
x, the coefficient of x^2 is $\frac{7}{16}$. Given that n is a positive integer,
(a) find the value of n
(b) evaluate the coefficient of x^3 in the expansion.　　　[E]

93 Giving your answers in radians to 2 decimal places, solve the
equation $\sin x - 3\cos 2x + 2 = 0$ for $0 < x \leqslant 2\pi$.　　　[E]

94 Given that $-\frac{\pi}{2} < \arctan x < \frac{\pi}{2}$ for $x \in \mathbb{R}$ find, to 2 decimal
places, the positive values of x for which

(a) $\arctan x = \dfrac{\pi}{8}$　　　(b) $\arctan x + \arctan 2x = \dfrac{\pi}{4}$.

95 Expand $(a + b)^6$, simplifying each coefficient.
By taking $a = 1$ and $b = -0.003$ and showing all your
working, find the value of $(0.997)^6$, giving your answer to 8
decimal places.
Evaluate $(0.003)^6$, giving your answer in the standard form
$p \times 10^{-q}$, where $1 \leqslant p < 10$ and q is an integer.
State the number of decimal places required to express the
exact value of $(0.997)^6$ when it is written as a decimal
number.　　　[E]

96 Simplify $\dfrac{y^2 - 49}{y^2 + 7y} \div \dfrac{y^2 - y - 12}{y^2 + 3y}$ giving your answer in the

form $\dfrac{y - p}{y - q}$ where p and q are numbers to be found.

97 Identify the type of sequence generated by the relation
$u_{n+1} = \frac{8}{9}u_n$, $u_1 = 9$ by considering the first few terms.

Hence find (a) $\displaystyle\sum_{r=1}^{6} u_n$　　　(b) $\displaystyle\sum_{r=1}^{\infty} u_n$.

98 By considering appropriate sketch graphs, or otherwise, find
the set of values of x for which
(a) $|2x - 1| > |x - 1|$
(b) $|\cos x| \geqslant \frac{1}{2}$, where $0 \leqslant x \leqslant 2\pi$.

Exponentials and logarithms

5

5.1 Exponential functions

A function of the form f: $x \mapsto a^x$ where x is real and a is a positive constant is called an **exponential function**. The word 'exponential' comes from the word **exponent**, which is another word for '**power**' or '**index**'. So for an exponential function f: $x \mapsto a^x$, $x \in \mathbb{R}$, the variable x is called the power, or the index, or the exponent.

For $a = 2$, 3, 4 here are the graphs of the corresponding exponential functions f: $x \mapsto a^x$:

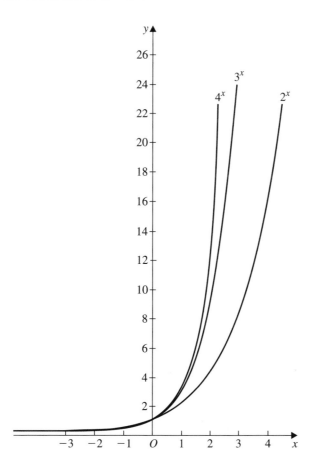

Notice that each graph passes through the point $(0, 1)$. It is also true that, as the value of a increases, so the gradient of the corresponding exponential graph increases: the graph of 4^x is much steeper at $x = 2$ than the graph of 2^x at $x = 2$. It can be shown that the gradient of the curve $y = 2^x$ at $(0, 1)$ is about 0.693, the gradient of the curve $y = 3^x$ at $(0, 1)$ is about 1.099, and that of the curve $y = 4^x$ at $(0, 1)$ is about 1.386.

As the value of a increases so the value of the gradient at $(0, 1)$ increases. If the gradient at $(0, 1)$ for the curve $y = 2^x$ is about 0.693 and the gradient for the curve $y = 3^x$ at the same point is about 1.099, there must be a value of a, lying between 2 and 3 at which the gradient of the exponential curve at $(0, 1)$ is exactly 1. It can be shown that this number is an irrational number that is approximately $2.718\,28\,\ldots$. The number is symbolised by e. So the gradient of the curve $y = e^x$ at the point $(0, 1)$ is exactly 1.

The function f: $x \mapsto e^x$, $x \in \mathbb{R}$ is called **the exponential function** (as opposed to *an* exponential function).

Exercise 5A

1 Draw the graph of $y = 2^x$. From your graph find, to 2 significant figures, the value of:

(a) $2^{1.7}$ (b) $2^{0.3}$ (c) $2^{3.3}$ (d) $2^{-0.8}$

2 Draw the graph of $y = 3^x$. From your graph find, to 2 significant figures, the value of:

(a) $3^{2.9}$ (b) $3^{-0.4}$

(c) $3^{1.3}$

3 Draw the graph of $y = e^x$. From your graph find, to 2 significant figures, the value of:

(a) $e^{-0.3}$ (b) $e^{1.9}$

(c) $e^{2.7}$

Find also the value of x for which:

(d) $e^x = 6.7$ (e) $e^x = 16.4$.

> You can check your answers using a calculator.

5.2 The natural logarithmic function

Here is the graph of the function f: $x \mapsto e^x$, $x \in \mathbb{R}$. You can see that the function is one–one. So it must have an inverse function.

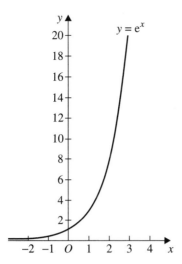

To find the inverse function write $x = e^y$ and try to make y the subject of the equation.

In the expression e^y, e is called the base and y is called the power, or index or exponent. A fourth name for y is the **logarithm**. So the expression $x = e^y$ can be interpreted as meaning that y is the logarithm of the number x in the base e. We write this as $y = \log_e x$ or more usually as $y = \ln x$.

Logarithms in base e are frequently called **natural logarithms**.

■ **The function g: $x \mapsto \ln x$, $x > 0$ is the inverse of the function f: $x \mapsto e^x$, $x \in \mathbb{R}$. That is, g $=$ f^{-1}.**

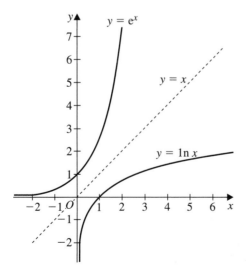

These are the graphs of e^x and of $\ln x$.
You can see that the graph of $y = \ln x$ is the reflection of the graph of $y = e^x$ in the line $y = x$.

Exercise 5B

1 Draw the graph of $y = \ln x$. Find from your graph the values of
   (a) $\ln 0.4$ (b) $\ln 0.8$ (c) $\ln 1.7$ (d) $\ln 3.3$
   (e) $\ln 4.7$ (f) e^{-1} (g) $e^{-0.6}$ (h) $e^{1.8}$

> You can check your answers using a calculator.

2 Draw on the same axes the graphs of:
   (a) $y = \ln x$ (b) $y = \ln 3x$ (c) $y = \ln 7x$
   What do you notice?

5.3 Laws of logarithms

You have seen in sections 5.1 and 5.2 that the words **power**, **index**, **exponent** and **logarithm** are synonymous: they are four different words to describe exactly the same thing.

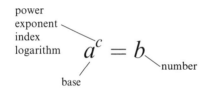

For the time being use the word 'logarithm' and take the base to be positive ($a > 0$). Then b must also be positive. Remember that the graph of $y = a^x (a > 0)$ looks like this:

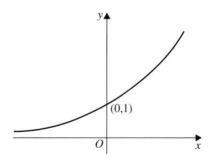

Now the statement $b = a^c$ reads 'the number b is equal to the base a raised to the logarithm c'. Another way of reading the statement is 'c is the logarithm of the number b to the base a'. This can be written

$$c = \log_a b$$

Example 1

Express the following in logarithm notation:

(a) $4^3 = 64$ (b) $27^{\frac{2}{3}} = 9$

(a) $4^3 = 64$ is equivalent to writing

$$\log_4 64 = 3$$

(b) $27^{\frac{2}{3}} = 9$ is equivalent to writing

$$\log_{27} 9 = \tfrac{2}{3}$$

Generalising then, you can say that

$$a^c = b \quad \text{and} \quad c = \log_a b$$

are **identical** and **interchangeable**.

Let $p = \log_a x$ and let $q = \log_a y$, where $a > 0$. Then these two statements can also be written as

$$x = a^p \quad \text{and} \quad y = a^q$$

Now $$xy = a^p \times a^q = a^{p+q}$$

But another way of writing $xy = a^{p+q}$ is

$$p + q = \log_a xy$$

However $$p = \log_a x \text{ and } q = \log_a y$$

■ $$\boldsymbol{\log_a xy = \log_a x + \log_a y}$$

Also: $$\frac{x}{y} = \frac{a^p}{a^q} = a^{p-q}$$

But $\dfrac{x}{y} = a^{p-q}$ can be written

$$p - q = \log_a \frac{x}{y}$$

■ $$\boldsymbol{\log_a \frac{x}{y} = \log_a x - \log_a y}$$

Now: $$x^n = (a^p)^n = a^{pn}$$

This statement can be written as

$$\log_a x^n = pn$$

But since $p = \log_a x$ then

■ $$\boldsymbol{\log_a x^n = n \log_a x}$$

If $r = \log_a a$ then: $\qquad a^r = a$

and this implies that $r = 1$.

■ $$\boldsymbol{\log_a a = 1}$$

If $r = \log_a 1$ then: $\qquad a^r = 1$

But $a^0 = 1$. So:

$$r = 0$$

■ $$\log_a 1 = 0$$

These five results are very important and you must memorise them.

There are two *common* bases for logarithms, 10 and e.

■ **$\log_{10} x$ is usually written $\lg x$.**

■ **$\log_e x$ is usually written $\ln x$.**

You should find a 'ln' button on your calculator which will evaluate logarithms to base e. However, many calculators do not have a 'lg' button but instead a button marked 'log'. This is, in fact, the button needed to evaluate logarithms to base 10.

Example 2
Find x if $\log_2 32 = x$.

$$\log_2 32 = x \Rightarrow 2^x = 32$$

But $$2^5 = 32$$

So: $$x = 5$$

Example 3
Find the value of $\log_3 243$.

If $y = \log_3 243$
then: $$3^y = 243$$

But $$3^5 = 243$$

So: $$y = 5$$

Example 4
Simplify:

$$\log_a 4 + 2\log_a 3 - \log_a 6$$

$$\log_a 4 + 2\log_a 3 - \log_a 6 = \log_a 4 + \log_a 3^2 - \log_a 6$$
$$= \log_a 4 + \log_a 9 - \log_a 6$$
$$= \log_a(4 \times 9) - \log_a 6$$
$$= \log_a \frac{36}{6}$$
$$= \log_a 6$$

Example 5

Express $\log_a \dfrac{x^3}{y^2 z}$ in terms of $\log_a x$, $\log_a y$ and $\log_a z$.

$$\log_a \frac{x^3}{y^2 z} = \log_a x^3 - \log_a y^2 z$$

$$= 3 \log_a x - [\log_a y^2 + \log_a z]$$

$$= 3 \log_a x - \log_a y^2 - \log_a z$$

$$= 3 \log_a x - 2 \log_a y - \log_a z$$

It is possible to express a logarithm written in one base as a logarithm in another base. This is particularly useful when, say, you need to calculate the value of a logarithm in base 7, for which there is no button on your calculator. If you can convert the logarithm from base 7 to base 10 or base e, then you can use your calculator to work out its value.

If $y = \log_a b$, then:

$$a^y = b$$

So, taking logarithms to base c gives

$$\log_c(a^y) = \log_c b$$

that is: $\qquad\qquad y \log_c a = \log_c b$

So: $\qquad\qquad y = \dfrac{\log_c b}{\log_c a}$

■ **Thus:** $\qquad\qquad \boldsymbol{\log_a b = \dfrac{\log_c b}{\log_c a}}$

Example 6

Calculate, to 3 significant figures, the value of $\log_4 7$.

$$\log_4 7 = \frac{\lg 7}{\lg 4} = \frac{0.845\,09 \ldots}{0.602\,05 \ldots}$$

$$= 1.40 \ (3 \text{ s.f.})$$

Example 7

Calculate, to 3 significant figures, the value of $\log_7 5$.

$$\log_7 5 = \frac{\ln 5}{\ln 7} = \frac{1.6094 \ldots}{1.9459 \ldots}$$

$$= 0.827 \ (3 \text{ s.f.})$$

Exercise 5C

Find the exact value of x, showing your working:

1 $\log_2 8 = x$ **2** $\log_3 27 = x$ **3** $\log_x 125 = 3$

4 $\log_x 36 = 0.5$ **5** $\log_2 x = 4$ **6** $\log_4 64 = x$

7 $\log_5 125 = x$ **8** $\log_x 9 = -2$ **9** $\log_5 x = -1$

10 $\log_9 x = 3\frac{1}{2}$

Find the value of:

11 $\log_3 81$ **12** $\log_4 256$ **13** $\log_3 3$

14 $\log_3 \frac{1}{9}$ **15** $\log_7 343$ **16** $\log_{64} 4$

17 $-\log_2\left(\frac{1}{8}\right)$ **18** $\log_5\left(\frac{1}{125}\right)$ **19** $\log_8 2$

20 $\log_{27} 3$

Calculate, to 3 significant figures, the value of:

21 $\log_4 9$ **22** $\log_5 22$ **23** $\log_6 3$

24 $\log_8 5$ **25** $\log_9 11$

Simplify:

26 $\log_3 7 + \log_3 2$ **27** $\lg 15 - \lg 5$

28 $\ln 5 + \ln 6 - \ln 10$ **29** $2\ln 8 - \ln 5 + 2\ln 10$

30 $2\log_a 3 - 3\log_a 2 + 4\log_a 1$ **31** $3\log_a 4 - \log_a 2 - 3\log_a 6$

32 $2\log_a 7 - 2\log_a a + 2\log_a 3$ **33** $\log_a 5 + \frac{1}{2}\log_a 16 - \log_a 2$

34 $5\log_a a + \frac{1}{3}\log_a 27 + \log_a 2$ **35** $\frac{1}{4}\log_a 81 + 3\log_a\left(\frac{1}{4}\right) - 2\log_a\left(\frac{3}{4}\right)$

Express in terms of $\log_a x$, $\log_a y$ and $\log_a z$:

36 $\log_a\left(\frac{xy}{z}\right)$ **37** $\log_a\left(\frac{x^2 y}{z^3}\right)$ **38** $\log_a xy^2 z^3$

39 $\log_a \sqrt{(xy^2 z)}$ **40** $\log_a \dfrac{xy}{\sqrt{z^3}}$

5.4 Equations of the form $a^x = b$

Although you can solve equations such as $3^x = 9$, $4^x = 64$, $2^x = 128$, and so on, because the value of x is an integer, in general you cannot solve such equations by inspection. It is time consuming to find a solution to $5^x = 67$ by trial and improvement.

The standard method for solving such equations (other than trial and improvement) is by taking logarithms.

So if $5^x = 67$

then
$$\lg 5^x = \lg 67$$
$$x\lg 5 = \lg 67$$

and hence
$$x = \frac{\lg 67}{\lg 5}$$

This can now be evaluated with the help of a calculator.

$$x = \frac{1.826\ 07\dots}{0.698\ 97\dots}$$
$$= 2.61 \text{ (3 s.f.)}$$

There is no particular reason to take logarithms to base 10. Natural logarithms would do just as well. These would lead to the solution

$$x = \frac{\ln 67}{\ln 5}$$

So:
$$x = \frac{4.204\ 69\dots}{1.609\ 43\dots}$$
$$= 2.61 \text{ (3 s.f.)}$$

Example 8
Solve the equation $4^{x+2} = 51$.

If $4^{x+2} = 51$

then:
$$\lg 4^{x+2} = \lg 51$$
$$(x+2)\lg 4 = \lg 51$$
$$x + 2 = \frac{\lg 51}{\lg 4}$$
$$x = \frac{\lg 51}{\lg 4} - 2$$
$$= 0.836 \text{ (3 s.f.)}$$

Example 9
Solve the equation $(0.3)^{5x} = 0.51$.

If $(0.3)^{5x} = 0.51$

then:
$$\lg(0.3)^{5x} = \lg 0.51$$
$$5x \lg 0.3 = \lg 0.51$$
$$5x = \frac{\lg 0.51}{\lg 0.3}$$
$$5x = 0.559\ 26\dots$$
$$x = 0.112 \text{ (3 s.f.)}$$

Example 10

Solve the equation $3^{2x} - 6(3^x) + 5 = 0$.

Let $y = 3^x$

Since $3^{2x} = (3^x)^2$ the equation becomes

$$y^2 - 6y + 5 = 0$$
$$(y - 5)(y - 1) = 0$$

So: $$y = 1 \text{ or } 5$$

That is $$3^x = 1 \text{ or } 3^x = 5$$

$$3^x = 1 = 3^0 \quad \text{or} \quad \lg 3^x = \lg 5$$
$$x \lg 3 = \lg 5$$
$$x = \frac{\lg 5}{\lg 3}$$

$$x = 0 \text{ or } x = 1.46 \text{ (3 s.f.)}$$

Example 11

Solve the equation $2(5^{2x}) - 5^x = 6$.

Let $y = 5^x$

Then: $$2y^2 - y = 6$$

or: $$2y^2 - y - 6 = 0$$
$$(2y + 3)(y - 2) = 0$$
$$y = -1\tfrac{1}{2} \text{ or } y = 2$$

So: $$5^x = -1\tfrac{1}{2} \text{ or } 5^x = 2$$

Since 5^x is always positive, $5^x = -1\tfrac{1}{2}$ gives no real value of x.

$$5^x = 2$$

gives $$\lg 5^x = \lg 2$$
$$x \lg 5 = \lg 2$$
$$x = \frac{\lg 2}{\lg 5}$$
$$x = 0.431 \text{ (3 s.f.)}$$

Exercise 5D

Solve the equations:

1 $2^x = 7$

2 $3^x = 19$

3 $4^x = 11$

4 $5^x = 9$

5 $7^x = 151$

6 $4^{-x} = 0.125$

7 $3^{x+1} = 23$

8 $5^{3x+2} = 43$

9 $2^{x+1} = 3^x$

10 $5^{x+3} = 3^{x-2}$

11 $6^{2x-1} = 9^{x+3}$

12 $4^{3x+2} = 7^{x-3}$

13 $2^{2x} - 5(2^x) + 6 = 0$ **14** $2(3^{2x}) - 9(3^x) + 4 = 0$

15 $3(4^{2x}) + 11(4^x) = 4$ **16** $3^{2x+1} = 3^x + 24$

17 $2^{2x+1} = 5(2^x) + 3$ **18** $4^{2x} + 48 = 4^{x+2}$

19 $2e^x + 2e^{-x} = 5$ **20** $25^x = 5^{x+1} - 6$

21 Find the values of x for which
$$\log_3 x - 2\log_x 3 = 1$$ [E]

22 Solve the equation
$$\log_3 (2 - 3x) = \log_9 (6x^2 - 19x + 2)$$ [E]

23 Find the possible values of x for which
$$2^{2x+1} = 3(2^x) - 1$$ [E]

24 If $xy = 64$ and $\log_x y + \log_y x = \frac{5}{2}$, find x and y.   [E]

25 Prove that if $a^x = b^y = (ab)^{xy}$, then
$$x + y = 1$$ [E]

SUMMARY OF KEY POINTS

1 A function $f : x \mapsto a^x$, where a is a constant, is called an exponential function.

2 The function $f : x \mapsto e^x$, $x \in \mathbb{R}$ is called *the* exponential function.

3 A logarithm is another name for a power or index or exponent.

4 Logarithms in base e are called natural logarithms.

5 $\log_e x$ is usually written as $\ln x$.

6 If $f : x \mapsto e^x$, $x \in \mathbb{R}$, then
$$f^{-1} : x \mapsto \ln x, x > 0$$

7 The laws of logarithms are:
$$\log_a xy = \log_a x + \log_a y$$
$$\log_a \frac{x}{y} = \log_a x - \log_a y$$
$$\log_a x^n = n \log_a x$$
$$\log_a a = 1$$
$$\log_a 1 = 0$$

8 $\log_{10} x$ is usually written $\lg x$.

9 $\log_a b = \dfrac{\log_c b}{\log_c a}$

10 An equation of the form $a^x = b$ is solved by taking logarithms of both sides.

Differentiation

6.1 The differentiation of e^x

You met the exponential function and the graph of $y = e^x$ in section 5.1. There you learned that the graph of $y = e^x$ has a gradient 1 at the point on the graph where $x = 0$. Now when $x = 0$ the value of y is $e^0 = 1$. In other words, at the point where $x = 0$ the value of y and the gradient of the curve are both 1. The surprising thing about the exponential function is that this is not true just for the point on the curve where $x = 1$. It is in fact true that at *any* point on the curve $y = e^x$, where $x = p$, the value of y is e^p and the gradient $\dfrac{dy}{dx}$ is also e^p. So at $x = 2$, $y = e^2$ and the gradient $\dfrac{dy}{dx} = e^2$. At $x = 5.6$, $y = e^{5.6}$ and the gradient $\dfrac{dy}{dx} = e^{5.6}$, etc.

■ **When $y = e^x$, $\dfrac{dy}{dx} = e^x$.**

When $y = ke^x$, $\dfrac{dy}{dx} = ke^x$, where k is a constant.

Example 1
Given that $f(x) = 3e^x$ find, to 3 significant figures, the value of $f'(2)$.

Since
$$f(x) = 3e^x$$
$$f'(x) = 3e^x$$

and
$$f'(2) = 3e^2$$
$$= 22.2 \quad (3 \text{ s.f.})$$

Example 2
Given that $f(x) = x^3 - \frac{1}{2}e^x$, find the value of $f'(1.5)$, giving your answer to 3 significant figures.

Since
$$f(x) = x^3 - \tfrac{1}{2}e^x$$
$$f'(x) = 3x^2 - \tfrac{1}{2}e^x$$
and
$$f'(1.5) = 3(1.5)^2 - \tfrac{1}{2}e^{1.5}$$
$$= 6.75 - 2.24\cdots$$
$$= 4.51 \quad (3 \text{ s.f.})$$

6.2 The differentiation of ln x, x > 0

The diagram shows the graphs of $y = e^x$ and $y = \ln x$ and you know from the work in chapter 5 that $\ln x$ is the inverse function of e^x. That is, $y = e^x$ is the reflection of $y = \ln x$ in the line $y = x$.

Consider the point $P(a, b)$ on the curve $y = \ln x$.

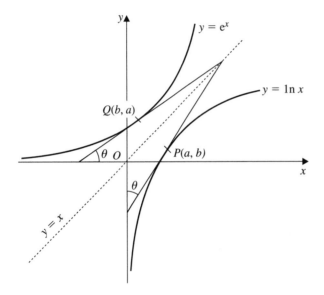

The tangent to the curve at P has gradient $\dfrac{dy}{dx}$. We want to find the derivative when $x = a$. In other words we want $\dfrac{dy}{dx}$ in terms of a.

Consider the point Q, which is the reflection of P in the line $y = x$. The point Q has coordinates (b, a) and lies on the curve $y = e^x$ because e^x is the inverse function of $\ln x$. For $y = e^x$, $\dfrac{dy}{dx} = e^x$ and the gradient of the tangent to the curve $y = e^x$ is e^b at $Q(b, a)$. But as Q is on the curve, we know that $a = e^b$. That is, the gradient of the curve $y = e^x$ at $Q(b, a)$ is a.

The curves $y = \ln x$ and $y = e^x$ are symmetrical about the line $y = x$. If the tangent to $y = e^x$ at (b, a) makes an angle θ with the

x-axis, then the tangent to the curve $y = \ln x$ at (a, b) will make an angle θ with the y-axis. The gradient of the curve $y = e^x$ at Q is $\tan\theta = a$. Because of symmetry, the gradient of the curve $y = \ln x$ at the point $P(a, b)$ is $\tan(90° - \theta)$.

But: $$\tan(90° - \theta) = \frac{1}{\tan\theta} = \frac{1}{a}$$

So the gradient of the curve $y = \ln x$ at P is $\frac{1}{a}$. That is, for $y = \ln x$, $\frac{dy}{dx} = \frac{1}{a}$ at the point (a, b).

The point (a, b) can represent *any* point on the curve $y = \ln x$, so this is an important result:

- **When $y = \ln x$, $\dfrac{dy}{dx} = \dfrac{1}{x}$**

Since $\ln kx = \ln k + \ln x$ (rules of logarithms),

$$\frac{d}{dx}(\ln kx) = \frac{d}{dx}(\ln k) + \frac{d}{dx}(\ln x)$$
$$= 0 + \frac{1}{x}$$
$$= \frac{1}{x} \quad \text{(provided that } k \text{ is a constant)}$$

Also from the change-of-base rule for logarithms:

$$\log_a x = \frac{\ln x}{\ln a}$$

and $$\frac{d}{dx}(\log_a x) = \frac{d}{dx}\left[\frac{\ln x}{\ln a}\right] = \frac{1}{\ln a}\frac{d}{dx}(\ln x)$$
$$= \frac{1}{\ln a}\left(\frac{1}{x}\right), \text{ where } a \text{ is a constant}$$

Memorise these results:

- $\dfrac{d}{dx}(\ln kx) = \dfrac{1}{x}$

- $\dfrac{d}{dx}(\log_a x) = \dfrac{1}{x\ln a}$

Example 3

Find (a) $\dfrac{d}{dx}(\ln 5x)$ (b) $\dfrac{d}{dx}(\log_4 x)$

(a) $\ln 5x = \ln 5 + \ln x$ (rules of logarithms)

$$\frac{d}{dx}(\ln 5x) = \frac{d}{dx}(\ln 5) + \frac{d}{dx}(\ln x) = 0 + \frac{1}{x} = \frac{1}{x}$$

(b) $\log_4 x = \dfrac{\ln x}{\ln 4}$ (change-of-base rule)

$$\frac{d}{dx}(\log_4 x) = \frac{1}{\ln 4}\frac{d}{dx}(\ln x) = \frac{1}{\ln 4}\cdot\frac{1}{x} = \frac{1}{x\ln 4}$$

Example 4

Given that $y = x^2 - 3\ln x$, find the value of $\dfrac{dy}{dx}$ at $x = 2$.

Differentiating with respect to x gives:

$$\frac{dy}{dx} = 2x - \frac{3}{x}$$

At $x = 2$,
$$\frac{dy}{dx} = 4 - \tfrac{3}{2}$$
$$= 2\tfrac{1}{2}$$

Example 5

Find the gradient of the curve with equation

$$y = \tfrac{1}{4}e^x - 2\ln x$$

at the point where $x = \tfrac{1}{3}$.

At any point on the curve:

$$\frac{dy}{dx} = \tfrac{1}{4}e^x - \frac{2}{x}$$

by differentiating with respect to x.

As $\dfrac{dy}{dx}$ is the gradient, at $x = \tfrac{1}{3}$ you have:

$$\text{gradient of curve} = \tfrac{1}{4}e^{\frac{1}{3}} - \frac{2}{\tfrac{1}{3}}$$
$$= \tfrac{1}{4}e^{\frac{1}{3}} - 6$$
$$= -5.65 \ (3 \text{ s.f.})$$

Exercise 6A

1 Differentiate these expressions with respect to x:
  (a) e^x (b) $-2e^x$ (c) $\tfrac{1}{2}e^x$ (d) $5e^x$

2 Differentiate these expressions with respect to x:

  (a) $2x^4 - e^x$ (b) $4(e^x - x^{\frac{3}{2}})$ (c) $\dfrac{e^x}{3} - \dfrac{5}{x^2}$

3 Find the gradient of the curve with equation $y = f(x)$ at the point where $x = \tfrac{1}{4}$ when $f(x) =$

  (a) $\sqrt{x} - 2e^x$ (b) $\dfrac{1}{\sqrt{x}} + \tfrac{1}{4}e^x$

  giving your answers to 3 significant figures.

4 Differentiate these expressions with respect to x:

(a) $2\ln x$ (b) $\ln x + 6$ (c) $4\ln 2x + x^{\frac{1}{2}}$

(d) $\frac{1}{2}\ln x^3 + \frac{1}{4}x^2$ (e) $\frac{1}{3}\ln x + 2e^x$ (f) $-5\ln x^2$

(g) $\ln x^{\frac{1}{2}} + 3x^2$ (h) $\frac{1}{2}e^x - 5\ln\dfrac{x}{5}$ (i) $\dfrac{2}{x} - 3\ln\dfrac{x^2}{3}$

(j) $4(\ln x - 3x^{-1})$ (k) $\log_3 x^2$ (l) $\lg x^3$

5 Sketch the graph of the curve with equation $y = 1 + \ln x$ for $x \geqslant 0$. The points A and B have x-coordinates 2 and 4. Giving your answers to 3 decimal places find:

(a) the y-coordinates of A and B

(b) the gradient of the curve with equation $y = 1 + \ln x$ at A and at B.

6 Find the value of $\dfrac{dy}{dx}$ for the curve with equation $y = f(x)$ at the point P whose x-coordinate is given in each case.

$f(x)$	x-coordinate of P
(a) $3\ln x$	1.5
(b) $x^2 + \frac{1}{3}\ln 4x$	2
(c) $-\ln\dfrac{x}{2}$	0.2
(d) $e^x - 6\ln x^3$	1
(e) $x^2 - 2\lg x$	0.8

7 For the exponential function $f: x \mapsto e^x + 1, x \in \mathbb{R}$:

(a) find the inverse function f^{-1} in a similar form

(b) sketch the graphs of f, f^{-1} and the line $y = x$ on the same diagram

(c) find the derived functions of f and f^{-1}.

6.3 Applications of differentiation

You are now able to extend the work on tangents and normals learned in Book P1, chapter 6, to the exponential and logarithm curves.

■ **For any point (a, b) on the curve with equation $y = f(x)$, the tangent has equation**

$$y - b = f'(a)(x - a)$$

and the normal has equation

$$y - b = -\frac{1}{f'(a)}(x - a)$$

Example 6

Find an equation of the tangent and of the normal to the curve with equation $y = 4e^x$ at the point where $x = -\frac{1}{2}$.

At $x = -\frac{1}{2}$, $y = 4e^{-\frac{1}{2}}$

So:
$$\frac{dy}{dx} = 4e^x = 4e^{-\frac{1}{2}}$$

The gradient of the tangent at $(-\frac{1}{2}, 4e^{-\frac{1}{2}})$ is $4e^{-\frac{1}{2}}$ and its equation is

$$y - 4e^{-\frac{1}{2}} = 4e^{-\frac{1}{2}}(x + \frac{1}{2})$$

The gradient of the normal at $(-\frac{1}{2}, 4e^{-\frac{1}{2}})$ is $-\dfrac{1}{4e^{-\frac{1}{2}}} = -\frac{1}{4}e^{\frac{1}{2}}$.

The equation of the normal is
$$y - 4e^{-\frac{1}{2}} = -\frac{1}{4}e^{\frac{1}{2}}(x + \frac{1}{2})$$

Notice that you do not need to simplify the equations of the tangent and normal further unless you are specifically told to do so.

Example 7

The tangent to the curve with equation $y = \ln 2x$ at the point P where $x = 1$ meets the coordinate axes at the points A and B. Find, to 3 significant figures, the length of AB.

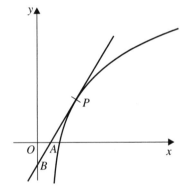

At P, $x = 1$, $y = \ln 2$.

Also:
$$y = \ln 2x = \ln 2 + \ln x$$
$$\frac{dy}{dx} = 0 + \frac{1}{x} = \frac{1}{x}$$

So at $(1, \ln 2)$, $\dfrac{dy}{dx} = 1$ and the gradient of the tangent is 1.

The equation of the tangent at P is

$$y - \ln 2 = 1(x - 1)$$

So the tangent meets the x-axis at $y = 0$, that is:

$$x = 1 - \ln 2$$

So A is the point $(1 - \ln 2, 0)$.
The tangent meets the y-axis at $x = 0$, that is:

$$y = \ln 2 - 1 = -(1 - \ln 2)$$

$$AB^2 = OA^2 + OB^2 \quad \text{(Pythagoras)}$$

$$= (1 - \ln 2)^2 + (1 - \ln 2)^2$$

$$AB = 0.434 \text{ units} \quad \text{(3 s.f.)}$$

Example 8

The normal at $Q(3, \ln\frac{3}{4})$ to the curve with equation $y = \ln\dfrac{x}{4}$ meets the x-axis at R. Find the length of QR, giving your answer to 3 significant figures.

$$y = \ln\frac{x}{4} = \ln x - \ln 4$$

$$\frac{dy}{dx} = \frac{1}{x} - 0 = \frac{1}{x}$$

So at $Q(3, \ln\frac{3}{4})$, $\dfrac{dy}{dx} = \frac{1}{3}$. The gradient of the normal at Q is $-\dfrac{1}{\frac{1}{3}} = -3$. The equation of the normal is

$$y - \ln\tfrac{3}{4} = -3(x - 3)$$

At R, $y = 0 \Rightarrow -\ln\tfrac{3}{4} = -3x + 9$

$$\Rightarrow 3x = 9 + \ln\tfrac{3}{4}$$

$$\Rightarrow x = \frac{9 + \ln\frac{3}{4}}{3}$$

$$= 3 + \tfrac{1}{3}\ln\tfrac{3}{4}$$

Using $d^2 = (x_1 - x_2)^2 + (y_1 - y_2)^2$ you have

$$QR^2 = [3 - (3 + \tfrac{1}{3}\ln\tfrac{3}{4})]^2 + [\ln\tfrac{3}{4} - 0]^2$$

$$= [3 - 3 - \tfrac{1}{3}\ln\tfrac{3}{4}]^2 + (\ln\tfrac{3}{4})^2$$

$$= \tfrac{1}{9}(\ln\tfrac{3}{4})^2 + (\ln\tfrac{3}{4})^2$$

$$= \tfrac{10}{9}(\ln\tfrac{3}{4})^2$$

So: $\qquad\qquad QR = 0.303$ units (3 s.f.)

Example 9

Find the coordinates and the nature of the turning point on the curve with equation $y = x^3 - 81 \ln x$.

$$\frac{dy}{dx} = 3x^2 - \frac{81}{x}$$

For a turning point, $\dfrac{dy}{dx} = 0$

That is: $\qquad\qquad 3x^2 = \dfrac{81}{x}$

So: $x^3 = 27$ and $x = 3$

At $x = 3$, $y = 27 - 81 \ln 3 \approx -62$

The turning point is at $(3, -62)$.

Now differentiate again with respect to x:

$$\frac{dy}{dx} = 3x^2 - 81x^{-1}$$

So:

$$\frac{d^2y}{dx^2} = 6x + 81x^{-2}$$

$$= 6x + \frac{81}{x^2}$$

At $x = 3$, $\frac{d^2y}{dx^2} = 18 + \frac{81}{9} = 27 > 0$.

Since $\frac{dy}{dx} = 0$ and $\frac{d^2y}{dx^2} > 0$ at $x = 3$, $y = -62$ is a minimum value.

Exercise 6B

1 Show that the tangent at $(0, 2)$ to the curve with equation $y = 2e^x$ passes through the point $(-1, 0)$.

2 Show that the tangent at $(e, e + 1)$ to the curve with equation $y = x + \ln x$ is of the form $y = kx$ and find the constant k in terms of e.

3 Find an equation of the normal at the point where $x = -1$ on the curve with equation $y = 3e^x$.

4 Find an equation of the normal at $(1, 0)$ to the curve with equation $y = \ln x^3$.

5 Prove that $\log_a x = (\ln x)(\log_a e)$.
Hence prove that $\frac{d}{dx}(\log_a x) = \frac{1}{x}\log_a e$.

6 Find an equation of the tangent at $(10, 1)$ to the curve with equation $y = \lg x$.

7 Find, to 2 decimal places, the y-coordinate of the point where the normal at $(e, 4)$ to the curve with equation $y = 4\ln x$ cuts the y-axis.

8 The tangent and normal to the curve with equation $y = 7x - e^x$ at the point P on the curve where $x = 2$ meet the y-axis at A and B respectively. Find the length of AB.

9 Show that the curve with equation $y = e^x - x$ has just one turning point and find its coordinates.

10 The curve C has equation $y = x^2 - \ln x$, $x > 0$. Show that C has just one turning point and find its coordinates.

11 Given that $y = 9x^3 - 8\ln x$, $x > 0$, find the value of x and the value of y when $\frac{dy}{dx} = 0$.

12 Given that $y = 8x - e^x$, find the value of x and the value of y

   when $\dfrac{dy}{dx} = 0$. State whether the value of y you have found is

   a maximum or a minimum.

13 Given that $f(x) = 4x^2 - 9e^x$, find the value of x for which
   $f''(x) = 0$ and the corresponding value of $f(x)$.

SUMMARY OF KEY POINTS

1 $\dfrac{d(e^x)}{dx} = e^x$ and $\dfrac{d(ke^x)}{dx} = ke^x$, where k is a constant

2 $\dfrac{d(\ln x)}{dx} = \dfrac{1}{x}$

3 $\dfrac{d(\ln kx)}{dx} = \dfrac{1}{x}$, where k is a constant

4 $\dfrac{d(\log_a x)}{dx} = \dfrac{1}{x \ln a}$

Integration

7

7.1 The integration of e^x

As integration is the reverse process to differentiation, you can use the result

$$\frac{d}{dx}(e^x) = e^x$$

to produce the result

■ $\int e^x dx = e^x + C$, where C is an arbitrary constant.

Also, since $\frac{d}{dx}(ke^x) = ke^x$, you have

■ $\int ke^x dx = ke^x + C$, where k is a constant and C is the arbitrary constant of integration.

Example 1

Evaluate $\displaystyle\int_0^3 e^x dx$

$$\int_0^3 e^x dx = \left[e^x\right]_0^3 = e^3 - e^0$$
$$= e^3 - 1$$

Note: Answers may often be left in terms of e, but always read the question carefully.

Example 2

Given that $\dfrac{dy}{dx} = e^x + x^{-\frac{1}{2}}$ and that $y = 2$ at $x = 1$, find the value of y at $x = 2$, giving your answer to 3 significant figures.

Since $\dfrac{dy}{dx} = e^x + x^{-\frac{1}{2}}$ you can write

$$y = \int (e^x + x^{-\frac{1}{2}}) \, dx$$

$$= \int e^x \, dx + \int x^{-\frac{1}{2}} \, dx$$

$$y = e^x + 2x^{\frac{1}{2}} + C, \text{ where } C \text{ is a constant.}$$

Since $y = 2$ at $x = 1$,

$$2 = e + 2 + C$$

That is: $\qquad\qquad\qquad C = -e$

Hence: $\qquad\qquad\qquad y = e^x + 2x^{\frac{1}{2}} - e$

At $x = 2$, $\qquad\qquad\qquad y = e^2 - e + 2\sqrt{2}$

$$y = 7.50 \ (3 \text{ s.f.})$$

7.2 The integration of $\dfrac{1}{x}$

As integration is the reverse process to differentiation, you can use the result that for $x > 0$,

$$\frac{d(\ln x)}{dx} = \frac{1}{x}$$

to produce the result for $x > 0$:

$$\int \frac{1}{x} \, dx = \ln x + C$$

where C is an arbitrary constant. (I)

Now $\qquad \dfrac{d(\ln kx)}{dx} = \dfrac{1}{x}$, where k is a constant

So for $x < 0$: $\qquad \dfrac{d[\ln(-x)]}{dx} = \dfrac{1}{x}$, putting $k = -1$

Thus for $x < 0$, $\qquad \displaystyle\int \frac{1}{x} \, dx = \ln(-x) + C$

where C is an arbitrary constant. (II)

So combining (I) and (II) we get:

■ $\qquad\qquad\qquad \displaystyle\int \frac{1}{x} \, dx = \ln|x| + C$

Example 3

Evaluate (a) $\int_3^8 \dfrac{1}{x}\,\mathrm{d}x$ (b) $\int_3^8 \dfrac{1}{6x}\,\mathrm{d}x$, giving your answers in the form of a single natural logarithm.

(a)
$$\int_3^8 \frac{1}{x}\,\mathrm{d}x = \Big[\ln|x|\Big]_3^8$$
$$= \ln|8| - \ln|3|$$
$$= \ln 8 - \ln 3$$

Using the rule $\log a - \log b = \log \dfrac{a}{b}$ you have

$$\int_3^8 \frac{1}{x}\,\mathrm{d}x = \ln 8 - \ln 3 = \ln \tfrac{8}{3}$$

(b) $\int_3^8 \dfrac{1}{6x}\,\mathrm{d}x = \int_3^8 \tfrac{1}{6}\cdot\dfrac{1}{x}\,\mathrm{d}x = \tfrac{1}{6}\int_3^8 \dfrac{1}{x}\,\mathrm{d}x$

So from (a) you have

$$\int_3^8 \frac{1}{6x}\,\mathrm{d}x = \tfrac{1}{6}\int_3^8 \frac{1}{x}\,\mathrm{d}x = \tfrac{1}{6}\ln \tfrac{8}{3}$$

Example 4

For $t \geqslant 1$, the variables x and t are related by the differential equation $\dfrac{\mathrm{d}x}{\mathrm{d}t} = \dfrac{2 + 4t^2}{t}$ and $x = 2$ when $t = 1$. Find x in terms of t.

$$\frac{\mathrm{d}x}{\mathrm{d}t} = \frac{2 + 4t^2}{t} = \frac{2}{t} + 4t$$

Integrating with respect to t:

$$x = 2\ln t + 2t^2 + C$$

where C is an arbitrary constant.

But $x = 2$ when $t = 1$, so

$$2 = 2\ln 1 + 2 + C$$

But $\ln 1 = 0$, so $C = 0$.

That gives the equation relating x and t as:

$$x = 2\ln t + 2t^2$$

Example 5

At any point $P(x, y)$ on a certain curve, the gradient, $\dfrac{\mathrm{d}y}{\mathrm{d}x}$, is inversely proportional to x. Given that $\dfrac{\mathrm{d}y}{\mathrm{d}x} = 2$ and $y = 2$ at $x = 4$, find y in terms of x.

As $\dfrac{dy}{dx}$ is inversely proportional to x, you can write:

$$\frac{dy}{dx} = \frac{k}{x}$$

where k is a constant.

But $\dfrac{dy}{dx} = 2$ at $x = 4$ so you have

$$2 = \frac{k}{4} \Rightarrow k = 8$$

That is:
$$\frac{dy}{dx} = \frac{8}{x}$$

Integrating with respect to x:

$$y = 8 \ln |x| + C$$

where C is a constant.

But $y = 2$ at $x = 4$ so you have

$$2 = 8 \ln 4 + C$$
$$\Rightarrow C = 2 - 8 \ln 4$$

Hence you can write

$$y = 8 \ln |x| + 2 - 8 \ln 4$$

which is
$$y = 2 + 8(\ln |x| - \ln 4)$$
$$= 2 + 8 \ln \left| \frac{x}{4} \right|$$

as the simplest way of expressing y in terms of x.

Exercise 7A

In questions 1–12 integrate with respect to x:

1 $4e^x$

2 $\frac{1}{2}e^x$

3 $x^{\frac{2}{3}} - \frac{2}{3}e^x$

4 $\dfrac{e^x + 7x + x^2}{3}$

5 $(e^{\frac{x}{2}} + 1)^2 + (e^{\frac{x}{2}} - 1)^2$

6 $7x^{-1}$

7 $-2x^{-1}$

8 $\dfrac{x^2 + 4x}{x^2}$

9 $x^{\frac{1}{3}} - \dfrac{1}{x^{\frac{1}{2}}}$

10 $\dfrac{6}{x} - \frac{1}{2}e^x + 3$

11 $\left(x^2 + \dfrac{4}{x} \right)^2$

12 $\left(x - \dfrac{1}{x} \right)^3$

In questions 13–20 evaluate:

13 $\displaystyle\int_{1}^{3} 2e^x \, dx$

14 $\displaystyle\int_{-2}^{0} \frac{e^x}{3} \, dx$

15 $\displaystyle\int_{2}^{5} \frac{4}{x} \, dx$

16 $\displaystyle\int_{3}^{6} \left(x - \frac{1}{x}\right) dx$

17 $\displaystyle\int_{-3}^{-1} \frac{1}{x} \, dx$

18 $\displaystyle\int_{2}^{3} (2x^{-1} - 3e^x) \, dx$

19 $\displaystyle\int_{e}^{e^2} \left(\frac{5}{x} + e\right) dx$

20 $\displaystyle\int_{1}^{e} \left(\frac{1}{x} + 2\right)^2 dx$

21 Given that $\dfrac{dy}{dx} = \dfrac{3}{2x}$ and $y = 3$ at $x = 1$, find y in terms of x.

22 Given that $\dfrac{dy}{dx} = 3e^x + 4$ and that $y = 6$ at $x = \frac{1}{2}$, find y in terms of x.

23 Given that $\dfrac{dy}{dx}$ is directly proportional to $\dfrac{x^2 + 1}{x}$ and $\dfrac{dy}{dx} = y = 4$ at $x = 1$, find y in terms of x.

24 $\dfrac{dy}{dx}$ is inversely proportional to x and $\dfrac{dy}{dx} = -4$ at $x = 2$. Also it is known that $y = 3$ at $x = 1$. Find y in terms of x.

25 Find y in terms of x, given that $e^{-x} \dfrac{dy}{dx} = 4.5$ and $y = 8$ at $x = 0$. Hence express x in terms of y.

7.3 Using integration to find areas and volumes

The area under a curve

The diagram shows part of the curve with equation $y = f(x)$ between the values $x = a$ and $x = b$. The finite region R is bounded by the curve, the lines $x = a$ and $x = b$ and the x-axis.

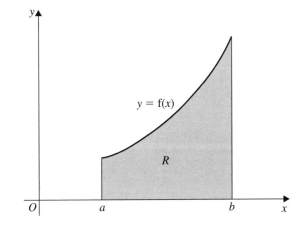

You can find an approximate value for the area of R by dividing R into small strips parallel to the y-axis as shown below.

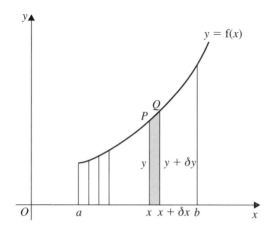

If you divide R into a *very* large number of thin strips (much more than can be shown in the diagram), the curved top of each strip will be almost a straight line. So each strip could be regarded as a trapezium and the area of R is approximately the sum of the areas of all the trapezia.

Take a typical strip by considering two neighbouring points $(x, 0)$ and $(x + \delta x, 0)$ on the x-axis. The corresponding points on the curve $y = f(x)$ are P and Q with coordinates (x, y) and $(x + \delta x, y + \delta y)$ respectively. δx and δy are very small quantities (increments). If you think of the strip as a trapezium, its area is:

$$\delta x \left(\frac{y + \delta y + y}{2} \right)$$
$$= y\delta x + \tfrac{1}{2}\delta y \delta x$$
$$\approx y\delta x$$

(because $\tfrac{1}{2}\delta y \delta x$ is so small that it can be left out).

Then:

$$\text{area of } R \approx \sum_{x=a}^{x=b} y\,\delta x$$

That is, the sum of the areas of all the strips from $x = a$ to $x = b$.

The more strips you take, the more accurate your approximation to the area of R will be. By using more advanced mathematics than you will find in an A-level course, it can be shown that, as you increase the number of strips indefinitely, that is, making $\delta x \to 0$,

$$\lim_{\delta x \to 0} \sum_{x=a}^{x=b} y\,\delta x = \int_a^b y\,dx = \int_a^b f(x)\,dx$$

In Book P1, chapter 6, you were given this formula in order to evaluate areas of regions. Now you have been given an explanation about where the formula comes from. That is, the summation tends to the value of the definite integral $\int_a^b f(x)\, dx$, which is the limiting value **and** the actual area of R exactly.

■ **Area of $R = \int_a^b f(x)\, dx$**

This result is often called the **fundamental theorem of integral calculus** and its importance is paramount because all integration theory is based on it. In your work, you are expected to assume the validity of this result, and to use it for the growing list of functions you are able to integrate.

In a similar way it can be shown that the area of the region bounded by the curve $x = g(y)$, the y-axis and the lines $y = p$ and $y = q$ is

■ $\int_p^q x\, dy = \int_p^q g(y)\, dy$

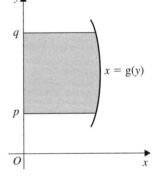

Example 6
Sketch a diagram to show the finite region bounded by the curve with equation $y = x^{-1}$, the lines $x = 0.5$ and $x = 4$, and the x-axis. Find the area of this region.

The sketch shows the region required.

The area of this region is:

$$\int_{0.5}^4 x^{-1}\, dx = \Big[\ln |x|\Big]_{0.5}^4$$

$$= \ln 4 - \ln 0.5$$

$$= 2.08 \ (2 \text{ d.p.})$$

Example 7

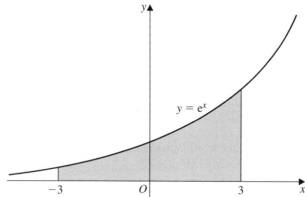

The diagram shows the shaded region bounded by the curve with equation $y = e^x$, the lines $x = -3$ and $x = 3$ and the x-axis. Find the area of the shaded region.

$$\text{Area required} = \int_{-3}^{3} e^x \, dx = \left[e^x \right]_{-3}^{3}$$

$$= e^3 - e^{-3}$$

$$= 20.04 \ (2 \text{ d.p.})$$

Volumes of revolution

You have seen that the area of the region R bounded by the curve with equation $y = f(x)$, the x-axis and the lines $x = a$ and $x = b$ can be found by dividing the region into elementary strips of width δx and summing the area of all the strips as $\delta x \rightarrow 0$. A typical strip is shown in the left-hand diagram below.

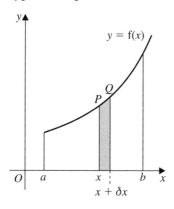
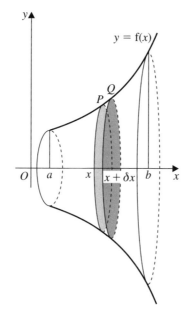

Suppose now that the region R is rotated completely (that is, through 2π radians) about the x-axis. A solid S will be formed as shown in the right-hand diagram. Each end of the solid is a circle, their radii being a and b.

Now think about what happens to the strip of length y and thickness δx when it is rotated completely about the x-axis. The rotating strip forms a circular disc of radius y and thickness δx. The volume of this disc is $\pi y^2 \delta x$.

The volume of S is the sum of all such discs from $x = a$ to $x = b$. As δx is made progressively smaller, the successive approximations to the volume of S approach the actual value of the volume and we can assume:

$$\text{Volume of } S = \lim_{\delta x \to 0} \sum_{x=a}^{x=b} \pi y^2 \, \delta x = \int_a^b \pi y^2 \, \mathrm{d}x$$

$$= \int_a^b \pi [\mathrm{f}(x)]^2 \, \mathrm{d}x$$

We have then

■ **Volume of $S = \displaystyle\int_a^b \pi [\mathrm{f}(x)]^2 \, \mathrm{d}x$**

In the same way, you can think about a region bounded by the curve with equation $x = \mathrm{g}(y)$, the y-axis and the lines $y = p$ and $y = q$. If this region is rotated completely about the y-axis, the solid formed has volume

$$\int_p^q \pi [\mathrm{g}(y)]^2 \, \mathrm{d}y$$

This volume is often referred to as the **volume of revolution** and is said to be *generated* by the rotation of the curve.

Example 8

The finite region bounded by the curve with equation $y = x - x^2$ and the x-axis is rotated through 2π radians about the x-axis. Find the volume of revolution so formed, leaving your answer in terms of π.

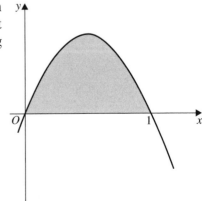

First, sketch the curve $y = x - x^2$:
The curve meets the x-axis at points where $x - x^2 = 0$;

that is: $\qquad\qquad\qquad x(1 - x) = 0$

So: $\qquad\qquad\qquad x = 0 \text{ and } x = 1$

The finite region is shown shaded.

$$\text{Volume of revolution} = \int_0^1 \pi y^2 \, dx$$

$$= \pi \int_0^1 (x - x^2)^2 \, dx$$

$$= \pi \int_0^1 (x^2 - 2x^3 + x^4) \, dx$$

$$= \pi \left[\frac{x^3}{3} - \frac{2x^4}{4} + \frac{x^5}{5} \right]_0^1$$

$$= \pi(\tfrac{1}{3} - \tfrac{1}{2} + \tfrac{1}{5}) = \frac{\pi}{30}$$

Example 9

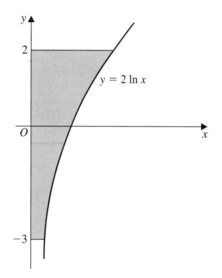

The shaded region is bounded by the curve with equation $y = 2\ln x$, the y-axis and the lines with equations $y = -3$ and $y = 2$. The region is rotated through $360°$ about the *y-axis* to form a solid of revolution S. Find, in terms of π and e, the volume of S.

If $y = 2\ln x$ then $\ln x = \dfrac{y}{2}$ and $x = e^{\frac{y}{2}}$.

$$\text{Volume of } S = \pi \int_{-3}^{2} x^2 \, dy$$

$$= \pi \int_{-3}^{2} \left[e^{\frac{y}{2}} \right]^2 dy$$

$$= \pi \int_{-3}^{2} e^y \, dy$$

Integrating with respect to y:

$$\text{Volume of } S = \pi \left[e^y \right]_{-3}^{2} = \pi(e^2 - e^{-3})$$

Exercise 7B

1 The diagram shows a sketch of the curve with equation $xy = 4$. Find the area of the region R bounded by the curve, the lines with equations $x = 1$ and $x = 5$ and the x-axis. Find also the volume of the solid formed when the region is rotated completely about the x-axis.

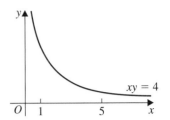

2 Sketch the curve with equation $y = 2 + 3e^x$. Find the area of the region bounded by the curve, the lines with equations $x = -2$ and $x = 3$ and the x-axis.

3 The points $A(-1, e^{-1})$ and $B(2, e^2)$ are on the curve with equation $y = e^x$. Find to 2 decimal places, the area of the region bounded by the curve and the line segment AB.

4 The diagram shows a sketch of the curve with equation $2y^2 = x^3$. Find the volume of the solid formed by the complete rotation *about the y-axis* of the region bounded by the curve, the y-axis and the line with equation $y = 2$, which lies in the first quadrant. Find also the volume formed when the region is rotated completely about the x-axis.

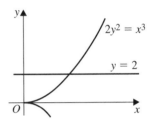

5 The diagram shows a sketch of the curve with equation $y = x + \dfrac{1}{x}$.

Find the area of the region R bounded by the curve, the lines with equations $x = \frac{1}{2}$, $x = 3$ and the x-axis.
Find also the volume of the solid formed when R is rotated through $180°$ about the x-axis.

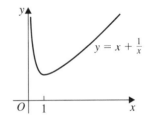

6 The diagram shows a sketch of the curve with equation $y = \dfrac{x^2 - 1}{x^2}$. Find the area of the finite region R bounded by the curve, the lines with equations $x = 1$ and $x = 3$ and the x-axis. Find
(a) the area of R
(b) the volume formed when R is rotated through $360°$ about the x-axis.

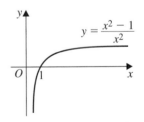

7 The diagram shows a sketch of the curve with equation $y^2 = 16x$. Find the area of the region in the first quadrant bounded by the curve, the y-axis and the line with equation $y = 8$. This region is rotated completely about the y-axis. Find the volume of the solid formed.

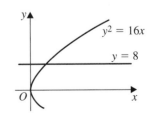

8 The normal to the curve with equation $y = 2e^x$ at the point $P(1, 2e)$ meets the x-axis at Q. Show that Q is the point $(4e^2 + 1, 0)$.

Find the area of the region R bounded by the coordinate axes, the normal and the curve $y = 2e^x$.

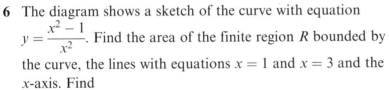

9 (a) Sketch the curve with equation $y = 2x^2 - 1$, showing on your sketch the coordinates of the points at which the curve meets the coordinate axes.

The finite region R is bounded by the curve and the line with equation $y = 0$.

(b) Find the area of R.

The region R is rotated through $180°$ about the y-axis to form a solid S.

(c) Find the volume of S.

10 Find an equation of the normal at $(3, 8)$ to the curve with equation $y = 2 + 5x - x^2$.

Show that this normal meets the curve again at the point $(1, 6)$.

Find the area of the finite region bounded by the normal and the curve.

11 The diagram shows a sketch of the curve with equation $y = x^3 - x$. The region R is bounded by the x-axis and the curve and lies in the second quadrant.

(a) Find the area of R.

(b) Find, in terms of π, the volume generated when R is rotated completely about the x-axis.

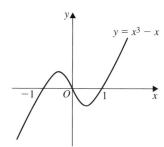

12 The diagram shows a sketch of the curve with equation $y = 3x - \dfrac{2}{x}$. The region R is bounded by the curve, the lines with equations $x = 1$ and $x = 4$, and the x-axis.

(a) Find the area of R.

(b) Find the volume generated when R is rotated through $360°$ about the x-axis.

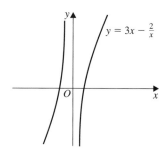

13 The part of the curve with equation $y = x(x - 3)$ between the lines with equations $x = 1$ and $x = 2$ is rotated completely about the x-axis.

Find the volume of revolution so formed.

14 The diagram shows a sketch of the curve with equation $y^3 = x$. Find the area of the region bounded by the curve, the lines with equations $y = 2$ and $y = 4$, and the y-axis.

This region is rotated completely about the y-axis.

Find the volume generated.

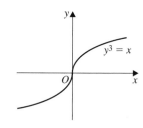

15 The finite region R lies in the first quadrant and is bounded by the curve with equation $y = f(x)$, the x-axis and the lines with equations $x = a$ and $x = b$.

Find the volume generated when R is rotated completely about the x-axis in the following cases. In each case, $f(x)$ is non-negative and finite for $a \leqslant x \leqslant b$.

(a) $f(x) = 2x^{\frac{1}{4}}, a = 1, b = 16$ (b) $f(x) = x^{-\frac{1}{2}}, a = 2, b = 5$

(c) $f(x) = x\sqrt{(4 - x^2)}, a = 0, b = 2$

(d) $f(x) = \dfrac{x + 1}{x}, a = 1, b = 4$

7.4 Numerical integration: the trapezium rule

We often need to evaluate definite integrals, in the evaluation of areas and volumes and in the solution of differential equations. Not all integrals, however, can be evaluated by direct integration leading to an exact answer. Here are two integrals which fall into this category:

$$\int_1^6 (\ln x)^{\frac{1}{2}} \, dx, \quad \int_0^3 e^{x^2} \, dx$$

If you draw graphs, you can see that the areas of these regions *do* exist:

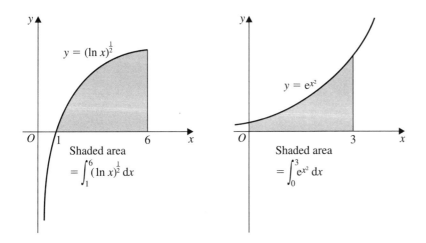

So you need to develop a strategy for finding approximations for these integrals.

The trapezium rule

For the curve with equation $y = f(x)$, suppose that y is positive for all values of x in the interval $a \leqslant x \leqslant b$. Then the area of the region bounded by $y = f(x)$, the lines with equations $x = a$, $x = b$ and the x-axis is given by the definite integral $\int_a^b f(x) \, dx$ and can be shown in the diagram by the shaded region.

In the diagram, the coordinates of P and Q are $(a, 0)$ and $(b, 0)$, $AP = f(a)$ and $BQ = f(b)$.

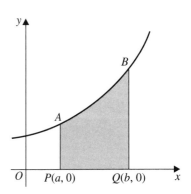

An estimate of the area of this region can be obtained by joining A to B with a straight line and then taking the area of the trapezium $APQB$ as an approximation to the area given by $\int_a^b f(x)\,dx$.

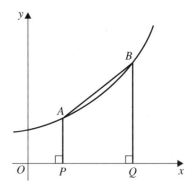

The area of the trapezium $APQB$ is given by the product of its width PQ and its average height $\left(\dfrac{AP + BQ}{2}\right)$.

So:

$$\text{area of trapezium} = \tfrac{1}{2}PQ(AP + BQ)$$
$$= \tfrac{1}{2}(b - a)[f(a) + f(b)]$$

That is, a crude approximation to the definite integral is given by

$$\int_a^b f(x)\,dx \approx \tfrac{1}{2}(b - a)[f(a) + f(b)]$$

To obtain a better approximation, divide the interval $a \leqslant x \leqslant b$ into n equal parts of length h, where $h = \dfrac{b - a}{n}$. The region is then divided into n strips of equal width $\dfrac{b - a}{n}$ by lines drawn parallel to the y-axis, as shown in the following diagram, where A_0 is $(a, 0)$, A_n is $(b, 0)$ and

$$A_0A_1 = A_1A_2 = A_2A_3 = \ldots = A_{n-2}A_{n-1} = A_{n-1}A_n = \frac{b - a}{n} = h$$

$$P_0A_0 = y_0, P_1A_1 = y_1, P_2A_2 = y_2 \ldots, P_nA_n = y_n$$

As the curve has equation $y = f(x)$, you can say also

$$y_0 = f(a), y_1 = f(a + h), y_2 = f(a + 2h) \ldots, y_n = f(b)$$

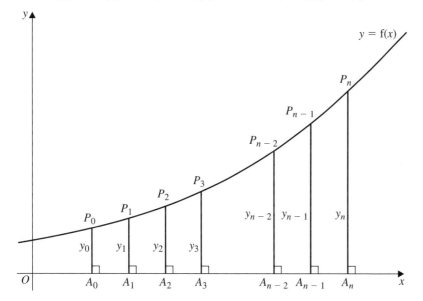

By joining P_0 and P_1, P_1 and P_2, P_2 and P_3, $\ldots P_{n-1}$ and P_n with straight lines you form n small trapezia. You can then approximate the area of the region given by $\int_a^b f(x)\,dx$ by finding the areas of each of these trapezia and adding them. So:

$$\int_a^b f(x)\,dx \approx \tfrac{1}{2}h(y_0 + y_1) + \tfrac{1}{2}h(y_1 + y_2) + \tfrac{1}{2}h(y_2 + y_3) + \ldots + \tfrac{1}{2}h(y_{n-1} + y_n)$$

That is:

■ $$\int_a^b f(x)\,dx \approx \frac{h}{2}[y_0 + 2y_1 + 2y_2 + 2y_3 + \ldots + 2y_{n-1} + y_n]$$

This summation of n trapezia to approximate to the area of the region given by $\int_a^b f(x)\,dx$ is known as the **trapezium rule**.

In order to apply the rule, remember that the curve $y = f(x)$ must remain on the same side of the x-axis, i.e. $y > 0$ OR $y < 0$ throughout the interval $a \leqslant x \leqslant b$.

You are now in a position to find estimates of integrals such as $\int_1^6 (\ln x)^{\frac{1}{2}}\,dx$ and $\int_0^3 e^{x^2}\,dx$.

Example 10

Using six equally spaced ordinates with the trapezium rule, find an estimate for $\int_1^6 (\ln x)^{\frac{1}{2}}\,dx$.

You can tabulate your working like this:

x values	y values (4 d.p.)	
1	$y_0 = (\ln 1)^{\frac{1}{2}} = 0$	$y_0 = 0$
2	$y_1 = (\ln 2)^{\frac{1}{2}} = 0.8326$	$2y_1 = 1.6652$
3	$y_2 = (\ln 3)^{\frac{1}{2}} = 1.0481$	$2y_2 = 2.0962$
4	$y_3 = (\ln 4)^{\frac{1}{2}} = 1.1774$	$2y_3 = 2.3548$
5	$y_4 = (\ln 5)^{\frac{1}{2}} = 1.2686$	$2y_4 = 2.5372$
6	$y_5 = (\ln 6)^{\frac{1}{2}} = 1.3386$	$y_5 = 1.3386$

Using the trapezium rule with $h = \dfrac{6 - 1}{5} = 1$ you have:

$$\int_1^6 (\ln x)^{\frac{1}{2}}\,dx \approx \frac{h}{2}[y_0 + 2y_1 + 2y_2 + 2y_3 + 2y_4 + 2y_5 + y_6]$$

$$\approx \tfrac{1}{2}[0 + 1.6652 + 2.0962 + 2.3548 + 2.5372 + 1.3386]$$

$$= 4.996$$

So $\int_1^6 (\ln x)^{\frac{1}{2}}\,dx \approx 5.0$ (2 s.f.)

Exercise 7C

In questions 1–8, use the trapezium rule with n intervals of equal width to find an estimate of the definite integral, giving your final answer to 3 decimal places.

1 $\displaystyle\int_0^{0.6} e^{-x^2}\,dx, \quad n = 6$

2 $\displaystyle\int_0^4 (16 - x^2)^{\frac{1}{2}}\,dx, \quad n = 4$

3 $\displaystyle\int_{\frac{\pi}{6}}^{\frac{\pi}{2}} \sin^{\frac{1}{2}}x\,dx, \quad n = 6$

4 $\displaystyle\int_0^{\frac{\pi}{4}} \ln\sec x\,dx, \quad n = 5$

5 $\displaystyle\int_{-2}^3 e^{x^2}\,dx, \quad n = 10$

6 $\displaystyle\int_1^2 \lg x\,dx, \quad n = 5$

7 $\displaystyle\int_0^\pi \sin^{\frac{3}{2}}x\,dx, \quad n = 8$

8 $\displaystyle\int_0^{\frac{\pi}{2}} \cos^{\frac{1}{3}}x\,dx, \quad n = 5$

9 The region R is bounded by the curve with equation $y = e^{\sqrt{x}}$, the lines with equations $x = 0$ and $x = 4$ and the x-axis. Use the trapezium rule with 6 intervals of equal width to estimate, to three decimal places
   (a) the area of R
   (b) the value generated when R is rotated completely about the x-axis.

10 The diagram shows a sketch of the region bounded by the curve with equation $y = (x^2 + 2)^{\frac{1}{2}}$, the lines with equations $x = -2$, $x = 2$ and $y = 0$. Use the trapezium rule with 5 equally spaced ordinates to estimate the area of the region, giving your answer to three decimal places.
    Find, in terms of π by direct integration, the volume generated when the region is rotated through $360°$ about the x-axis.

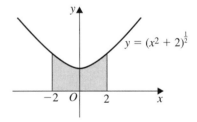

11

x	0	$\dfrac{\pi}{6}$	$\dfrac{\pi}{3}$	$\dfrac{\pi}{2}$
$\sin(\sin x)$	0	0.48	0.76	0.84

The table gives four values of x and the corresponding values of $\sin(\sin x)$, corrected to two decimal places. Use the trapezium rule with four ordinates and only the values in the table, to estimate, to one decimal place, a value of

$$\int_0^{\frac{\pi}{2}} \sin(\sin x)\,dx \qquad\qquad \text{[E]}$$

12 Use the trapezium rule with 5 strips of equal width to find, to three decimal places, the value of

$$\int_0^1 10^x \, \mathrm{d}x$$ [E]

13 The table gives the values of a function f(x) for certain values of x.

x	1	1.5	2	2.5	3	3.5	4
f(x)	4.1	4.7	5.1	4.8	5.1	5.4	5.9

Use the trapezium rule with 6 intervals of equal width to estimate the value of $\int_1^4 \mathrm{f}(x)\,\mathrm{d}x$. [E]

SUMMARY OF KEY POINTS

1 $\int \mathrm{e}^x \, \mathrm{d}x = \mathrm{e}^x + C$

2 $\int k\mathrm{e}^x \, \mathrm{d}x = k\mathrm{e}^x + C$, where k is a constant

3 $\int \dfrac{1}{x} \mathrm{d}x = \ln|x| + C$

4 The volume generated when R is rotated completely about the x-axis is

$$\pi \int_a^b [\mathrm{f}(x)]^2 \mathrm{d}x$$

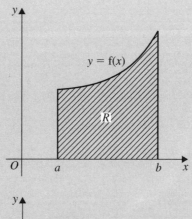

5 The volume generated when R is rotated completely about the y-axis is

$$\pi \int_p^q [\mathrm{g}(y)]^2 \mathrm{d}y$$

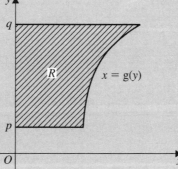

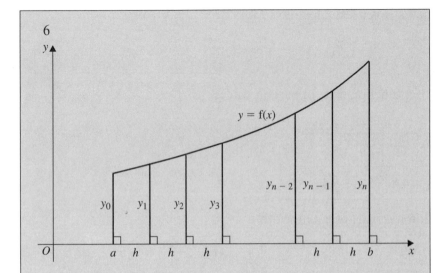

The trapezium rule states that the area of the region bounded by the curve with equation $y = f(x)$, the x-axis and the ordinates $x = a$ and $x = b$ is approximately

$$\frac{h}{2}[y_0 + 2y_1 + 2y_2 + 2y_3 + \ldots + 2y_{n-2} + 2y_{n-1} + y_n]$$

Numerical methods

8

8.1 Locating the roots of f(x) = 0

You know how to solve linear equations (such as $4x - 2 = 0$) and quadratic equations (such as $3x^2 - 2x - 1 = 0$). For polynomials of degree higher than two it is not always possible to find a factor, or factors. So trying to factorise the left-hand side of a polynomial equation is not a good way of finding the roots of the equation. This is particularly true when the roots are not integers, as trying to guess factors that are decimals is a very difficult exercise. There is also no simple algebraic method of finding the roots of equations which involve e^x, $\ln x$, $\sin x$, $\cos x$, etc. These are sometimes called **transcendental** equations.

For these types of equations you have to find out approximately where a root lies. Then you can use numerical methods to find closer and closer approximations to the root.

Example 1
Locate the roots of $x^2 - 3x - 10 = 0$.
Consider the function $f(x) \equiv x^2 - 3x - 10$. If you put $y = f(x)$, so that $y = x^2 - 3x - 10$, you can draw the graph of the function. It looks like this:

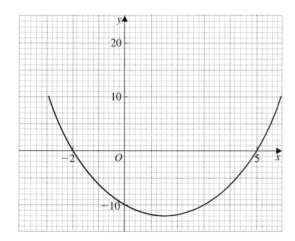

To find the roots of the equation $x^2 - 3x - 10 = 0$ you need to find points on the curve $y = x^2 - 3x - 10$ at which $y = 0$. Now on the graph the line $y = 0$ is the x-axis. So for the roots of the equation $x^2 - 3x - 10 = 0$ you need to find where the graph of $y = x^2 - 3x - 10$ cuts the x-axis. The graph cuts the x-axis at $x = -2$ and $x = 5$ so the roots of the equation are -2 and 5.

This procedure is one that works in general. To find the roots of $f(x) = 0$ first consider the graph of $y = f(x)$. It might look like this:

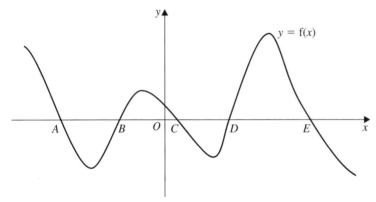

But for the equation $f(x) = 0$ you need to consider the curve $y = f(x)$ together with the line $y = 0$ (the x-axis). In this case the equation $f(x) = 0$ has five real roots which are given by the x-coordinates of the points A, B, C, D and E. It would be very time-consuming and impractical to draw a graph each time you wish to find the roots of an equation $f(x) = 0$ which you cannot solve algebraically. To find a better method, let's look at the graph of $y = f(x)$ to see what happens near a root.

To the left of point A on the graph the values of y are positive because the curve lies above the x-axis at these points. Just to the right of point A the values of y for points on the curve are negative because the curve is below the x-axis at these points. Just to the left of point B the values of y for points on the curve are negative and just to the right they are positive.

So the values of y for points on the graph of $y = f(x)$ *change sign* from positive to negative or negative to positive as the curve crosses the x-axis. This is when it passes through a root of the equation $f(x) = 0$. The graph shows that the same is true for points C, D and E.

In general, if you can find two values of x, one for which $f(x)$ is positive and one for which $f(x)$ is negative, then you know that the curve of $y = f(x)$ must have crossed the x-axis and so must have passed through a root of the equation $f(x) = 0$. So if $f(x_1) > 0$ and $f(x_2) < 0$ you know that there is at least one value of x lying between x_1 and x_2 which is a root of $f(x) = 0$. Similarly, if $f(x_3) < 0$ and $f(x_4) > 0$ there has been change of sign so at least one root of $f(x) = 0$ must lie between x_3 and x_4.

The only times this piece of detection does not work is where the graph looks like one of the following:

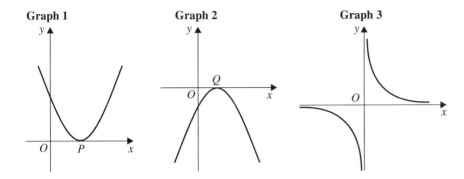

Graph 1

Graph 2

Graph 3

In Graph 1 there is a root of $f(x) = 0$ at P, but $f(x) > 0$ to the left of P and $f(x) > 0$ to the right of P.

Similarly, in Graph 2, $f(x) < 0$ to the left of Q and $f(x) < 0$ to the right of Q.

In Graph 3, the curve contains a **discontinuity** – a point at which the curve does not move continuously from one y value to the next. The curve never crosses the x-axis so no root exists. However, just to the left of the y-axis $f(x) < 0$ and just to the right of it $f(x) > 0$.

In the first two graphs the root cannot be detected by looking for a change in the sign of the value y. In Graph 3 you may think wrongly that a finite root exists because $f(x) < 0$ for $x < 0$ and $f(x) > 0$ for $x > 0$. However, the method does work in the overwhelming majority of cases.

Example 2

Show that $3 + 4x - x^4 = 0$ has a root somewhere between $x = 1$ and $x = 2$.

Let $f(x) \equiv 3 + 4x - x^4$

$f(1) = 3 + (4 \times 1) - 1^4 = 3 + 4 - 1 = 6 > 0$

$f(2) = 3 + (4 \times 2) - 2^4 = 3 + 8 - 16 = -5 < 0$

Because $f(1) > 0$ and $f(2) < 0$ there is a root of $3 + 4x - x^4$ between $x = 1$ and $x = 2$.

Example 3

Show that $\ln(1 + x) = e^{-x} + 1$ has a root near $x = 2$.

Rewrite the equation $\ln(1 + x) = e^{-x} + 1$ as:

$$\ln(1 + x) - e^{-x} - 1 = 0$$

and let:
$$f(x) \equiv \ln(1 + x) - e^{-x} - 1$$
$$f(1.5) = \ln 2.5 - e^{-1.5} - 1$$
$$\approx 0.916 - 0.223 - 1$$
$$= -0.307 < 0$$

$$f(2.5) = \ln 3.5 - e^{-2.5} - 1$$
$$\approx 1.253 - 0.082 - 1$$
$$= 0.171 > 0$$

As $f(1.5) < 0$ and $f(2.5) > 0$ there is a root of $\ln(1 + x) = e^{-x} + 1$ somewhere between $x = 1.5$ and $x = 2.5$.

Exercise 8A

1 Show that the equation $x^3 - 12x + 7 = 0$ has one negative real root and two positive real roots. Show that one of the roots lies between $x = \frac{1}{2}$ and $x = 1$. [E]

2 Show that $x^3 - x + 3 = 0$ has a root between $x = -3$ and $x = +3$.

3 Given that $f(x) \equiv 3 + 4x - x^4$, show that the equation $f(x) = 0$ has a root $x = a$, where a is in the interval $1 \leqslant a \leqslant 2$. [E]

4 Show that $x^3 + 2x - 4 = 0$ has a root in the vicinity of $x = 1.2$.

5 Show that a root of $x^3 + 8x - 28 = 0$ lies near 2.

6 Show that the equation $\sin x - \ln x = 0$ has a root lying between $x = 2$ and $x = 3$. Given that this root lies between $\dfrac{a}{10}$ and $\dfrac{a+1}{10}$, where a is an integer, find the value of a. [E]

7 Show graphically or otherwise that the equation $x \ln x = 1 + x$ has only one real root and prove that this root lies between 3.5 and 3.8. [E]

8 Show by means of a sketch that the equation $x^2 - 1 = e^{\frac{x}{2}}$ has three real roots. Show that one root lies in the interval $(-1.5, -1)$. [E]

9 Show that the equation $e^x \cos 2x - 1 = 0$ has a root between 0.4 and 0.45. [E]

10 Given that $f(x) \equiv 4x - e^x$, show that the equation $f(x) = 0$ has a root in the interval $0.3 \leqslant x \leqslant 0.4$. [E]

11 It is given that $f(x) \equiv x - (\sin x + \cos x)^{\frac{1}{2}}, 0 \leqslant x \leqslant \frac{3}{4}\pi$. Show that the equation $f(x) = 0$ has a root lying between 1.1 and 1.2. [E]

12 By means of a sketch of the graphs $y = 8e^{-x}$ and $y = x^3$ show that the equation $8e^{-x} = x^3$ has exactly one real root.
Denoting this real root by α find the integer n such that $n < \alpha < n + 1$. [E]

13 $f(x) \equiv x - \pi(1 - \tan x), |x| < \frac{1}{2}\pi$.
Calculate values for $f(0.6)$ and $f(0.7)$ and hence deduce that the equation $f(x) = 0$ has a root α, where $0.6 < \alpha < 0.7$. [E]

14 In the diagram, O is the centre of a circle, radius $10\,\text{cm}$, and the points A and B are situated on the circumference so that $\angle AOB = 2\theta$ radians. The area of the shaded segment is $44\,\text{cm}^2$. Show that $2\theta - \sin 2\theta - 0.88 = 0$.
Show further that a root of this equation lies between 0.9 and 1. [E]

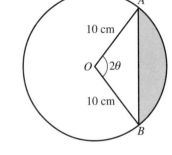

15 (a) Using the same axes, sketch the graphs of $y = e^x$ and $y = \dfrac{1}{x}$.

(b) Deduce the number of real solutions of the equation
$$e^x = \frac{1}{x}$$
and show that this equation may be written in the form
$$x - e^{-x} = 0$$

(c) Show that the equation $x - e^{-x} = 0$ has a root in the interval $0.5 < x < 0.6$. [E]

16 Using the same axes, sketch for $0 < x < 2\pi$ the graphs of $y = \sin x$ and $y = \ln x$.

x	1.5	2.0	2.5
$\sin x$			
$\ln x$			

Copy the table and use your calculator to complete the entries. By choosing further values of x and extending the table, find an estimate, to 1 decimal place, for the root of the equation
$$\sin x = \ln x$$

17 (a) Sketch, for $0 < x < \frac{\pi}{2}$, the curve with equation $y = \tan x$.
By using your sketch, show that the equation $\tan x = \dfrac{1}{x}$ has one and only one root in $0 < x < \frac{\pi}{2}$.

(b) Show further that this root lies between 0.85 and 0.87. [E]

8.2 Simple iterative methods

Consider the equation $x^2 - 5x + 2 = 0$. The graph of $y = x^2 - 5x + 2$ is shown below.

As you can see, one root of the equation $x^2 - 5x + 2 = 0$ lies between 0 and 1 and another between 4 and 5. You could also have found this by the methods shown in section 8.1. That is, if $f(x) \equiv x^2 - 5x + 2$, then

$f(0) = 2 > 0$ and $f(1) = -2 < 0$, so a root lies between 0 and 1.

$f(4) = -2 < 0$, $f(5) = +2 > 0$, so a root lies between 4 and 5.

Rearrange the equation $x^2 - 5x + 2 = 0$ so that:

$$x^2 = 5x - 2$$

and hence

$$x = \pm\sqrt{(5x - 2)}$$

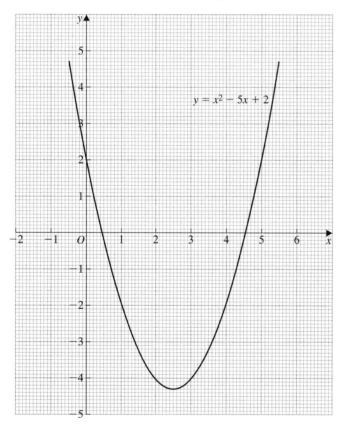

Take the positive root and form the iteration formula

$$x_{n+1} = \sqrt{(5x_n - 2)}$$

Using the formula, you can now find a sequence of approximations $x_0, x_1, x_2, \ldots$ that gets progressively closer to one of the roots of the equation $x^2 - 5x + 2 = 0$. As one root lies between 4 and 5, you could take the starting value as $x_0 = 4$.

Using the iteration formula:

$$x_1 = \sqrt{[(5 \times 4) - 2]} = \sqrt{18} = 4.242\,640\,687$$
$$x_2 = \sqrt{[(5 \times 4.242\,640\,687) - 2]} = 4.383\,286\,83$$
$$x_3 = 4.462\,783\,229$$
$$x_4 = 4.507\,096\,199$$
$$x_5 = 4.531\,609\,095$$
$$x_6 = 4.545\,112\,262$$
$$x_7 = 4.552\,533\,505$$
$$x_8 = 4.556\,607\,019$$
$$x_9 = 4.558\,841\,42$$
$$x_{10} = 4.560\,066\,568$$
$$x_{11} = 4.560\,738\,19$$

where the calculations are given to 9-figure accuracy.

So one root of the equation is 4.56 (2 decimal places), which is the same as can be obtained by using the quadratic formula.

The question now arises as to why this method works. The graphs of $y = \sqrt{(5x - 2)}$ and $y = x$ look like this:

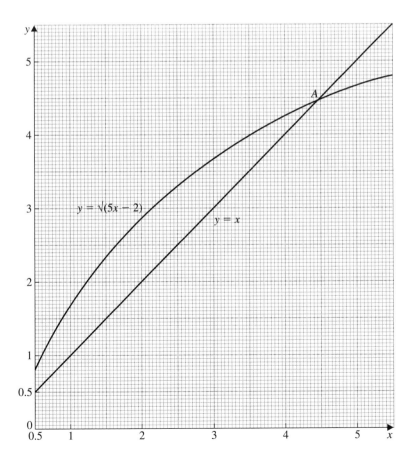

Given that the equation $x = \sqrt{(5x - 2)}$ is another form of the equation $x^2 - 5x + 2 = 0$, a solution of $x^2 - 5x + 2 = 0$ occurs where the graph of $y = x$ crosses the graph of $y = \sqrt{(5x - 2)}$, because when these two equations are satisfied simultaneously then $x = \sqrt{(5x - 2)}$. So you need to find a sequence of approximations that gets closer and closer to the x-coordinate of the point A.

Consider those parts of the graphs that lie between $x = 4$ and the point A:

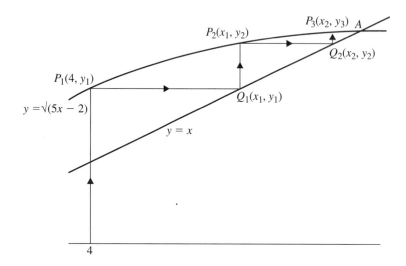

We started with $x_0 = 4$ and substituted this into $y = \sqrt{(5x - 2)}$ to give $y_1 = 4.242\,640\,687$. So we went from $x = 4$ to the point P_1 on the graph of $y = \sqrt{(5x - 2)}$. Then we put $x_1 = 4.242\,640\,687$. That is we put the value $y_1 = x_1$. So we went horizontally from P_1 to Q_1 on the graph of $y = x$. Thus the point Q_1 has coordinates $(4.242\,640\,687, 4.242\,640\,687)$. We then substituted $x_1 = 4.242\,640\,687$ into $y = \sqrt{(5x - 2)}$ to give $y_2 = 4.383\,286\,83$. So we went from Q_1 to P_2. At this point we put $x_2 = 4.383\,286\,83$. That is, we put $y_2 = x_2$ and so we moved from P_2 to Q_2 on the graph. Then we moved to P_3, and so on, and, as you can see, we got closer and closer to the point A.

This method clearly involves going vertically up to the graph of $y = \sqrt{(5x - 2)}$ and then going horizontally across to the graph of $y = x$. It depends on one of the graphs having equation $y = x$. So of the two graphs, one must have equation $y = x$ and the other $y = \mathrm{f}(x)$.

■ **When trying to solve an equation $\mathbf{f}(x) = 0$ by an iterative method, you first rearrange $\mathbf{f}(x) = 0$ into a form $x = \mathbf{g}(x)$. The iteration formula is then**

$$x_{n+1} = \mathbf{g}(x_n)$$

This is all very well, but there is no unique form $x = g(x)$ into which the equation $f(x) = 0$ can be rearranged. We rearranged the equation $x^2 - 5x + 2 = 0$ above into the form $x = \sqrt{(5x - 2)}$. However, we could have rearranged it into the form

$$5x = x^2 + 2 \text{ and hence } x = \frac{x^2 + 2}{5}$$

OR $\qquad\qquad x^2 = 5x - 2 \text{ and hence } x = 5 - \dfrac{2}{x}$

OR $\qquad\qquad x(x - 5) = -2 \text{ and hence } x = \dfrac{-2}{x - 5}$

This raises the question of whether it matters how we rearrange the equation.

We know that the formula $x_{n+1} = \sqrt{(5x_n - 2)}$, starting with $x_0 = 4$, converges to the larger root, which is 4.56 (2 d.p.).

Let's try $x_{n+1} = \dfrac{x_n^2 + 2}{5}$, starting with $x_0 = 4$. Then:

$$x_1 = 3.6$$
$$x_2 = 2.992$$
$$x_3 = 2.190\,412\,8$$
$$x_4 = 1.359\,581\,647$$
$$x_5 = 0.769\,692\,45$$
$$x_6 = 0.518\,485\,293$$
$$x_7 = 0.453\,765\,4$$
$$x_8 = 0.441\,180\,607$$
$$x_9 = 0.438\,928\,065$$
$$x_{10} = 0.438\,531\,569$$

This root is 0.44 (2 d.p.).

So this iteration formula, starting at $x_0 = 4$, leads to the *smaller* root of the equation $x^2 - 5x + 2 = 0$.

Now try $x_{n+1} = 5 - \dfrac{2}{x_n}$ starting at $x_0 = 4$:

$$x_1 = 4.5$$
$$x_2 = 4.555\,555\,56$$
$$x_3 = 4.560\,975\,61$$
$$x_4 = 4.561\,497\,326$$
$$x_5 = 4.561\,547\,479$$

That is 4.56 (2 d.p.), and so we are back to the first root again.

Finally, consider $x_{n+1} = \dfrac{-2}{x_n - 5}$ starting at $x_0 = 4$:

$$x_1 = 2$$
$$x_2 = 0.666\,666\,666$$
$$x_3 = 0.461\,538\,461$$
$$x_4 = 0.440\,677\,966$$
$$x_5 = 0.438\,661\,71$$
$$x_6 = 0.438\,467\,807$$

That is 0.44 (2 d.p.) and you are back to the other root.

So some of the iteration formulae lead to one root and some to the second root, even though you have the same starting point. Of course, using each iteration formula with a given starting point will only ever lead to at most *one* root of the equation. If an equation has three roots, you will need to find at least three iterative sequences to obtain all of them. If an equation has four roots, you will need to find at least four iterative sequences to obtain all of them, and so on.

Example 4

Show that the equation $x^3 - 3x - 5 = 0$ can be written in the form $x = \sqrt[3]{(3x + 5)}$.

Using the formula $x_{n+1} = \sqrt[3]{(3x_n + 5)}$, find, to 3 decimal places, a root of the equation $x^3 - 3x - 5 = 0$, starting with $x_0 = 2$.

$$x^3 - 3x - 5 = 0 \Rightarrow x^3 = 3x + 5$$

So: $$x = \sqrt[3]{(3x + 5)}$$

Using $x_{n+1} = \sqrt[3]{(3x_n + 5)}$ and $x_0 = 2$:

$$x_1 = 2.223\,980\,091$$
$$x_2 = 2.268\,372\,388$$
$$x_3 = 2.276\,967\,161$$
$$x_4 = 2.278\,623\,713$$
$$x_5 = 2.278\,942\,719$$

So a root of the equation is 2.279 (3 d.p.)

Starting points for iteration

At the beginning of section 8.2 you considered the graph of $y = x^2 - 5x + 2$ and you were able to see that one root of the equation $x^2 - 5x + 2 = 0$ lay between 0 and 1 and the other between 4 and 5. This then allowed you to say that since 4 was close to a root we could use $x_0 = 4$ as a starting point for the iteration.

When you select a starting point for the iteration it is sensible to choose a point that lies reasonably close to the root. The further the starting point is from the root, the more calculating you are likely to have to do. It is therefore going to save you time and energy if you choose a point reasonably close to the root.

As a general rule, try to find an interval in which a root lies and then choose as a starting point, x_0, either

(i) one of the end-points of the interval, or

(ii) the mean value of the two end-points of the interval.

However, it is not sensible, in general, to draw the graph of $y = f(x)$ in order to find an interval within which a root lies: this is time-consuming and, if the graph is drawn 'accurately', you may be tempted to try to read the value of the root from the graph! Instead you should always use the result you were shown in section 8.1, i.e. if $f(a) < 0$ and $f(b) > 0$, or if $f(a) > 0$ and $f(b) < 0$ then generally a root of $f(x) = 0$ lies in the interval $[a, b]$.

Convergence

The equation $x^3 - 3x - 5 = 0$ in example 4 could be rearranged so that $3x = x^3 - 5$ and hence

$$x = \frac{x^3 - 5}{3}$$

Using the iteration formula

$$x_{n+1} = \frac{x_n^3 - 5}{3}$$

and the starting point $x_0 = 2$, you obtain

$$x_1 = 1$$
$$x_2 = -1.333\,333\,333$$
$$x_3 = -2.456\,790\,123$$
$$x_4 = -6.609\,579\,113$$
$$x_5 = -97.916\,538\,71$$
$$x_6 = -312\,931.4535$$

It should be obvious to you by now that, far from getting close to a root of the equation $x^3 - 3x - 5 = 0$, in fact the sequence of values $x_0, x_1, x_2, x_3, \ldots$ is getting further and further away from a root. The sequence is not convergent. It is a divergent sequence. Successive members of the sequence are increasing negatively without limit.

So not only do you not know when you start using an iteration formula which root of the equation you are likely to end up with, in fact you do not know whether you are going to get to a root at all!

Example 5

Show that the equation $\ln x - x + 2 = 0$ can be written in the form $x = 2 + \ln x$.

Using the iteration formula $x_{n+1} = 2 + \ln x_n$ and starting with $x_0 = 2$, find, to 3 significant figures, a root of the equation $\ln x - x + 2 = 0$.

$$\ln x - x + 2 = 0$$
$$\Rightarrow \qquad -x = -2 - \ln x$$
$$\Rightarrow \qquad x = 2 + \ln x$$

If $x_{n+1} = 2 + \ln x_n$ then:

$$x_0 = 2$$
$$x_1 = 2.693\,147\,181$$
$$x_2 = 2.990\,710\,465$$
$$x_3 = 3.095\,510\,973$$
$$x_4 = 3.129\,952\,989$$
$$x_5 = 3.141\,017\,985$$
$$x_6 = 3.144\,546\,946$$
$$x_7 = 3.145\,669\,825$$
$$x_8 = 3.146\,026\,848$$
$$x_9 = 3.146\,140\,339$$

So a root is 3.15 (3 s.f.)

Example 6

Starting with $x_0 = 0$ and using the iteration formula $x_{n+1} = \sin x_n - 0.5$, find, to 4 significant figures, a root of the equation $\sin x - x = 0.5$.

In this question you must first realise that any calculations will only make sense if x is measured in radians.

$$x_0 = 0$$
$$x_1 = -0.5$$
$$x_2 = -0.979\,425\,538$$
$$x_3 = -1.330\,177\,246$$
$$x_4 = -1.471\,190\,631$$
$$x_5 = -1.495\,043\,453$$
$$x_6 = -1.497\,132\,123$$
$$x_7 = -1.497\,288\,019$$
$$x_8 = -1.497\,299\,481$$

So a root is -1.497 (4 s.f.)

Example 7

Show that the equation $x \ln x + x - 3 = 0$ has a root lying in the interval [1, 2]. Using a suitable iteration formula, find this root to three significant figures.

Rearrange the equation

$$x \ln x + x - 3 = 0$$

as

$$x(\ln x + 1) - 3 = 0$$

$$x(\ln x + 1) = 3$$

$$x = \frac{3}{1 + \ln x}$$

and so try the iteration formula $x_{n+1} = \dfrac{3}{1 + \ln x_n}$

$$x_0 = 2$$
$$x_1 = 1.771\,848\,327$$
$$x_2 = 1.908\,368\,716$$
$$x_3 = 1.822\,324\,789$$
$$x_4 = 1.874\,867\,538$$
$$x_5 = 1.842\,143\,064$$
$$x_6 = 1.862\,278\,771$$
$$x_7 = 1.849\,795\,515$$
$$x_8 = 1.857\,498\,762$$
$$x_9 = 1.852\,731\,52$$
$$x_{10} = 1.855\,676\,553$$
$$x_{11} = 1.853\,855\,219$$
$$x_{12} = 1.854\,980\,846$$
$$x_{13} = 1.854\,284\,891$$
$$x_{14} = 1.854\,715\,076$$

So the root is 1.85 (3 s.f.)

How to check the degree of accuracy of a root

In example 7, the iteration produces values

$$x_0, x_1, x_2, x_3 \ldots$$

which form an **alternating sequence** around the true value of the root, each one closer to the root than its predecessors. So you can state with absolute confidence that the value is 1.85 *correct* to 3 significant figures because you know that the root lies in the interval $(1.8542 \ldots, 1.8547 \ldots)$

In example 5, the iteration produces values

$$x_0, x_1, x_2, x_3, \ldots$$

which form an **increasing sequence** whose limit is the root. All these values are on the lower side of the root and getting progressively nearer to it. In order to test the accuracy of an approximation to the root, you need to choose an interval which encloses the approximation and then test each end of the interval to see if a sign change is occurring. Consider, in example 5, the approximation 3.146 to the root of $f(x) = 0$, where $f(x) = \ln x - x + 2$.

Now 3.146 is enclosed in the interval

$$(3.1455, 3.1465)$$

and any value in that interval takes the value 3.146 *correct* to 3 decimal places.

Using your calculator you find that

$$f(3.1455) > 0$$
$$f(3.1465) < 0$$

which shows a sign change for $f(x)$ and this implies that the true value of the root lies in the interval because the curve $y = f(x)$ must cross the x-axis somewhere in this interval.

So you can conclude that the root is 3.146 *correct* to 3 decimal places.

Exercise 8B

1 (a) Show that $x^2 - 3x + 1 = 0$ has one root lying between 0 and 1 and another lying between 2 and 3.

(b) Show that $x^2 - 3x + 1 = 0$ can be rearranged into the form

(i) $x = \dfrac{x^2 + p}{q}$, where p and q are constants.

(ii) $x = r + \dfrac{s}{x}$, where r and s are constants

and state the values of p, q, r and s.

(c) Using the iteration formula

$$x_{n+1} = \frac{x_n^2 + p}{q}$$

together with your values of p and q and starting at $x_0 = 0.5$ find, to 3 decimal places, one root of the equation $x^2 - 3x + 1 = 0$.

(d) Using the iteration formula

$$x_{n+1} = r + \frac{s}{x_n}$$

together with your values of r and s find, to 3 decimal places, the second root of $x^2 - 3x + 1 = 0$.

2 (a) Show that $x^3 = 14$ has a root lying between 2 and 3.

(b) Show further that $x^3 = 14$ can be rearranged into the form

$$x = \frac{p}{x^2} + \frac{x}{2}$$

where p is a constant and state the value of p.

(c) Using the iteration formula

$$x_{n+1} = \frac{p}{x_n^2} + \frac{x_n}{2}$$

together with your value of p and starting with $x_0 = 2.5$, find, to 3 significant figures, a root of $x^3 = 14$.

3 Using the iteration formula

$$x_{n+1} = 2 + \frac{1}{x_n^2}$$

and starting with $x_0 = 2$, find the value, to 4 significant figures, to which the sequence $x_0, x_1, x_2, \ldots$ tends. This sequence leads to one root of an equation. State the equation.

4 Show that the equation $x^3 + 6x^2 - 9x + 2 = 0$ has a root lying between 0 and 0.5. Use the iteration formula

$$x_{n+1} = \frac{6x_n^2 + 2}{9 - x_n^2}$$

with $x_0 = 0$ to find this root to 3 decimal places.

5 Show that $1 + x^2 - x^3 = 0$ has a root lying between 1 and 2. Using the iteration formula

$$x_{n+1} = \sqrt[3]{(1 + x_n^2)}$$

with $x_0 = 1$, find this root to 3 significant figures.

6 Show that $x^2 = \sin x$ has a root lying between 0 and 1. Using the iteration formula

$$x_{n+1} = \frac{\sin x_n}{x_n}$$

find this root to 3 decimal places.

7 By considering the roots of the equation $f'(x) = 0$, or otherwise, prove that the equation $f(x) = 0$, where $f(x) \equiv x^3 + 2x + 4$, has only one real root. Show that this root lies in the interval $-2 < x < -1$.

Use the iteration formula

$$x_{n+1} = -\tfrac{1}{6}(x_n^3 - 4x_n + 4), \quad x_0 = -1$$

to find two further approximations to this root of the equation, giving your final answer to 2 decimal places. [E]

8 Show that the equation $2^x = 8x$ has two roots, one lying between 0 and 1 and the other lying between 5 and 6. Use the iteration formula

$$x_{n+1} = \frac{2^{x_n}}{8}, \quad x_0 = 1$$

to find, to 4 decimal places, the root which lies between 0 and 1.

9 Using the iteration formula

$$x_{n+1} = (22x_n + 50)^{\frac{1}{4}} \quad \text{and} \quad x_0 = 3.5$$

find a root of $x^4 - 22x - 50 = 0$ to 4 significant figures. Check that your answer is *correct* to 4 significant figures.

10 Show that $x \sin \sqrt{x} = 1$ has a root lying between 1 and 2. Using the iteration formula

$$x_{n+1} = \frac{1}{\sin \sqrt{x_n}}$$

find, to 4 decimal places, the value of this root.

11 Use the iteration formula

$$x_{n+1} = 3^{\frac{1}{x_n}} \quad \text{with} \quad x_0 = 1.5$$

to find the value, to 3 significant figures, to which the sequence $x_0, x_1, x_2, \ldots$ tends. This sequence leads to one root of an equation. State the equation.

12 Use the iteration formula

$$x_{n+1} = \tfrac{2}{3}x_n + \frac{5}{x_n^2}, \quad x_0 = 2$$

to solve the equation $x^3 = 15$, giving your answer *correct* to 3 significant figures.

13 Show that the equation $x^3 - x - 1 = 0$ has a real root α in the interval $(1, 1.5)$. Use the iteration formula $x_{n+1} = (1 + x_n)^{\frac{1}{3}}$ to find α, correct to 3 decimal places. Prove that the answer you have found is, in fact, correct to 3 decimal places.

14 Prove that the negative root of the equation $x^3 - 10x + 1 = 0$ is -3.211 *correct* to 3 decimal places. Show that this equation has further roots in the intervals $(0, 1)$ and $(3, 4)$. Using a suitable iteration, find the larger root to 3 decimal places.

SUMMARY OF KEY POINTS

1 If $f(x_1) > 0$ and $f(x_2) < 0$ or if $f(x_1) < 0$ and $f(x_2) > 0$ and if f is continuous in the interval between x_1 and x_2, then the equation $f(x) = 0$ has a root in the interval between x_1 and x_2.

2 In order to find a root of the equation $f(x) = 0$ by iteration, the equation must first be rearranged in the form $x = g(x)$. The iteration formula is then $x_{n+1} = g(x_n)$.

3 Each iteration formula with a given starting point can only lead to one root of the equation at most.

4 Sometimes an iterative procedure with a given starting point will *not* lead to a root of the equation. The sequence $x_0, x_1, x_2, \ldots$ will instead diverge.

Proof

9

In chapter 7 of Book P1 you were introduced to proofs using a direct method. That is, you start at a well defined point and follow this with a number of valid, logical steps which lead to the required conclusion. This method of proof permeates all of mathematics and you will already have written many such proofs in your solutions to work covered in both this book and P1. Many more similar questions on newly introduced topics will come your way as you work through the contents of Books P3, P4, P5 and P6. It must become part of your daily skills that you can write direct proofs with clarity and confidence. Also, it is vital that you can spot flaws and errors when reading mathematical statements. In this chapter you will meet proof by contradiction and disproof by counter-example.

9.1 Proof by contradiction

For some statements, p and q, it is possible to prove that $p \Rightarrow q$ by assuming that $p \Rightarrow$ 'not' q and showing that this leads to a contradiction. If this happens, then you can conclude that since $p \not\Rightarrow$ 'not' q, then $p \Rightarrow q$. Some famous proofs in the history of mathematics have been established in this way. The method is often called an **indirect proof**. Here is an example from over 2000 years ago.

Example 1
Prove that the number of prime numbers is infinite.

You start by assuming that the number of prime numbers is finite and that the largest prime number is A, say. Consider the number N formed by multiplying together all the primes and adding the number 1 to the product. That is:

$$N = (2)(3)(5)(7)\ldots(A) + 1$$

Clearly $2 \times 3 \times 5 \times 7 \times \ldots \times A$ is even, since it has a factor 2. So N is not divisible by 2 because it is an odd number; N is not divisible by 3, 5, 7, ..., A because, in each case, it leaves a remainder of 1.

Thus N has no prime factors and it is greater than the largest prime number A. Hence the assumption that the number of primes is finite is false, leading to a contradiction. Therefore, the number of primes is infinite.

Example 2
Given that x and y are positive integers, show that if xy is an odd number, then both x and y are odd numbers.

Start by assuming that x and y are not both odd. So let x be even and equal to $2m$ where m is an integer.

Now $xy = 2my$ and $2my$ is an even number, which is contrary to what is required. Hence x cannot be even and nor can y if xy is to be odd.

Example 3
Prove that the product of four consecutive positive integers cannot be a perfect square.

Let the integers be N, $N+1$, $N+2$ and $N+3$ and assume that $N(N+1)(N+2)(N+3) = p^2$, say, where p is a positive integer.

Now
$$\begin{aligned}
N(N+1)(N+2)(N+3) &= [(N+1)(N+2)][N(N+3)] \\
&= [N^2 + 3N + 2][N^2 + 3N] \\
&= N^2(N^2 + 3N) + 3N(N^2 + 3N) + 2(N^2 + 3N) \\
&= (N^2 + 3N)^2 + 2(N^2 + 3N)
\end{aligned}$$

Complete the square on this and you obtain:
$$(N^2 + 3N)^2 + 2(N^2 + 3N) + 1 - 1$$
$$= (N^2 + 3N + 1)^2 - 1$$

So we have
$$(N^2 + 3N + 1)^2 - 1 = p^2$$

That is, the square of one integer minus 1 is equal to the square of another integer and this is impossible.

This contradiction leads you to conclude that the product of four consecutive positive integers cannot be a perfect square.

9.2 Disproof by counter-example

If a statement, or proposition, is suspected of being false, then *one single counter-example* is sufficient to prove this is so.

It is important to realise that endless checking of particular cases will not prove a proposition generally. For example, the correct statement

$$\sum_{r=1}^{n} r = \tfrac{1}{2}n(n+1)$$

cannot be proved generally by saying

$$n = 1, \sum r = 1$$
$$n = 2, \sum r = 1 + 2 = 3$$
$$n = 3, \sum r = 1 + 2 + 3 = 6$$

and so on...

all of which agree with using $\tfrac{1}{2}n(n+1)$ with $n = 1, 2, 3, \ldots$

On the other hand, just one single counter-example is sufficient to prove that a proposition is false.

Example 4

Give a counter-example to show that the following statement is false: 'The product of two unequal positive irrational numbers is irrational'.

Here is a counter-example: take one number as $\sqrt{2}$ and the other as $\sqrt{8}$. The product is

$$(\sqrt{2})(\sqrt{8}) = \sqrt{16} = 4$$

which is rational.

Another counter-example could be $3 - \sqrt{2}$ and $3 + \sqrt{2}$, whose product is

$$(3 - \sqrt{2})(3 + \sqrt{2}) = 3^2 - (\sqrt{2})^2 = 7$$

So the original statement is false.

Example 5

Find a counter-example to disprove the assertion that $f(n) = n^2 + n + 1$ is either a prime number or a multiple of 3 for all positive integral values of n.

By direct evaluation you have
$f(1) = 3, f(2) = 7, f(3) = 13, f(4) = 21, f(5) = 31, f(6) = 43, f(7) = 57,$
$f(8) = 73, f(9) = 91 = 7 \times 13$
So the assertion breaks down for $n = 9$ and is therefore disproved.

Example 6

Let $f(x) \equiv x^3 - 27x + k$, $k \in \mathbb{R}^+$.

Find a counter-example to disprove the assertion that the equation $f(x) = 0$ has 3 real roots for all values of k.

Consider a sketch of the curve with equation $y = x^3 - 27x$. This curve passes through the origin O and cuts the x-axis where $x^2 - 27 = 0 \Rightarrow x = \pm 3\sqrt{3}$.

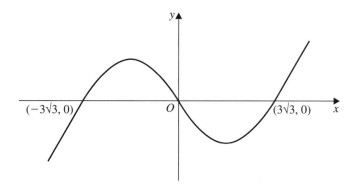

The stationary points are given by $f'(x) = 0$, that is:

$$3x^2 - 27 = 0 \Rightarrow x = \pm 3$$
$$y = 3^3 - 27(3) \text{ or } (-3)^3 - 27(-3)$$
$$= -54 \qquad \text{or } 54$$

If a line is drawn parallel to the x-axis higher than than $y = 54$ or lower than $y = -54$ then this line cuts the curve $y = x^3 - 27x$ in just one point. This implies that the equation $x^3 - 27x + k = 0$ will only have one root if $|k| > 54$.

So any value of k for which $|k| > 54$ will suffice as a counter-example to disprove the assertion that the equation $x^3 - 27x + k = 0$ has 3 real roots for all values of k.

Notice here that you need to use a logical mathematical approach to finding the counter-example. Mere substitution of $k = 1, 2, \ldots$ etc. is not to be recommended.

Exercise 9A

In questions 1–10, find a counter-example to disprove the assertion being made.

1 If $0 < x < 2\pi$, the only solution of the equation $\sin x = \frac{1}{2}$ is $\frac{\pi}{6}$.

2 $u > v$ and $x > y \Rightarrow ux > vy$, where u, x, v and y are real numbers.

3 x is real and $x < 4 \Rightarrow x^2 < 16$.

4 The equation $x^2 + x - a = 0$ has real roots for all real values of a.

5 The complete set of values of x for which
$$x^2 + 5x > -6$$
is $-2 < x < 3$.

6 $f(n) \equiv n^2 + n + 41$ is a prime number for all integral values of n.

7 The equation $ax^2 + bx + c = 0$ only has real roots if $b^2 > 4ac$, where a, b and c are real numbers.

8 A quadrilateral with all its interior angles equal also has all its sides equal and conversely.

9 $f(n) \equiv (n + 1)(n + 2)(n + 3)$ is divisible by 12 for all positive integral n.

10 For all real values of x and y,
$$\sin x > \sin y \Rightarrow x > y$$

In questions 11–15, use a proof by contradiction in each case.

11 For all $x > 1$, $x + \dfrac{1}{x} > 2$.

12 Given that $x^2 < 2x$ then $0 < x < 2$.

13 Prove that there are no integers p and q such that $\dfrac{p^2}{q^2} = 2$.

14 Prove that there are an infinite number of rational numbers between 0 and 1.

15 Prove that $\sqrt{3}$ is irrational.

16 The equation $x^3 - 3x^2 - 2x + 3 = 0$ has a root in the interval $(N, N + 1)$ where N is an integer. Prove that there are three possible values of N.

17 Prove that $\displaystyle\sum_{r=1}^{n} (2r - 1) = n^2$.

18 Prove that the complete solution of the inequality
$$x^2 + 4x + 5 > 0$$
is the set of real numbers.

19 Prove that the sum to infinity of the geometric series
$$\tfrac{1}{3} - (\tfrac{1}{3})^3 + (\tfrac{1}{3})^5 - \dots$$
is $\tfrac{3}{10}$.

20 The sum of the first n terms of a sequence is $\dfrac{n}{n^2 + 1}$.

Prove that:

(a) all the terms after the first are negative

(b) as $n \to \infty$, the nth term of the sequence $\to 0$.

SUMMARY OF KEY POINTS

1 If an assertion or proposition is suspected of being false, then one single counter-example is sufficient to prove that the assertion is false.

2 In some circumstances it is possible to prove that an assertion is true by assuming first that it is false, and showing that this assumption leads to a contradiction.

Review exercise 2

1 Solve the equations
  (a) $e^x = 3$
  (b) $2^{-x} = 6$
  (c) $2^{2x} - 8(2^x) + 15 = 0$
  giving answers to 3 significant figures.

2 The tangent to the curve with equation $y = e^x$ at $(2, e^2)$ meets the x-axis at A and the y-axis at B. Find the length of AB, giving your answer to 2 decimal places.

3 A root of the equation $e^x - 7x = 0$ lies in the interval $N < x < N + 1$, where N is an integer. Find two values for N.
  [E]

4 Evaluate (a) $\displaystyle\int_{-0.5}^{0.5} (4 + 4e^x)\, dx$ (b) $\displaystyle\int_{1}^{2} \left(\frac{4}{x} + \frac{4}{x^2} \right) dx$.

5 The function f is defined by

$$\text{f} : x \mapsto -\ln(x - 2), \; x \in \mathbb{R}, \; x > 2$$

The figure shows a sketch of the curve with equation $y = \text{f}(x)$. The curve crosses the x-axis at the point $P(p, 0)$. The curve has an asymptote, shown by a broken line in the diagram, whose equation is $x = q$.

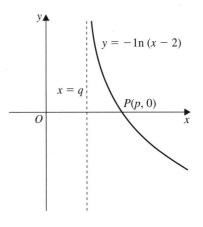

  (a) Write down the value of p and the value of q.
  (b) Find the function f^{-1} and state its domain.
  (c) Sketch the curve with equation $y = \text{f}^{-1}(x)$ and its asymptote.
  Write on your sketch the coordinates of any point where the curve crosses the coordinate axes and the equation of the asymptote.
  [E]

6 Evaluate (a) $\displaystyle\int_1^{16} x^{-\frac{3}{4}}\,dx$ (b) $\displaystyle\int_2^5 \left(x - \frac{2}{x}\right)^2 dx$

(c) $\displaystyle\int_4^5 \frac{e^x}{5}\,dx$ **[E]**

7 Find, to 2 decimal places, the value of x for which $3^{x-2} = 2^x$.

8

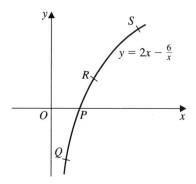

The diagram shows the curve with equation $y = 2x - \dfrac{6}{x}$,

which cuts the positive x-axis at the point P. At Q, R and S on the curve $x = 1$, 3, 6 respectively.

(a) Find the gradient of the line QR.

(b) Show that the gradient of the curve at P is equal to the gradient of QR.

(c) Find the area of the region bounded by the curve and the line RS.

9 The function f is given by

$$f : x \mapsto \ln(4 - 2x),\ x < 2$$

(a) Find an expression for $f^{-1}(x)$.

(b) Sketch the curve with equation $y = f^{-1}(x)$, showing the coordinates of the points where the curve meets the axes.

(c) State the range of f^{-1}.

The function g is given by

$$g : x \mapsto e^x,\ x \in \mathbb{R}.$$

(d) Find the value of gf(0.5).   **[E]**

10 Solve the equation

$$\lg(5x + 8) + \lg(2x + 1) - 2\lg(x + 1) = 1$$

11
$$f(x) \equiv \frac{(2\sqrt{x} + 3)^2}{x}, \quad x > 0$$

(a) Show that f(x) can be expressed as $A + Bx^{-\frac{1}{2}} + Cx^{-1}$, giving the values of the constants A, B and C.

(b) Find $\displaystyle\int f(x)\,dx$

(c) Find the area of the finite region bounded by the curve with equation $y = f(x)$ and the lines with equations $x = 4$, $x = 9$ and $y = 0$, giving your answer in terms of natural logarithms.　　　**[E]**

> f(x) is finite and positive for $4 \leqslant x \leqslant 9$.

12 Find an equation of the tangent and of the normal at the point where $x = 2$ on the curve with equation $y = x^3 - 18\ln x$.

13 The functions f and g are defined over the set of real numbers by
$$f : x \mapsto 3x - 5$$
$$g : x \mapsto e^{-2x}$$

(a) State the range of g.

(b) Sketch the graphs of the inverse functions f^{-1} and g^{-1} and write on your sketches the coordinates of any points at which a graph meets the coordinates axes.

(c) State, giving a reason, the number of roots of the equation
$$f^{-1}(x) = g^{-1}(x).$$

(d) Evaluate $fg(-\frac{1}{3})$, giving your answer to 2 decimal places.

14 Given that $p = \lg 2$ and $q = \lg 3$ express in terms of p and q
(a) $\lg 6$　　(b) $\lg 4.5$　　(c) $\lg 24$　　(d) $\lg 648$　　(e) $\log_2 3$.

15 The region R is bounded by the curve with equation $y = x^3$, the x-axis and the lines with equations $x = 2$ and $x = 4$.

(a) Find the area of R.

(b) Find the volume generated by rotating R through $360°$ about the x-axis.

16
$$f(x) \equiv 3 - \frac{x^2}{4} + \ln\frac{x}{2}, \quad x > 0$$

(a) Show that there is a root α of $f(x) = 0$, such that $0.09 < \alpha < 0.1$.

(b) Find $f'(x)$.

(c) Obtain the value of β such that $f'(\beta) = 0$.　　　**[E]**

17 The function f is defined by $f : x \mapsto e^x + k, \ x \in \mathbb{R}$ and k is a positive constant.

(a) State the range of f.

(b) Find $f(\ln k)$, simplifying your answer.

(c) Find f^{-1}, the inverse function of f, in the form $f^{-1} : x \mapsto \ldots$, stating its domain.

(d) On the same axes, sketch the curves with equations $y = f(x)$, and $y = f^{-1}(x)$, giving the coordinates of all points where the graphs cut the axes. [E]

18 A function f is given by
$$f(x) \equiv -2x^3 + 3x^2 + 12x - 5, \ x \in \mathbb{R}.$$

(a) By calculation, show that the equation $f(x) = 0$ has a root in the interval $(0, 1)$.

(b) By calculation, find the negative integer, N, for which a root of the equation $f(x) = 0$ lies in the interval $(N, N + 1)$. Show sufficient working to justify your answer.

(c) By using a calculus method, find the complete set of values of x for which f is an increasing function. [E]

19 A formula used to calculate the power gain of an amplifier has the form
$$G = h \ln \left(\frac{p_2}{p_1} \right)$$

Given that $G = 16$, $h = 4.3$ and $p_1 = 8$,

(a) calculate, to the nearest whole number, the value of p_2.

Given that the values of G and p_1 are exact but that the value of h has been given to one decimal place,

(b) find the range of possible values of p_2. [E]

20 Show that the equation $e^x - 3x = 0$ has one root in the interval $(0, 1)$ and another root in the interval $(1, 2)$. Prove that the larger root is 1.51 *correct* to 2 decimal places.

21 Solve the equation
$$\ln(5x + 6) = 2 \ln(5x - 6) \qquad \text{[E]}$$

22 The function f is defined by

$$f : x \mapsto \ln(5x - 2), \ x > \tfrac{2}{5}$$

(a) Find an expression for $f^{-1}(x)$.

(b) Write down the domain of f^{-1}.

(c) Solve, giving your answer to 3 decimal places,

$$\ln(5x - 2) = 2 \qquad\qquad \text{[E]}$$

23 Integrate with respect to x: (a) $x^{\frac{2}{3}} - \tfrac{2}{3}e^x$ (b) $\left(x - \dfrac{2}{x}\right)^3$

24 The curve C has equation $y = \tfrac{1}{2}x^{\frac{3}{2}} - \ln 3x$. Find an equation of the normal to C at the point where $x = 1$.

25 It is given that $y = x^{\frac{3}{2}} + \dfrac{48}{x}, \ x > 0$.

(a) Find the value of x and the value of y when $\dfrac{dy}{dx} = 0$.

(b) Show that the value of y which you found in (a) is a minimum.

The finite region R lies in the first quadrant and is bounded by the curve with equation $y = x^{\frac{3}{2}} + \dfrac{48}{x}$, the lines $x = 1$, $x = 4$ and the x-axis.

(c) Find, by integration, the area of R giving your answer in the form $p + q \ln r$, where the numbers p, q and r are to be found. [E]

26 Show that the equation

$$6^x + 70 = 10(2^x) + 7(3^x)$$

can be rewritten as

$$(2^x - 7)(3^x - 10) = 0$$

Hence find the solutions of the equation, giving your answers to 2 decimal places.

27 Given that $f(x) \equiv 3 + 4x - x^4$, show that the equation $f(x) = 0$ has a root $x = a$, where a is in the interval $1 \leqslant a \leqslant 2$. It may be assumed that if x_n is an approximation to a, then a better approximation is given by x_{n+1}, where

$$x_{n+1} = (3 + 4x_n)^{\frac{1}{4}}$$

Starting with $x_0 = 1.75$, use this result twice to obtain the value of a to 2 decimal places. [E]

28 Find the values of x for which

$$2 \ln 2x - 6 \ln 2 = \ln (x - 3)$$

29 The function f is defined by

$$f : x \mapsto x + \frac{9}{x}, x \in \mathbb{R}, x \neq 0.$$

(a) Find the values of x for which $f(x) = \frac{15}{2}$.

(b) Find $f'(x)$.

(c) Find the set of values of x for which f is an increasing function.

The finite region R lies in the first quadrant and is enclosed by the curve with equation $y = f(x)$, the lines with equations $x = 1$ and $x = e$, and the x-axis.

(d) Use integration to find the area of R, giving your answer in terms of e. [E]

30 (a) Show that the equation $x = \ln (x + 4)$ has a root between 1 and 2.

(b) Use the iteration formula $x_{n+1} = \ln (x_n + 4)$, $x_0 = 2$ to find this root correct to 5 decimal places. Show all your intermediate results clearly.

31 Differentiate with respect to x

(a) $(x^3 + 1)^2$ (b) $\ln x^2$ (c) $\ln \left[\dfrac{e^{x^2}}{x^2} \right]$

32

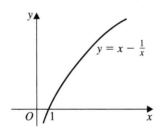

The diagram shows a sketch of the graph with equation $y = x - \dfrac{1}{x}$. The region bounded by the x-axis, the lines with equations $x = 2$ and $x = 3$ and the curve is rotated through $360°$ about the x-axis. Calculate, in terms of π, the volume of the solid formed. [E]

33

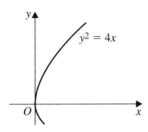

The diagram shows a sketch of the graph with equation
$y^2 = 4x$.
The region R is bounded by the curve, the lines with
equations $y = 1$ and $y = 2$ and the y-axis.
(a) Find the area of R.
(b) Find the volume of the solid formed when R is rotated
completely about the y-axis.

34 Use the trapezium rule with five intervals of equal width to
estimate the value of $\displaystyle\int_0^{\frac{\pi}{6}} \sqrt{\sin x}\, dx$, giving your answer to
3 decimal places.

35 Obtain the equation of the normal to the curve with equation
$$y = x + \frac{4}{x}$$
at the point $(1, 5)$. Find also the equations of the two tangents
to the curve which are parallel to the normal and show that
the perpendicular distance between them is $\frac{8}{5}\sqrt{15}$.   [E]

36

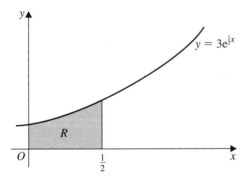

In the diagram, the shaded region, R, is bounded by the curve
with equation $y = 3e^{\frac{1}{2}x}$, the line with equation $x = \frac{1}{2}$ and the
coordinate axes. The region R is rotated through $360°$ about
the x-axis. Find, in terms of e and π, the volume of the solid
generated.   [E]

37 Prove that the tangent at $P(1, e)$ to the curve with equation $y = e^x$ passes through the origin O. Find, in terms of e, the area of the finite region bounded by the curve, the line OP and the y-axis.

38 The tangent at $P(x_n, x_n^2 - 2)$, where $x_n > 0$, to the curve with equation $y = x^2 - 2$ meets the x-axis at the point $Q(x_{n+1}, 0)$. Show that

$$x_{n+1} = \frac{x_n^2 + 2}{2x_n}$$

This relationship between x_{n+1} and x_n is used, starting with $x_1 = 2$, to find successive approximations for the positive root of the equation $x^2 - 2 = 0$. Find x_2 and x_3 as fractions and show that $x_4 = \frac{577}{408}$. [E]

39 Given that $f(x) \equiv x^2 - 6x + 10$, show that $f(x) > 0$ for all real values of x.
Using the same axes sketch the graphs of $y = f(x)$, $y = 3f(x)$, $y = f(x - 3)$. [E]

40 (a) Sketch the graph of $y = 8 - 2x^2$, indicating clearly any points of intersection with the coordinate axes.
(b) Find an equation of the tangent to this curve at the point where $x = a$.
(c) Find the value of a for which this tangent is parallel to the line with equation $y = 3x + 6$.
The finite region bounded by the curve and the x-axis is rotated through π radians about the y-axis.
(d) Calculate the volume of the solid formed, leaving your answer in terms of π. [E]

41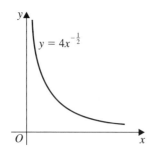

The diagram shows a sketch of the graph with equation $y = 4x^{-\frac{1}{2}}$.

The region R is bounded by the curve, and the lines with equations $x = 1$, $x = 4$ and $y = 0$.

(a) Find the area of R.

(b) Find the volume of the solid formed when R is rotated completely about the x-axis.

42 Use the trapezium rule with six intervals of equal width to find an estimate for $\int_2^8 \frac{1}{x}\,\mathrm{d}x$, giving your answer to 3 decimal places.

Evaluate $\int_2^8 \frac{1}{x}\,\mathrm{d}x$ exactly and hence find the percentage error in your estimate when using the trapezium rule, giving your answer to 2 decimal places.

43 The part of the curve $y = x(x - 3)$ between the ordinates, $x = 1$ and $x = 2$ is rotated completely about the x-axis. Calculate, in terms of π, the volume so formed. [E]

44 Show that the equation

$$3x - 1 - \cos 2x = 0$$

has only one real root and that this root lies between 0.4 and 0.6. The iterative procedure

$$x_{n+1} = \tfrac{1}{3}(1 + \cos 2x_n)$$

is to be used to find further approximations to the root, starting with the initial value $x = 0.5$. Calculate the value of the root giving your answer to 3 decimal places. [E]

45 Use the trapezium rule with 5 intervals of equal width to find an estimate for $\int_1^2 10^x\,\mathrm{d}x$, giving your answer to 2 decimal places.

46 In the figure AB is a sketch of part of the curve with equation $10y = x^2$. The curved surface of an open bowl with a flat circular base is traced out by the complete revolution of the arc AB about the y-axis. The radius of the base is 10 cm and the radius of the top rim of the bowl is 20 cm.

(a) Calculate the capacity of this bowl, in litres to 1 decimal place.

The point C lies on the arc AB. The curved surface of another bowl is traced out by rotating the arc AC through a complete revolution about the y-axis.

The capacity of this bowl is 10 litres.

(b) Calculate the depth of this bowl, in cm to 1 decimal place. [E]

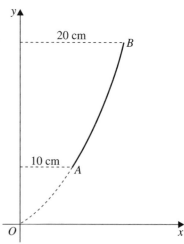

47

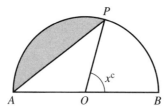

The figure shows a semicircle with O the mid-point of the diameter AB. The point P on the semicircle is such that the area of sector POB is equal to the area of the shaded segment. Angle POB is x radians.

(a) Show that $x = \frac{1}{2}(\pi - \sin x)$.

The iterative method based on the relation $x_{n+1} = \frac{1}{2}(\pi - \sin x_n)$ can be used to evaluate x.

(b) Starting with $x_1 = 1$ perform two iterations to find the values of x_2 and x_3, giving your answers to two decimal places. [E]

48 Given that

$$x + y = 2 \text{ and } 3^x = 4^y$$

show that $x = \dfrac{\ln 16}{\ln 12}$ and find y in a similar form.

49 The diagram shows the region R, bounded by the curve with equation $xy = 4 + x^2$, the lines with equations $x = 1$ and $x = 4$ and the x-axis.

(a) Find the area of R.

(b) Find the volume generated when R is rotated through $360°$ about the x-axis.

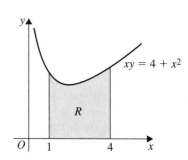

50 Find an equation of the tangent and of the normal at the point where $x = \frac{2}{5}$ on the curve with equation $y = \ln 5x$.

51

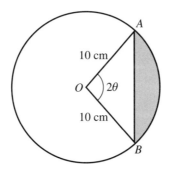

In the figure, O is the centre of a circle, radius 10 cm, and the points A and B are situated on the circumference so that $\angle AOB = 2\theta$ radians. The area of the shaded segment is 44 cm². Show that

$$2\theta - \sin 2\theta - 0.88 = 0$$

Show further that a root of this equation lies between 0.9 and 1.

By taking 0.9 as a first approximation to this root, use the iterative procedure

$$\theta_{n+1} = \tfrac{1}{2}(\sin 2\theta_n + 0.88)$$

to find this root, giving your answer to 3 decimal places.   [E]

52 Solve the equations, giving answers to 3 significant figures

(a) $5^x = 7^{x-1}$ (b) $\ln(x+1) - \ln x = e$

53 A right circular cone is formed by rotating the right-angled triangle bounded by the lines with equations $y = \dfrac{r}{h}x$ and $x = r$ and the x-axis through 360° about the x-axis.

Prove that the volume of the cone is $\frac{1}{3}\pi r^2 h$. Given that h and r can vary, find the maximum volume of the cone if $h + r = 12c$, where c is a constant.

54 Solve the differential equation $\dfrac{\mathrm{d}y}{\mathrm{d}x} = 6 - 2e^x$, given that $y = 3$ at $x = \ln 2$.

55 Sketch the curve with equation $y = \ln x$.

Show that the equation

$$x + \ln x - 3 = 0$$

has just one real root, and that this root lies between 2 and 2.5.

The sequence defined by the iteration formula

$$x_{n+1} = 3 - \ln x_n, \quad x_1 = 2$$

is known to converge. Use this sequence to calculate the root of the equation $x + \ln x - 3 = 0$ to two decimal places.　　[E]

56 Find the value, or values, of p for which

$$\lg(p + 6) = 2\lg(p - 6)$$

57 Show, graphically or otherwise, that the equation

$$x^3 + 2x - 2 = 0$$

has only one real root. Show also that this root lies between 0.7 and 1. Working to 3 decimal places, obtain approximations to this root by performing two iterations, using the procedure defined by

$$x_{n+1} = \frac{2 - x_n^3}{2}$$

and starting with $x_1 = 0.8$.　　[E]

58 The figure shows the shaded region R which is bounded by the curves with equations $y = x^2$ and $y = 8 - x^2$. Find
(a) the coordinates of the points A, B and C
(b) the area of R
(c) the volume generated when R is rotated through π radians about the y-axis.　　[E]

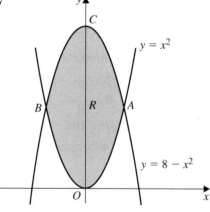

59 Solve for p and q the simultaneous equations

$$\lg p - \lg(q + 1) = 1$$
$$\log_2(p - 14q) = 3$$

60 Find an equation of the tangent and of the normal to the curve with equation $y = -2e^x$ at the point on the curve where $x = -1$.

61 The curve with equation $y = 2x(3 - x)$ crosses the x-axis at O and A.

(a) State the coordinates of the point A.

A straight line, which crosses the y-axis at the point B with coordinates $(0, 5)$, meets the curve at the points C and D, as shown in the figure. The coordinates of the point D are (k, k).

(b) Show that the value of k is $2\frac{1}{2}$.

(c) Find an equation of the straight line passing through B and D.

(d) Show that the x-coordinate of the point C is 1.

(e) Calculate the area of the shaded region R.

(f) Calculate, in terms of π, the volume generated when the shaded region S, bounded by the curve, the x-axis and the line with equation $x = 1$, is rotated through $360°$ about the x-axis. [E]

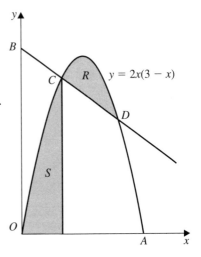

62 The equation of a curve is $y = ax^n$, where a and n are constants. Given that the points $(3, 11)$ and $(4, 5)$ lie on the curve, find, to 3 significant figures, the values of a and n.

63 Solve the equations

(a) $\log_2 x + 4\log_x 2 = 5$

(b) $\log_3 (2 - 3x) = \log_9 (6x^2 - 19x + 2)$ [E]

64 The table below gives values of a function $f(x)$ for certain values of x:

x	1	1.5	2	2.5	3	3.5	4
$f(x)$	4.1	4.7	5.1	4.8	5.1	5.4	5.9

Use the trapezium rule with six intervals to estimate $\int_1^4 [f(x)]^2 \, dx$.

65 (a) (i) Given that $\log_3 x = 2$, determine the value of x.

(ii) Calculate the value of y for which

$$2 \log_3 y - \log_3 (y + 4) = 2$$

(iii) Calculate the values of z for which

$$\log_3 z = 4 \log_z 3$$

(b) (i) Express $\log_a (p^2 q)$ in terms of $\log_a p$ and $\log_a q$.

(ii) Given that $\log_a (pq) = 5$ and $\log_a (p^2 q) = 9$, find the values of $\log_a p$ and $\log_a q$. [E]

66

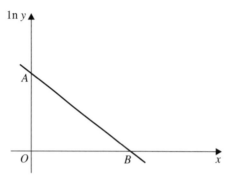

The diagram shows a straight line graph of $\ln y$ against x. The line crosses the axes at points $A(0, 2)$ and $B(3, 0)$. Given that $y = pq^x$, where p and q are constants, find, to one decimal place, the values of p and q. [E]

67 A sequence of numbers $u_1, u_2, u_3, \ldots u_n, \ldots$ is given by the relation

$$u_n = 3(\tfrac{2}{3})^n - 1$$

where n is a positive integer.
Prove that $3u_{n+1} = 2u_n - 1$

68 The finite region R is bounded by the curve with equation $y = x^2 + 1$, the lines with equations $x = 1$ and $x = 2$ and the x-axis.

The region R is rotated through 2π about the x-axis. Find the volume of the solid generated. [E]

69 The points P and Q lie on the curve with equation $y = e^{\frac{1}{2}x}$.
The x-coordinates of P and Q are $\ln 4$ and $\ln 16$ respectively.

(a) Find an equation of the line PQ.

(b) Show that this line passes through the origin O.

(c) Calculate the length, to 3 significant figures, of the line segment PQ.

The finite region R is bounded by the arc of the curve with equation $y = e^{\frac{1}{2}x}$ between P and Q, the lines with equations $x = \ln 4$ and $x = \ln 16$ and the x-axis. The region R is rotated through $360°$ about the x-axis.

(d) Find the volume of the solid so formed. [E]

70 The temperature, $\theta\,°C$, of a hot drink t minutes ($t \geqslant 0$) after it has been made is given by

$$\theta = 20 + 40e^{-0.05t}$$

(a) Find, in $°C$, the temperature of the drink at the instant at which it is made.

(b) Calculate, in $°C$ to 3 significant figures, the temperature of the drink 10 minutes after it was made.

(c) Calculate, to the nearest whole number, the value of t when the temperature of the drink is $40°C$. [E]

71 (a) (i) Solve the equation $z^2 - 9z + 18 = 0$.

(ii) By substituting $z = 3^x$ into the equation

$$3^{2x-1} - 3^{x+1} + 6 = 0$$

show that $z^2 - 9z + 18 = 0$.

(iii) Hence, or otherwise, solve, to 3 decimal places where appropriate, the equation

$$3^{2x-1} - 3^{x+1} + 6 = 0$$

(b) (i) Show that $\log_2 w = 2\log_4 w$.

(ii) Hence solve the simultaneous equations

$$\log_4 t^2 - \log_2 u^2 = (\log_{\frac{1}{2}} 9) - 1$$
$$4^t = 2^{u-2}$$

where $u > 0$ and $t > 0$. [E]

72

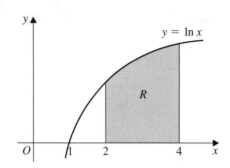

The shaded region R, as shown in the figure, is bounded by the lines with equations $x = 2$, $x = 4$ and $y = 0$ and the curve with equation $y = \ln x$. Use the trapezium rule, with three equally spaced ordinates, to find an approximation for the area of R. Give your answer to 3 significant figures. [E]

73 (a) Given that $\log_m x = p$, express in terms of p,

(i) $\log_m (x^4)$

(ii) $\log_m \left(\dfrac{1}{x^2} \right)$

(iii) $\log_m (mx)$.

(b) Solve $6(5^{2x}) - 20(5^x) + 14 = 0$ giving each answer, where appropriate, to 3 significant figures.

(c) Given that

$$2\log_2 x = y \text{ and } \log_2 (2x) = y + 4$$

find the value of x. [E]

74

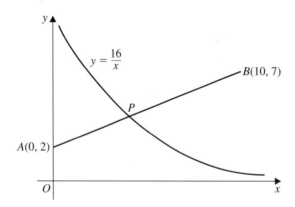

The diagram shows part of the curve with equation $y = \dfrac{16}{x}$.

The line AB joins the point A, with coordinates $(0, 2)$, to the point B, with coordinates $(10, 7)$, and crosses the curve at the point P.

(a) Find an equation of the line AB.

(b) Find the coordinates of the point P.

(c) Show that the normal to the curve at P passes through the origin.

The finite region bounded by the line OP, the curve with equation $y = \dfrac{16}{x}$, the line with equation $x = 8$, and the x-axis is rotated through $360°$ about the x-axis.

(d) Find, in terms of π, the volume of the solid generated.   [E]

75 Given that $x = 2^p$, $y = 4^q$

(a) express $4xy$ as a power of 2

(b) find $\log_2 (xy^3)$ in terms of p and q

(c) find $\log_8 (x^2y)$ in terms of p and q

Given further that $64(2^p) = 4^q$,

(d) express p in terms of q.

76 (a) Show that $\log_4 3 = \log_2 \sqrt{3}$.

(b) Hence or otherwise solve the simultaneous equations

$$2 \log_2 y = \log_4 3 + \log_2 x$$
$$3^y = 9^x$$

given that x and y are positive.   [E]

77 (a) Write down the common ratio of the geometric series G,

$$e + e^{\frac{1}{2}} + 1 + \ldots$$

(b) Calculate, to 3 significant figures, the sum of the first six terms of the series.

(c) Write down, in its simplest form, the common difference of the arithmetic series A,

$$\log_3 2 + \log_3 6 + \log_3 18 + \ldots$$

(d) Show that the sum of the first ten terms of A is $10 \log_3 2 + 45$ and evaluate this to 2 decimal places.

(e) One of these two series has a sum to infinity. Calculate, to 2 decimal places, this sum.   [E]

78 Evaluate:

(a) $\displaystyle\int_0^1 7(e^x + x^2)\,dx$ in terms of e

(b) $\displaystyle\int_0^2 e^{x^2}\,dx$, using the trapezium rule with 4 intervals of equal width, giving your answer to 3 significant figures.

79 Solve the simultaneous equations

$$\log_2 x - \log_4 y = 4$$
$$\log_2 (x - 2y) = 5 \qquad\qquad [E]$$

80 The function f is given by

$$f : x \mapsto e^{-2x},\ x \in \mathbb{R}$$

(a) State the range of f.

(b) Define the inverse function f^{-1} in a similar manner to f.

(c) Sketch the curve with equation $y = f^{-1}(x)$. $\qquad$ [E]

81

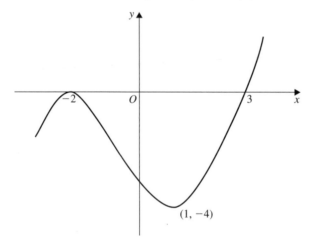

The diagram shows a sketch of the curve with equation $y = f(x)$. This curve has turning points at $(-2, 0)$ and $(1, -4)$ and it also cuts the x-axis at the point $(3, 0)$.

Using separate axes, sketch the curves with equations

(a) $y = |f(x)|$ $\qquad$ (b) $y = 4 - f(x)$

Mark on your sketches the coordinates of the turning points of your curves. $\qquad$ [E]

82 (a) Solve the equation $3^x = 5$, giving your answer to 3 significant figures.

(b) Use the substitution $y = 3^x$ to solve, to 2 decimal places, the equation

$$2(3^{2x}) - 7(3^x) + 6 = 0$$

83 By means of a sketch of the graphs of $y = 8e^{-x}$ and $y = x^3$ show that the equation

$$8e^{-x} = x^3$$

has exactly one real root.

Denoting this real root by α, find the integer n such that $n < \alpha < n + 1$.

Use the iterative formula $x_{n+1} = (8e^{-x_n})^{\frac{1}{3}}$, $x_0 = 2$ to find α correct to 2 decimal places.

84 (a) Solve the equation

$$2^{2x} - 5(2^{x+1}) + 16 = 0$$

(b) Given that b and c are non-zero constants and that the equations $x^2 + bx + c = 0$ and $7x^2 + 2bx - 3c = 0$ have a common root, prove that $b^2 = 4c$.   [E]

85 (a) Calculate the area of the finite region bounded by the curve with equation $y = x(4 - 3x)$ and the straight line with equation $y = x$.

(b) Find also the volume generated when this region is rotated completely about the x-axis, giving your answer in terms of π. [E]

86 The following pairs of values of two related variables x and y are given in the table.

x	10	20	30	40	50
y	1.21	3.98	7.97	13.08	19.22

Using the trapezium rule with 4 intervals of equal width find an estimate for $\int_{10}^{50} y \, dx$.

87 Find equations for the tangent and the normal at $P(\ln 2, 2k)$ on the curve with equation $y = ke^x$, where k is a constant.

88 Solve, giving your answers to 3 decimal places, the equations
(a) $3^x = 5$ (b) $\log_y 2 = \log_4 32$.   [E]

89 It is given that

$$f(x) \equiv x - (\sin x + \cos x)^{\frac{1}{2}}, \ 0 \leqslant x \leqslant \tfrac{3}{4}\pi$$

(a) Show that the equation $f(x) = 0$ has a root α lying between 1.1 and 1.2.

(b) Prove that $\alpha = 1.15$ *correct* to 2 decimal places.   [E]

90 Solve the simultaneous equations

$$\log_y x - 4\log_x y = 0$$
$$\lg x + \lg y = 1 \qquad\qquad [E]$$

91 Given that $y = e^x + x^2$, prove that

$$\frac{d^2y}{dx^2} = y + 2 - x^2$$

Find also an equation of the normal to the curve with equation $y = e^x + x^2$ at the point where $x = 1$.

92 (a) Use the trapezium rule with 3 intervals of equal width to find an estimate for

$$\int_{\frac{1}{2}}^{2} \frac{1}{x} dx$$

(b) Find the exact value of $\int_{\frac{1}{2}}^{2} \frac{1}{x} dx$ in terms of natural logs.

(c) Hence find the percentage error in the estimate found in part (a).

93 Show that for $a \in \mathbb{N}$, $a > 1$ and $p, q > 0$,

$$\log_a p^2, \ 2\log_a pq \quad \text{and} \quad 2\log_a pq^2$$

are three successive terms of an arithmetic sequence whose common difference is $2\log_a q$.

Given that $pq^2 = a$, show that the sum of the first 5 terms of the arithmetic sequence with first term $\log_a p^2$ and common difference $2\log_a q$ is 10. $\qquad [E]$

94 Use the trapezium rule with 3 equally spaced ordinates to estimate the value of

$$\int_0^1 e^{\sqrt{x}} dx$$

giving your answer to 3 significant figures. $\qquad [E]$

95 Solve the simultaneous equations

$$x + y = 35$$
$$\log_2 x - \log_4 y = 1$$

96 (a) Given that, for positive x,

$$\lg x + \lg 25 = \lg x^3$$

calculate the value of x, without using a calculator.

(b) Solve the equation

$$2^x = 5$$

giving your answer to 3 significant figures. [E]

97 Given that $y = x^{-2} + \ln x^3$, $x > 0$, prove that

$$x^4 \frac{d^2 y}{dx^2} = 3(2 - x^2).$$

98 Given that $\frac{dy}{dx} = 5e^x - \frac{4}{x}$ and that $y = 0$ at $x = 1$, find the value of y, to one decimal place, at $x = 2$.

99 State which of the following equations can be solved by considering the intersection of the graph of $y = \ln x$ with a suitable straight line.

(a) $2x + 3 = \ln\left(\frac{1}{x}\right)$

(b) $x + 1 + \ln(x^2) = 0$

(c) $e^{-3x} = x^3$

(d) $e^x = x + e$

100 The tangent to the curve with equation $y = 2\ln x - x + 1$ at the point on the curve where $x = 3$ meets the x-axis at P. Find the distance OP, where O is the origin.

Examination style paper

P2

Answer all questions   **Time allowed: 90 minutes**

1. Solve the simultaneous equations:

$$\lg x + \lg y = 1000,$$
$$\lg (3x + y) = 1. \qquad \textbf{(6 marks)}$$

2. (a) Expand $(3 - 2x)^7$ in ascending powers of x up to and including the term in x^3, simplifying each coefficient. **(4 marks)**
(b) Find the coefficient of the term in x^3 in the expansion of $(1 + x^2)(3 - 2x)^7$. **(3 marks)**

3. Given that $f(x) \equiv 5 \sin x - 2x$, show that the equation $f(x) = 0$ has a root α in the interval $[2, 2.2]$ **(3 marks)**

Use the iteration formula

$$x_{n+1} = \pi - \arcsin \left(\tfrac{2}{5} x_n \right)$$

with $x_0 = 2.1$ to find α *correct* to two decimal places. **(5 marks)**

4. (a) Sketch the graph of $y = f(x)$, where

$$f : x \mapsto x^2 - 3x - 4,\ x \in \mathbb{R},\ -3 \leqslant x \leqslant 5,$$

showing the coordinates of its end points and where it meets the coordinate axes. **(4 marks)**
(b) Find the range of f. **(2 marks)**
(c) Sketch the graph of $y = |f(x)|$ for $-3 \leqslant x \leqslant 5$. **(3 marks)**

5. The finite region R is bounded by the curve with equation $y = 3e^{\frac{x}{2}}$, the lines with equations $x = 1$ and $x = 4$ and the x-axis.
(a) Find an estimate, to two decimal places, of the area of R using the trapezium rule with 7 equally spaced ordinates. **(4 marks)**
(b) State, with a reason, whether your estimate is over, or under, the true value for the area. **(2 marks)**
(c) The region R is rotated through $360°$ about the x-axis. Using integration, find the volume of the solid so formed, leaving your answer in terms of π and e. **(4 marks)**

6.

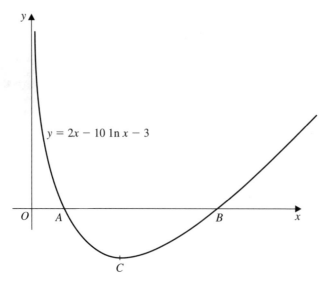

$y = 2x - 10 \ln x - 3$

The diagram shows a sketch of the curve with equation $y = 2x - 10 \ln x - 3$ which crosses the x-axis at A and B. At the point C y takes its minimum value.

(a) Show that the x-coordinate of A lies in the interval $[\frac{1}{2}, 1]$. **(3 marks)**

(b) Given that the x-coordinate of B lies in the interval $[N, N + 1]$ where N is an integer, find the value of N. **(3 marks)**

(c) Determine the coordinates of C. **(5 marks)**

7. Starting with the identity

$$\cos(A + B) \equiv \cos A \cos B - \sin A \sin B,$$

prove that $\cos 2A \equiv 2\cos^2 A - 1$. **(3 marks)**

Assuming also a similar identity for $\sin(A + B)$,

prove that $\cos 3A \equiv 4\cos^3 A - 3\cos A$. **(3 marks)**

Hence find, in terms of π, those values of x in the interval $[0, 3\pi]$ for which

$$\cos 3x - \cos 2x = 2\cos^2 x + 1$$ **(6 marks)**

8. Given that $24\cos\theta - 7\sin\theta \equiv R\cos(\theta + \alpha)$ where $R > 0$ and $0 < \alpha < \dfrac{\pi}{2}$, find

(a) the value of R, **(2 marks)**

(b) the value of α to two decimal places, **(2 marks)**

(c) the values of x in $(0, 2\pi)$ for which

$$24\cos x - 7\sin x = 14,$$

giving your answers to two decimal places, **(4 marks)**

(d) the greatest and the least values of

$$24\cos y - 7\sin y + 30$$

as y varies. **(4 marks)**

Answers

Exercise 1A

1 $\dfrac{x-3}{2x+6}$ **2** $\dfrac{x+5}{2x-4}$

3 $\dfrac{x-1}{x+3}$ **4** $\dfrac{2x-4}{x-4}$

5 $\dfrac{4}{3x^3(x+2)}$ **6** $\dfrac{6}{(x-4)(x+1)}$

7 $\dfrac{3(1-x)x}{2(7+x)(3-2x)}$ **8** $\dfrac{x+3}{2(x+2)}$

9 $\dfrac{2x^2(x-6)(x-5)(x+1)}{(2x+1)(x-3)}$

10 $\dfrac{10x}{3(x-5)(3x-2)}$ **11** $\dfrac{x(2-x)(2+x)}{6(x+4)(2x-3)}$

12 $\dfrac{20x^2}{7(x+1)(3x-2)}$ **13** $\dfrac{(x+3)(2x+3)}{5x^3(x-3)}$

14 $\dfrac{(x+2)(2x-1)}{(x-2)(x+3)}$ **15** $\dfrac{x+2}{4(x-2)}$

16 $\dfrac{5x+5}{(2x+1)(x+3)}$ **17** $\dfrac{7x-14}{(4x-5)(x-3)}$

18 $\dfrac{11+42x-8x^2}{2(4x+3)(2x-1)}$ **19** $\dfrac{9}{2x-3}$

20 $\dfrac{3x^2+16x+7}{(x+1)(x+3)(2x-1)}$

21 $\dfrac{-3x^2+6x+2}{(x-1)(2x+1)(x+4)}$

22 $\dfrac{-13x^2-38x-12}{(5-2x)(6+x)(1-x)}$

23 $\dfrac{9x^2+28x-2}{10(x-2)(x+2)(x+3)}$

24 $\dfrac{28-59x-14x^2}{(3-x)(7+x)(1-2x)}$

Exercise 1B

1 $1, -3$ **2** $\frac{1}{2}, -\frac{3}{4}$ **3** 3 or 5

4 $1, 8$ **5** $\frac{1}{6}(1 \pm \sqrt{13})$

6 $\dfrac{3}{(x-4)(x-1)}, \dfrac{5 \pm \sqrt{17}}{2}$

7 30 **8** 10 **9** 60 mph

10 $m = 8, n = 5$ **11** $1.62, -0.62$

Exercise 2A

1 $-3 \leqslant y \leqslant 9$ **2** $2 \leqslant y \leqslant 6$ **3** $0 \leqslant y \leqslant 16$

4 $\frac{1}{10} \leqslant y \leqslant \frac{1}{2}$ **5** $\frac{1}{4} \leqslant y \leqslant 16$

6 (a) $\frac{1}{5}$ (b) $\frac{1}{2}$ (c) 1 **7** $\frac{1}{8} \leqslant y \leqslant 1$

8 $-1 \leqslant x \leqslant \frac{8}{3}$ **9** $-3 \leqslant x \leqslant 6$

Exercise 2B

1 (a) (i) $\text{fg}: x \mapsto 9 - 8x, x \in \mathbb{R}$
  (ii) $\text{gf}: x \mapsto 27 - 8x, x \in \mathbb{R}$
  (iii) $\text{fh}: x \mapsto 13 - 6x, x \in \mathbb{R}$
  (iv) $\text{hf}: x \mapsto 18 - 6x, x \in \mathbb{R}$
  (v) $\text{gh}: x \mapsto 12x - 13, x \in \mathbb{R}$
  (vi) $\text{hg}: x \mapsto 12x - 6, x \in \mathbb{R}$
 (b) (i) -31 (ii) -15 (iii) -13
  (iv) -12 (v) -39 (vi) -1
 (c) (i) 3 (ii) 2 (iii) -1

2 (a) $1\frac{1}{2}$ (b) $\frac{5}{6}$ (c) $2\frac{2}{3}$ $x = -\frac{1}{4}$ or 4

3 (a) 0 (b) 8 (c) 35 (d) 3

4 $\text{p}(x) = x^3, \text{q}(x) = x + 2 \rightarrow \text{qp} = \text{f}$
 $\text{p}(x) = \dfrac{1}{x}, \text{q}(x) = x - 3 \rightarrow \text{qp} = \text{g}$
 $\text{fg}(2) = -13\frac{5}{8}$ $\text{gf}(2) = -2\frac{9}{10}$

5 $a + b = 1$

6 (a) $1 + \dfrac{x^2}{2}$ (b) $\left(1 + \dfrac{x}{2}\right)^2$ (c) $\dfrac{x+6}{4}$

8 $fg(x) = 18x^2 - 24x + 9$

$gf(x) = 6x^2 + 1$

$ff(x) = 8x^4 + 8x^2 + 3$

$gg(x) = 9x - 8$

Exercise 2C

1 $f^{-1}(x) = \frac{1}{2}x$ **2** $f^{-1}(x) = \dfrac{x-3}{2}$

3 $f^{-1}(x) = \dfrac{1-x}{2}$ **4** $f^{-1}(x) = -x^{\frac{1}{2}}$

5 $f^{-1}(x) = \dfrac{1}{x}$ ($f(x) = \dfrac{1}{x}$ is a self-inverse function)

6 $x - p$ **7** $\dfrac{x}{p}$ **8** $p - x$ (self-inverse)

9 $\dfrac{x-q}{p}$

10 $\dfrac{p}{x} (x \neq 0)$ (self-inverse)

11 $\dfrac{1-qx}{px} (x \neq 0)$

12 $y \in \mathbb{R}^+; \dfrac{1}{x^{\frac{1}{2}}}$ **13** $0 < y < 1; \dfrac{1-x}{x}$

14 $y \in \mathbb{R}^+; (x+1)^{\frac{1}{2}} - 1$ **15** $y > 5; (x-1)^{\frac{1}{2}} - 2$

16 $A = 5, B = 4; k = 5, y \geqslant 4;$

$f^{-1}(x) = (x-4)^{\frac{1}{2}} + 5; x \geqslant 4$

17 $g^{-1}(x) = \dfrac{1}{x} + 4, x \neq 0$

18 $f^{-1}(x) = \dfrac{x}{2-x}, x \in \mathbb{R}, x \neq 2$

19 (a) $\dfrac{13x+1}{x+5}$ (b) $\dfrac{3x+1}{x-5}$

Exercise 2D

3 (a) $y = x^2, y = x^4$ (b) $y = x^3$

4 $(\frac{1}{2}, \frac{1}{2})$ and $(1, 1)$

9 $(\frac{1}{7}, \frac{23}{7})$ and $(\frac{7}{3}, \frac{23}{3})$

10 $-3, 2$

11 (c) $2 \pm 2\sqrt{2}, 2$ (d) $\pm 1, \pm 3$

12 (a) $-\frac{5}{8}, \frac{5}{2}$ (b) $\frac{1}{4}, 3$ (c) $\pm 1, \pm 4$

13 $\pm 1, \pm 2$

15 (a) $2.35, -2.55$ (b) $2.25, -2.45$

16 (a) $2x^2 - 3x - 12 = 0$ (d) $-1.8, 3.3$

17 (a) 1.67 (b) $-1.88, 0.35, 1.53$

18 (a) -2.35 (b) $-3.6, -1.2, 2.9$

19 (a) -1.7 (b) $-2.6, 0.2$

Exercise 3A

1 $3, 2, 0, -4 \ldots$: divergent

2 $3, 10, 24, 52 \ldots$: divergent

3 $0, 1, \frac{3}{2}, \frac{7}{4} \ldots$: converges to 2

4 $3, 2, \frac{5}{3}, \frac{14}{9} \ldots$: converges to $1\frac{1}{2}$

5 $2, \frac{1}{5}, -\frac{4}{25}, -\frac{29}{125} \ldots$: converges to $-\frac{1}{4}$

6 $\frac{3}{2}, \frac{7}{5}, \frac{17}{12} \ldots$: limiting value $\sqrt{2}$

7 $33, 63, 153$

8 $u_7 = 16, u_{11} = 64, u_{14} = 320$

9 (a) diverges   (b) converges to zero

    (c) oscillates   (d) converges to zero

10 -6

11 limiting value 1 in both cases

12 $u_n = u_{n-1}u_{n-2}, u_1 = 1, u_2 = 3$

10th term $= 3^{34}$, 13th term $= 3^{144}$

Exercise 3B

1 (a) $1 + 6x + 9x^2$ (b) $1 - 10x + 25x^2$

   (c) $1 - 2x^2 + x^4$ (d) $1 + 4x^3 + 4x^6$

   (e) $9 - 24x + 22x^2 - 8x^3 + x^4$

2 (a) $1 + 6y + 12y^2 + 8y^3$

   (b) $1 - 3x^3 + 3x^6 - x^9$

   (c) $1 + 9x^{-1} + 27x^{-2} + 27x^{-3}$

3 (a) $1 + 4x + 6x^2 + 4x^3 + x^4$

   (b) $1 + 5x + 10x^2 + 10x^3 + 5x^4 + x^5$

4 (a) $1 - 12x + 54x^2 - 108x^3 + 81x^4$

   (b) $1 + 10x + 40x^2 + 80x^3 + 80x^4 + 32x^5$

Exercise 3C

1 $1 + 15x + 75x^2 + 125x^3; 2 + 150x^2$

2 $1 - x + \frac{1}{4}x^2, 1 - \frac{3}{2}x + \frac{3}{4}x^2 - \frac{1}{8}x^3,$

$1 - 2x + \frac{3}{2}x^2 - \frac{1}{2}x^3 + \frac{1}{16}x^4$

3 $8 - 36x + 54x^2 - 27x^3,$

$27 + 54x + 36x^2 + 8x^3,$

$-30 - 216x + 90x^2 - 97x^3$

4 (a) $1 - 12x + 60x^2 - 160x^3$

   (b) $128 - 448x + 672x^2 - 560x^3$

5 $-524\,288y^9 - 1\,179\,648y^7 - 258\,048y^5$

6 $0.850\,763\,0$

7 (a) $1.049\,070\,08$ (b) $0.953\,041\,92$

8 $37 - 252x - 36x^2 - 91x^3$

9 $625x^4 - 1000x^3 + 600x^2$

10 $m = 6$, $A = 2$, $B = 240$

11 (a) 56 (b) 98

12 $z^9 - 9z^7 + 36z^5 - 84z^3 + 126z - 126z^{-1}$
$+ 84z^{-3} - 36z^5 + 9z^{-7} - z^{-9}$

13 (a) 364 (b) 1080 (c) −80
(d) 86 016

14 −20 **15** $6\frac{19}{35}$

Exercise 3D

1 $1 - 23x + 253x^2$ **2** $A = 15$, $B = 105$,
$C = 455$

3 $78\,125x^7 - 328\,125x^6 + 590\,625x^5$

4 $162 + 432x^2 + 32x^4$

5 (a) $1 - 40y + 700y^2 - 7000y^3$
(b) $1 - 44y + 860y^2 - 9800y^3$

6 $1 + 10x + 45x^2 + 120x^3$, 0.980 179 04

7 $40x^8 + 1920x^4 + 16\,128$

8 $a = -780$, $b = 1351$

9 6726 **10** (a) 27 (b) 3 247 695

11 (a) 1.012 066 22
(b) 998 501 049 500 000

12 $n = 22$, $k = 2$, 12 320

13 $1 + 7ax + 21a^2x^2 + 35a^3x^3$; $a = 2$, $b = 5$;
434; 1484

15 $k = 2$, $n = 7$; 280, 560

16 $18\,564y^6$, 5.543×10^{10} (4 s.f.)

17 $1 + 6y + 15y^2 + 20y^3 + 15y^4 + 6y^5 + y^6$,
1.062 15

18 $a = 2$, $b = \frac{1}{2}$; $5x^3 + \frac{5}{8}x^4 + \frac{x}{32}$

19 $x^{80} + 40x^{78} + 780x^{76} + 9880x^{74}$

20 $k = \frac{1}{4}$, $n = 17$; $\frac{85}{8}x^3$, $\frac{595}{64}x^4$

Exercise 4A

1 (a) 1.235 (b) 1.466 (c) 1.122
(d) 1.086 (e) −1.664 (f) −1.662
(g) −3.420 (h) 1.287 (i) −0.5774
(j) −1.026

2 (a) −0.02921 (b) −1.034 (c) 1.341
(d) −0.08784 (e) −1.043 (f) 1.041
(g) 1.293 (h) −1.516 (i) 1.171
(j) 1.075

3 (a) 56.5, 303.5 (b) 207.5, 332.5

(c) 140.9, 320.9 (d) 153.9, 206.1
(e) 152.1, 207.9 (f) 81.6, 261.6
(g) 51.7, 308.3 (h) 33.4, 146.6
(i) 39.5, 219.5 (j) 61.1, 118.9

4 (a) 0.907, 5.376 (b) 3.805, 5.621
(c) 0.948, 4.090 (d) 2.114, 4.169
(e) 0.519, 2.623 (f) 2.660, 5.802
(g) 0.714, 5.569 (h) 3.745, 5.680
(i) 1.883, 5.025 (j) 2.080, 4.204

5 (a) $\frac{\pi}{2}$ (b) $-\frac{\pi}{3}$ (c) $\frac{\pi}{6}$
(d) $\frac{\pi}{2}$ (e) $-\frac{\pi}{3}$ (f) $\frac{5\pi}{12}$

6 (a) 0.85 (b) 1.43 (c) 2.40
(d) −1.45 (e) 1.68 (f) −0.34

10 (a) $\frac{\pi}{6}$ (b) $\frac{\pi}{12} + \frac{3}{2}$ (c) $\frac{\pi}{4}$

21 $p = 8$, $\theta = \frac{\pi}{6}$

22 $q = 15$, $\alpha = 1.08$ (2 d.p.)

23 $\frac{d^2}{16} = 1 + \frac{c^2}{9}$

24 $m = 6.72$, $\beta = 0.28$ (2 d.p.)

Exercise 4B

1 (a) $\frac{\sqrt{3} + 1}{2\sqrt{2}}$ (b) $\frac{\sqrt{3} - 1}{2\sqrt{2}}$

(c) $\frac{1 + \sqrt{3}}{1 - \sqrt{3}}$ (d) $\frac{\sqrt{3} - 1}{2\sqrt{2}}$

(e) $\frac{1 - \sqrt{3}}{2\sqrt{2}}$ (f) $\frac{\sqrt{3} - 1}{\sqrt{3} + 1}$

(g) $\frac{\sqrt{3} - 1}{2\sqrt{2}}$ (h) $-\frac{\sqrt{3} + 1}{2\sqrt{2}}$

2 (a) 1 (b) $\frac{1}{2}$ (c) $-\sqrt{3}$ (d) $\frac{1}{2}$
(e) $\frac{1}{2}$ (f) $\frac{1}{\sqrt{3}}$

3 (a) $\sin 4\theta$ (b) $\cos 3\theta$ (c) $\tan 2\theta$
(d) $3\sin 5\theta$ (e) $4\cos 2\theta$ (f) $2\cos 3\theta$

4 (a) $\frac{63}{65}$ (b) $\frac{56}{65}$ (c) $-\frac{63}{16}$ (d) $-\frac{56}{33}$

5 (a) $\frac{63}{65}$ (b) $-\frac{65}{56}$ (c) $\frac{63}{16}$ (d) $\frac{56}{33}$

6 (a) $\frac{36}{325}$ (b) $-\frac{325}{204}$ (c) $\frac{253}{325}$
(d) $-\frac{325}{323}$ (e) $-\frac{204}{253}$ (f) $-\frac{323}{36}$

7 (a) (i) 1 when $\theta = 20°$
(ii) −1 when $\theta = 200°$
(b) (i) 1 when $\theta = 110°$
(ii) −1 when $\theta = 290°$

(c) (i) 1 when $\theta = 65°$

(ii) -1 when $\theta = 245°$

8 (a) -1 when $\theta = 230°$

(b) -1 when $\theta = 223°$

(c) -3 when $\theta = 75°$

Exercise 4C

1 (a) $\frac{1}{2}$ (b) $\frac{1}{\sqrt{2}}$ (c) -1 (d) $\frac{\sqrt{3}}{2}$

(e) $1 - \frac{\sqrt{3}}{2}$ (f) $-2\sqrt{2}$ (g) $2\sqrt{3}$

(h) $\frac{1}{2} + \frac{\sqrt{3}}{4}$

2 (a) $\frac{24}{25}$ (b) $-\frac{7}{25}$ (c) $-\frac{24}{7}$

3 (a) $\frac{120}{169}$ (b) $-\frac{119}{169}$ (c) $-\frac{120}{119}$

4 (a) $-\frac{336}{625}$ (b) $\frac{625}{527}$ (c) $-\frac{527}{336}$

5 (a) $\frac{25}{7}$ (b) $-\frac{25}{24}$ (c) $-\frac{24}{7}$

6 (a) $\frac{1}{\sqrt{2}}$ (b) $\frac{1}{\sqrt{2}}$ (c) 1

7 $\frac{1}{3}$ or -3 8 $\frac{1}{7}$ or -7

9 $\sin 3\theta \equiv 3 \sin \theta - 4 \sin^3 \theta; \frac{47}{128}$

10 $\cos 3\theta = 4 \cos^3 \theta - 3 \cos \theta; -\frac{11}{16}$

11 (a) $(x - 2)^2 = 4y^2(1 - y^2)$

(b) $y = 3(2x^2 - 4x + 1)$

(c) $x(1 - y^2) = 2y$

(d) $x - 3 = \frac{2}{y^2} - 1$

(e) $x^2 y = 2$

Exercise 4D

1 $2 \sin 58° \cos 18°$ 2 $2 \cos 28° \sin 12°$

3 $2 \cos 78° \cos 22°$ 4 $-2 \sin 65° \sin 7°$

5 $2 \sin 29.6° \sin 21.1°$ 6 $\sin 60° - \sin 34°$

7 $\cos 34° - \cos 60°$

8 $\frac{1}{2}(\sin 197° + \sin 59°)$

9 $\frac{1}{2}(\cos 380° + \cos 120°)$

10 $\frac{1}{2}(\sin 70° - \sin 10°)$

11 $8.6°, 141.4°$ 12 $68.5°, 225.5°$

13 $170.7°, 350.7°$ 14 $169.6°, 349.6°$

15 $60°, 240°$ 16 $126.2°, 306.2°$

17 $85.9°, 265.9°$

18 $22.5°, 112.5°, 202.5°, 292.5°$

19 $0, 60°, 180°, 300°, 360°$

20 $0, 120°, 180°, 240°, 360°$

21 $21.5°, 158.5°$

22 $0, 60°, 120°, 180°, 240°, 300°$

23 $19.5°, 160.5°, 270°$

24 $33.7°, 63.4°, 213.7°, 243.4°$

25 $33.7°, 153.4°, 213.7°, 333.4°$

26 $30°, 90°, 150°, 270°$

27 $120°, 240°$

28 $15°, 75°, 195°, 255°$

29 $0, 180°, 360°, 60°, 300°, 120°, 240°$

30 $0, 180°, 360°, 45°, 135°, 225°, 315°$

31 $45°, 225°, 26.6°, 206.6°$

32 $51.3°, 128.7°$

33 $105°, 165°, 285°, 345°$

34 $30°, 150°, 180°$

35 $22.5°, 112.5°, 202.5°, 292.5°$

36 $45°, 225°, 121°, 301°$

37 $14.2°, 74.2°, 134.2, 194.2, 254.2, 314.2$

38 $0, 180°, 360°, 138.6°, 221.4°$

39 $0, 45°, 90°, 135°, 180°, 225°, 270°, 315°, 360°$

40 $22.5°, 45°, 67.5°, 112.5°, 135°, 157.5°$
$202.5°, 225°, 247.5°, 292.5°, 315°, 337.5°$

41 $0, 36°, 72°, 108°, 144°, 180°$
$216°, 252°, 288°, 324°, 360°$
$30°, 150°, 270°, 90°, 210°, 330°$

42 $0°, 90°, 180°, 270°, 360°$

43 $45°, 60°, 135°, 225°, 300°, 315°$

Exercise 4E

1 $17, 61.9°$ 2 $13, 67.4°$

3 $\sqrt{10}, 18.4°$ 4 $10, 53.1°$

5 $\sqrt{2}, 45°$

6 $17, 298.1°; -17, 118.1°$

7 $13, 22.6°; -13, 202.6°$

8 $\sqrt{10}, 108.4°; -\sqrt{10}, 288.4°$

9 $10, 53.1°; -10, 233.1°$

10 $\sqrt{2}, 315°; -\sqrt{2}, 135°$

11 $66.9°$ or $186.9°$ 12 $4.9°$ or $129.9°$

13 $114.3°$ or $335.7°$

14 $39.0°, 162.8°, 219.0°, 342.8°$

15 $110.6°, 230.6°, 350.6°$

16 $0, 4.71, 6.28$ 17 $1.57, 6.00$

18 $3.36, 5.09$

19 $0.34, 1.40, 3.48, 4.54$

20 2.67

21 $226.3°$, $346.3°$; -25, $106.3°$

22 $\sqrt{10}$, $18.4°$; $57.7°$, $159.2°$, $417.7°$, $519.2°$

23 $-336.9°$, $-276.9°$, $23.1°$, $83.1°$

24 (a) $-\dfrac{1}{\sqrt{13}}$, 1.031

    (b) 0, 0.49, 2.06, 3.63, 5.20, 1.57, 3.14,

       4.71, 6.28

25 (a) $\frac{1}{7}$, $\frac{1}{17}$ (b) 2.36, 2.64, 5.50, 5.78

Review exercise 1

1 $\dfrac{1}{2x-1}$

2 (a) $f^{-1}(x) = x^{\frac{1}{2}}$, $g^{-1}(x) = 2(x-1)$

3 (a) $81 + 1080x + 5400x^2 + 12\,000x^3$
    $+ 10\,000x^4$

    (b) $x = 100$, $1\,012\,054\,108\,081$

4 (a) $15.6°$, $195.6°$

    (b) $\dfrac{\pi}{6}$, $\dfrac{5\pi}{6}$, $\dfrac{7\pi}{6}$, $\dfrac{11\pi}{6}$

5 $\dfrac{3x-7}{x(x-1)(x-2)}$

6 (a) $\frac{1}{5}$ (b) $\dfrac{1}{x}$, $(x \neq 0)$ (c) $2, -1$

7 142\,506, 142\,506

8 (b) 0.6, 0.8

9 $\dfrac{1}{x-1}$

10 (i) (a) $x^3 + 3x + 3x^{-1} + x^{-3}$

    (b) $x^5 + 5x^3 + 10x + 10x^{-1} + 5x^{-3} + x^{-5}$,

    123

    (ii) $A = 45$, $B = 945$, $C = 12\,285$

11 (a) 1, 4   (b) $\dfrac{3x}{2-x}$, $(x \neq 2)$

12 $53.1°$, $323.1°$ **13** $-3, 1$

14 (a) $f^{-1} : x \mapsto \dfrac{x+1}{6}$

    (b) $fg : x \mapsto \dfrac{25-x}{x-1}$, $x \neq 1$

    (c) $\frac{3}{2}$ or $-\frac{1}{3}$

15 3

17 (a) $1 \leqslant f < 25$ (b) $f^{-1} : x \mapsto \dfrac{x+1}{6}$, $x \in \mathbb{R}$

(c) $fg : x \mapsto \dfrac{25-x}{x-1}$, $x \in \mathbb{R}$, $x \neq +1$

(d) $-\frac{1}{3}$, $\frac{3}{2}$

18 $1 + 8ax + 28a^2x^2$; $a = 1$, $b = -8$

19 (a) $k = -4$, greatest $y = 6$

    (b) $56.3°$, $236.3°$, $116.6°$, $296.6°$

20 (a) $A = 16$, $B = 2$, $C = 3$

    (b) (i) $f \leqslant 16$ (ii) $x > \frac{1}{2}$ or $x < -\frac{7}{2}$

21 $\dfrac{19x^2 + x - 31}{(x-3)(2x+5)(3x+2)}$

22 $R = 5\sqrt{2}$, $\alpha = 0.14$; 1.23, 4.77

23 (a) $fg : x \mapsto (2x+1)^2 + 3$ (b) $fg(x) \geqslant 3$

    (c) 3

24 $16 + 32x + 24x^2 + 8x^3 + x^4$;

    $16 - 32x + 24x^2 - 8x^3 + x^4$

25 (a) $90°$, $270°$, $26.6°$, $206.6°$

    (b) $\dfrac{5\pi}{6}$, $\dfrac{7\pi}{6}$, $\dfrac{\pi}{6}$, $\dfrac{11\pi}{6}$

26 (a) $k = \frac{3}{2}$, $p = 63$, $q = 189$ (b) 126

27 $1 - 14x + 84x^2$, $a = -15$, $b = 98$

28 (a) 1 or 9   (b) $\dfrac{x+2}{3}$, $9x - 8$ (c) 4

    (d) $9x^2 - 12x + 4$ (e) 2.54 or -1.04

29 $\alpha = 60°$; $255°$, $345°$

30 (a) $\dfrac{7 - 11x}{2(x+1)(x-1)(x-2)}$

    (b) (i) 12   (ii) $\frac{1}{27}$ (iii) 1   (c) $\frac{52}{5}$

31 (a) 3   (b) 540

32 (a) $\frac{\pi}{3}$, $\frac{4\pi}{3}$

    (b) (ii) -0.464, 2.68, -0.322, 2.820

33 (b) 5.76   (c) 0.40, 4.84

34 (a) $15 - 4k$ (b) $-8k^2 + 30k - 30$

    (c) 4 and $-\frac{1}{4}$

35 $A = \pm16$, $a = \pm2$

36 $\sqrt{3}$, $\sqrt{3}$, 0, $-\sqrt{3}$, $-\sqrt{3}$, 0 – periodic
sequence

37 $\sqrt{13}\cos(x - 33.69°)$; $74.0°$, $353.4°$

38 $x > 2$

39 (a) $f^{-1} : x \mapsto 2 + (x+4)^{\frac{1}{2}}$, $x \in \mathbb{R}$, $x \geqslant -3$

    (b) $\frac{1}{18}(1 \pm \sqrt{145})$

40 $1 - \frac{21}{2}x + \frac{105}{2}x^2 - \frac{665}{4}x^3$

41 2197, -2197

42 $1 + 10y + 45y^2 + 120y^3$

(a) $1 + 10x + 35x^2 + 30x^3$

(b) 0.90438

43 4, 6, 8; $4n^2 + 2n$

44 $-\frac{7}{5}$

45 (a) (i) $\frac{1}{2}$ (ii) $\frac{1}{2}$ (iii) $\frac{1}{\sqrt{3}}$

(b) 23.8, 203.8

46 $n^2 - n + 1, n^2 + n - 1$

47 (a) $\frac{\pi}{6}, \frac{\pi}{2}, \frac{5\pi}{6}$

(b) $0, \pm\frac{\pi}{3}, \pm\frac{\pi}{2}, \pm\pi$

48 0, 48.6, 131.4, 180, 270, 360

49 $-5.01, -1.27, 2.01, 4.28$

50 (a) $-\frac{7}{18}$ (b) $n = 7$

51 $x = \frac{1}{2}$ or $x = -2$

52 (b) (i) $\frac{\pi}{4}, \frac{\pi}{2}, \frac{3\pi}{4}, \frac{5\pi}{4}, \frac{3\pi}{2}, \frac{7\pi}{4}$ (ii) $\frac{\pi}{2}$

(c) 33.6

53 (c) $(-\beta, 0), (\alpha, 0), (0, -\alpha\beta); (-\alpha - \beta, 0), (0, 0)$

(d) $x = \dfrac{\alpha - \beta}{2}; x = \dfrac{-\alpha - \beta}{2}$

54 (b) 3 (c) $1 + \frac{7}{3}x + \frac{7}{3}x^2$

55 (b) ± 8

56 (c) $0, \frac{\pi}{18}, \frac{5\pi}{18}, \frac{13\pi}{18}, \frac{17\pi}{18}, \pi$

57 All curves touch or cross the x-axis in the range $-3 \leqslant x \leqslant 3$ at $(0, 0)$ only.

58 (b) $\frac{1}{3}$ (c) 7

59 (a) $f(x) \geqslant -1, y = x^2 - 4x + 3$

(c) (i) $(-1, 0), (1, 0), (0, -1)$

(ii) $(\frac{1}{2}, 0), (\frac{3}{2}, 0), (1, -1)$

60 $0, \frac{\pi}{3}, \frac{2\pi}{3}, \pi$

61 (a) $\dfrac{1}{1 - x}$ (b) x (c) $\dfrac{1}{1 - x}$

62 (b) -4 and 0

63 $\pm\frac{1}{3}$

64 (b) $(-a, 0), (a, 0), (0, a^2)$ (c) 5

65 (a) $(0, 0), (5, 0)$

(b) $(-1, 0), (4, 0), (0, -1.5)$

66 (b) $\frac{1}{2}, 1\frac{1}{2}$

67 $-148.8, -31.2, 31.2, 148.8$

68 $\pm\frac{3\pi}{4}, \pm\frac{\pi}{4}$

69 (b) $(gf)^{-1} : x \mapsto \dfrac{2x}{x - 2}, x \in \mathbb{R}, x \neq 2$

70 52.6, 105.9, 254.1, 307.4

71 Oscillating finite sequence

72 $0.62, -1.62$

73 0.75, 3

75 (a) $g(x) \geqslant 0$ (b) 0, 8 (c) 6, 2

76 (a) $gf(x) = 4 - 9x^2$ (c) $gf(x) \leqslant 4$

(d) 0.4

77 $90°, 450°, 143.1°, 503.1°$

79 $x^6 + 6x^5y + 15x^4y^2 + 20x^3y^3 + 15x^2y^4 + 6xy^5 + y^6; 4158$

80 $\dfrac{3}{2x - 1}$

81 0, 2.30, 3.98, 6.28

82 58.2, 76.8, 148.2, 166.8, 238.2, 256.8, 328.2, 346.8

83 (a) $1 + 11kx + 55k^2x^2 + 165k^3x^3 + \ldots$

(b) $\frac{1}{3}$ (c) $\frac{55}{9}$

84 5 or 4

85 1.23, 5.05

86 (a) $\frac{17}{8}$ (b) $-\frac{240}{289}$ (c) $-\frac{240}{161}$

87 $\dfrac{2(y - 2)}{y + 2}$

88 0.46, 3.61, 2.90, 6.04

90 (a) $fg : x \mapsto \dfrac{x + 2}{3x}, x \neq 0$

(b) $g^{-1} : x \mapsto \dfrac{4 + 2x}{1 - x}, x \neq 1$

91 (a) $f_2; (0, 0), (1, 0), (2, 0)$

(b) $f_4; (0, 0), (1, 0)$ (c) $f_3; (1, 0), (0, -1)$

(d) $f_1; (2, 0), (0, 2)$

92 (a) 8 (b) $\frac{7}{64}$

93 0.34, 2.80, 3.67, 5.76

94 (a) 0.37 (b) 0.28

95 $a^6 + 6a^5b + 15a^4b^2 + 20a^3b^3 + 15a^2b^4 + 6ab^5 + b^6, 0.98213446, 7.29 \times 10^{-16}, 18$

96 $\dfrac{y - 7}{y - 4}$

97 Geometric, common ratio $\frac{8}{9}$

(a) $\frac{269\,297}{6561}$ (b) 81

98 (a) $x < 0$ or $x > \frac{2}{3}$

(b) $0 \leqslant x \leqslant \frac{\pi}{3}$ or $\frac{2\pi}{3} \leqslant x \leqslant \frac{4\pi}{3}$ or $\frac{5\pi}{3} \leqslant x \leqslant 2\pi$

Exercise 5A

1 (a) 3.2 (b) 1.2 (c) 9.8 (d) 0.57
2 (a) 24 (b) 0.64 (c) 4.2
3 (a) 0.74 (b) 6.7 (c) 15 (d) 1.9
   (e) 2.8

Exercise 5B

1 (a) -0.92 (b) -0.22 (c) 0.53
   (d) 1.19 (e) 1.55 (f) 0.37
   (g) 0.55 (h) 6.05
2 (b) and (c) are translations of (a) in the direction of Oy.

Exercise 5C

1 3   **2** 3   **3** 5   **4** 1296
5 1   **6** 3   **7** 3   **8** $\frac{1}{3}$
9 $\frac{1}{5}$ **10** 2187   **11** 4   **12** 4
13 1   **14** -2 **15** 3   **16** $\frac{1}{3}$
17 3   **18** -3 **19** $\frac{1}{3}$ **20** $\frac{1}{3}$
21 1.58   **22** 1.92   **23** 0.613   **24** 0.774
25 1.09   **26** $\log_3 14$ **27** $\lg 3$
28 $\ln 3$ **29** $\ln 1280$ **30** $\log_a \frac{9}{8}$
31 $\log_a \frac{4}{27}$ **32** $\log_a 441 - 2$
33 $\log_a 10$ **34** $5 + \log_a 6$ **35** $-\log_a 12$
36 $\log_a x + \log_a y - \log_a z$
37 $2\log_a x + \log_a y - 3\log_a z$
38 $\log_a x + 2\log_a y + 3\log_a z$
39 $\frac{1}{2}\log_a x + \log_a y + \frac{1}{2}\log_a z$
40 $\log_a x + \log_a y - \frac{3}{2}\log_a z$

Exercise 5D

1 2.81   **2** 2.68   **3** 1.73   **4** 1.37
5 2.58   **6** 1.5   **7** 1.85   **8** 0.112
9 1.71   **10** -13.8 **11** 6.05   **12** -3.89
13 1 or 1.58   **14** -0.631 or 1.26
15 -0.792 **16** 1   **17** 1.58
18 1 or 1.79   **19** ± 0.693
20 0.431 or 0.683   **21** 9
22 $-\frac{1}{3}$ or -2 **23** 0 or -1
24 (4, 16) or (16, 4)

Exercise 6A

1 (a) e^x (b) $-2e^x$
   (c) $\frac{1}{2}e^x$ (d) $5e^x$
2 (a) $8x^3 - e^x$ (b) $4e^x - 6x^{\frac{1}{2}}$
   (c) $\frac{1}{3}e^x + \frac{10}{x^3}$
3 (a) -1.57 (b) -3.68
4 (a) $\frac{2}{x}$ (b) $\frac{1}{x}$
   (c) $\frac{4}{x} + \frac{1}{2\sqrt{x}}$ (d) $\frac{3}{2x} + \frac{x}{2}$
   (e) $\frac{1}{3x} + 2e^x$ (f) $\frac{-10}{x}$
   (g) $\frac{1}{2x} + 6x$ (h) $\frac{e^x}{2} - \frac{5}{x}$
   (i) $\frac{-2}{x^2} - \frac{6}{x}$ (j) $\frac{4}{x} + \frac{12}{x^2}$
   (k) $\frac{2}{x\ln 3}$ (l) $\frac{3}{x\ln 10}$
5 (a) 1.69, 2.39 (b) 0.5, 0.25
6 (a) 2 (b) $4\frac{1}{6}$ (c) -5
   (d) -15.28 (e) 0.51
7 (a) $f^{-1} : x \mapsto \ln(x-1), x \in \mathbb{R}, x > 1$
   (c) $\frac{df}{dx} : x \mapsto e^x, \frac{df^{-1}}{dx} : x \mapsto \frac{1}{x-1}, x > 1$

Exercise 6B

1 $k = 1 + \dfrac{1}{e}$
3 $y - \dfrac{3}{e} = -\dfrac{e}{3}(x+1)$
4 $y = -\frac{1}{3}(x-1)$
6 $y - 1 = \dfrac{1}{10\ln 10}(x - 10)$
7 5.85   **8** 5.92
9 (0, 1)   **10** $\left(\dfrac{1}{\sqrt{2}}, \frac{1}{2} + \frac{1}{2}\ln 2 \right)$
11 $x = \frac{2}{3}, y = \frac{8}{3} - 8\ln\frac{2}{3}$
12 $x = \ln 8, y = 8\ln 8 - 8$; maximum
13 $\ln\frac{8}{9}, -7.94$

Exercise 7A

1 $4e^x + C$ **2** $\frac{1}{2}e^x + C$
3 $\frac{3}{5}x^{\frac{5}{3}} - \frac{2}{3}e^x + C$

4 $\dfrac{e^x}{3} + \dfrac{7}{6}x^2 + \dfrac{x^3}{9} + C$ **5** $2e^x + 2x + C$

6 $7\ln x + C$ **7** $-2\ln x + C$

8 $x + 4\ln x + C$ **9** $\frac{3}{4}x^{\frac{4}{3}} - 2x^{\frac{1}{2}} + C$

10 $6\ln x - \frac{1}{2}e^x + 3x + C$

11 $\dfrac{x^5}{5} + 4x^2 - 16x^{-1} + C$

12 $\dfrac{x^4}{4} - \frac{3}{2}x^2 + 3\ln x + \frac{1}{2}x^{-2} + C$

13 $2e^3 - 2e$ **14** $\frac{1}{3} - \dfrac{e^{-2}}{3}$ **15** $4\ln\frac{5}{2}$

16 $\frac{27}{2} - \ln 2$ **17** $-\ln 3$

18 $2\ln\frac{3}{2} - 3e^3 + 3e^2$ **19** $e^3 - e^2 + 5$

20 $4e + 1 - e^{-1}$ **21** $y = \frac{3}{2}\ln x + 3$

22 $y = 3e^x + 4x + 4 - 3e^{\frac{1}{2}}$

23 $y = x^2 + 2\ln x + 3$ **24** $y = 3 - 8\ln x$

25 $y = 4.5e^x + 3.5 \Rightarrow x = \ln\left(\dfrac{2y-7}{9}\right)$

Exercise 7B

1 $4\ln 5, \frac{64\pi}{5}$ **2** $10 + 3e^3 - 3e^{-2}$

3 $\dfrac{e^2}{2} + \frac{5}{2}e^{-1}$ **4** $\frac{24\pi}{7}, 6\pi$

5 $\frac{35}{8} + \ln 6, \frac{125}{16}\pi$ **6** $\frac{4}{3}, \frac{80}{81}\pi$

7 $\frac{32}{3}, \frac{128}{5}\pi$ **8** $4e^3 + 2e - 2$

9 (b) $\frac{2\sqrt{2}}{3}$ (c) $\frac{\pi}{4}$ **10** $y = x + 5, \frac{4}{3}$

11 (a) $\frac{1}{4}$ (b) $\frac{8\pi}{105}$

12 (a) 19.7 (b) 156π

13 4.7π **14** $60, \frac{16\,256}{7}\pi$

15 (a) 168π (b) $\pi\ln\frac{5}{2}$

  (c) $\frac{64}{15}\pi$ (d) $\dfrac{\pi}{4}[15 + 8\ln 4]$

Exercise 7C

1 0.534 **2** 11.983 **3** 0.946

4 0.088 **5** 2339.716 **6** 0.167

7 1.743 **8** 1.234

9 $16.713, 261.052$ **10** $7.378, \frac{40}{3}\pi$

11 0.9 **12** 3.977 **13** 15.05

Exercise 8A

6 $a = 22$ **12** 1

15 (b) 1 **16** 2.2

Exercise 8B

1 (b) (i) $p = 1, q = 3$ (ii) $r = 3, s = -1$
  (c) 0.382 (d) 2.618

2 (b) 7 (c) 2.410

3 $2.206, x^3 - 2x^2 - 1 = 0$ **4** 0.275

5 1.47 **6** 0.877 **7** -1.18 **8** 0.1375

9 3.332 **10** 1.1411 **11** $1.83, x = 3^{\frac{1}{x}}$

12 2.47 **13** 1.325 **14** 3.111

Exercise 9A

1 $\dfrac{5\pi}{6}$ is a solution.

2 There are plenty of simple counter-examples, e.g. $-5 > -7$ and $3 > 2 \not\Rightarrow ux > vy$.

3 Take $x \leqslant -4$ and result proposed is false.

4 For any number $a < -\frac{1}{4}$, proposition is false.

5 Solution set should be $x < -3$ or $x > -2$.

6 Breaks down for $n = 40$ when $f(40) = 41^2$ for example.

7 Has real roots for $b^2 = 4ac$ too.

8 Untrue in both cases – compare with rectangle and rhombus.

9 Not true for $n = 4$ and many others.

10 Untrue in second quadrant.

Review exercise 2

1 (a) 1.10 (b) -2.58 (c) 2.32 or 1.58

2 7.46 **3** $0, 3$

4 (a) $4(e^{\frac{1}{2}} + 1 - e^{-\frac{1}{2}})$ (b) $4\ln 2 + 2$

5 (a) $p = 3, q = 2$
  (b) $f^{-1}: x \mapsto e^{-x} + 2, x \in \mathbb{R}$

6 (a) 4 (b) 28.2 (c) 18.8

7 5.42

8 (a) 4 (c) $4.5 - 6\ln 2$

9 (a) $\frac{1}{2}(4 - e^x)$ (c) $f^{-1}(x) < 2$ (d) 3

10 2

11 (a) $4 + 12x^{-\frac{1}{2}} + 9x^{-1}$
  (b) $4x + 24x^{\frac{1}{2}} + 9\ln x + C$
  (c) $44 + 9\ln\frac{9}{4}$

12 $y = 3x + 2 - 18\ln 2, 3y + x = 26 - 54\ln 2$

13 (a) $g(x) > 0$ (c) 1 root   (d) 0.84

14 (a) $p + q$ (b) $2q - p$ (c) $3p + q$

(d) $3p + 4q$　　(e) $\dfrac{q}{p}$

15 (a) 60　　(b) $16\frac{256}{7}\pi$

16 (b) $-\dfrac{x}{2} + \dfrac{1}{x}$　　(c) $\sqrt{2}$

17 (a) $y > k$　　(b) $2k$

(c) $f^{-1}(x) = \ln(x - k), \, x > k$

18 (b) -3　　(c) $-1 < x < 2$

19 (a) 330　　(b) $8e^{\frac{1600}{435}} < p_2 < 8e^{\frac{1600}{425}}$

21 2 (note that 0.6 is not possible)

22 (a) $\dfrac{e^x + 2}{5}$　　(b) $\mathbb{R}$　　(c) 1.878

23 (a) $\frac{3}{5}x^{\frac{5}{3}} - \frac{2}{3}e^x + C$

(b) $\dfrac{x^4}{4} - 3x^2 + 12\ln x + \dfrac{4}{x^2} + C$

24 $y = 4(x - 1) + \frac{1}{2} - \ln 3$

25 (a) $(4, 20)$　　(c) $\frac{62}{5} + 48\ln 4$

26 2.81, 2.10　　　　**27** 1.78

28 4 or 12

29 (a) $\frac{3}{2}, 6$　　(b) $1 - 9x^{-2}$

(c) $x > 3, \, x < -3$　　(d) $\frac{1}{2}(e^2 + 17)$

30 1.749 03

31 (a) $6x^5 + 6x^2$　　(b) $\dfrac{2}{x}$　　(c) $2x - \dfrac{2}{x}$

32 $\frac{9}{2}\pi$

33 (a) $\frac{7}{12}$　　(b) $\frac{31}{80}\pi$

34 0.244

35 $3y = x + 14; \, y - \dfrac{10}{\sqrt{6}} = \frac{1}{3}(x - \sqrt{6})$,

$y + \dfrac{10}{\sqrt{6}} = \frac{1}{3}(x + \sqrt{6})$

36 $9\pi(e^{\frac{1}{2}} - 1)$

37 $\frac{1}{2}e - 1$

38 $\frac{3}{2}, \frac{17}{12}$

40 (b) $y + 4ax = 2a^2 + 8$　　(c) $-\frac{3}{4}$

(d) 16π

41 (a) 8　　(b) $16\pi\ln 4$

42 1.405, $\ln 4$, 1.35%

43 4.7π　　　**44** 0.509　　　**45** 39.77

46 (a) 23.6 litres　　(b) 17.1 cm

47 (b) $x_2 = 1.15, \, x_3 = 1.11$

48 $\dfrac{\ln 9}{\ln 12}$

49 (a) $\frac{15}{2} + 4\ln 4$　　(b) 57π

50 $y - \ln 2 = \frac{5}{2}(x - \frac{2}{5}); \, y - \ln 2 = -\frac{2}{5}(x - \frac{2}{5})$

51 0.922

52 (a) 5.78　　(b) 0.0707

53 $\dfrac{256\pi c^3}{3}$

54 $y = 6x - 2e^x + 7 - 6\ln 2$

55 2.21　　　　**56** 10 (3 doesn't apply)

57 0.744, 0.794

58 $(2, 4), (-2, 4), (0, 8)$　　(b) $\frac{64}{3}$　　(c) 16π

59 $p = 15, \, q = \frac{1}{2}$

60 $y + 2e^{-1} = -2e^{-1}(x + 1), \, y + 2e^{-1} = \dfrac{e}{2}(x + 1)$

61 (a) $(3, 0)$　　(c) $x + y = 5$

(e) 1.125　　(f) $\frac{34\pi}{5}$

62 223, -2.74

63 (a) 2 or 16　　(b) $-\frac{1}{3}, \, -2$

64 76.06

65 (a) (i) 9　　(ii) 12　　(iii) 9 or $\frac{1}{9}$

(b) (i) $2\log_a p + \log_a q$

(ii) $\log_a p = 4, \, \log_a q = 1$

66 $p = 7.4, \, q = 0.5$

68 $\frac{178\pi}{15}$

69 (a) $x - y\ln 2 = 0$　　(c) 2.43

(d) 12π

70 (a) $60\,°C$　　(b) $44.3\,°C$　　(c) 14

71 (a) (i) 3, 6　　(iii) 1, 1.631

(b) (iii) $u = 3, \, t = \frac{1}{2}$ and $u = 6, \, t = 2$

72 2.14

73 (a) (i) $4p$　　(ii) $-2p$　　(iii) $1 + p$

(b) 0, 0.526　　(c) $\frac{1}{8}$

74 (a) $y - 2 = \frac{1}{2}x$　　(b) $(4, 4)$

(d) $\frac{160\pi}{3}$

75 (a) $2^{2 + p + 2q}$　　(b) $p + 6q$

(c) $\frac{2}{3}(p + q)$　　(d) $p = 2q - 6$

76 (b) $x = \frac{\sqrt{3}}{4}, \, y = \frac{\sqrt{3}}{2}$

77 (a) $e^{\frac{1}{2}}$　　(b) 6.56　　(c) 1

(d) 51.31　　(e) 6.91

78 (a) $7e - \frac{14}{3}$　　(b) 20.6

79 $x = 64, \, y = 16$

80 (a) $f(x) > 0$

(b) $f^{-1} : x \mapsto -\frac{1}{2}\ln x, \, x > 0$

81 (a) $(-2, 0), (1, 4), (3, 0)$

(b) $(-2, 0), (1, 4)$

82 (a) 1.46   (b) 0.37, 0.63

83 $n = 1, 1.30$

84 (a) 1, 3

85 (a) $\frac{1}{2}$ (b) $\frac{4}{5}\pi$

86 352.45

87 Tangent $y - 2k = 2k(x - \ln 2)$

Normal $y - 2k = -\dfrac{1}{2k}(x - \ln 2)$

88 (a) 1.465   (b) 1.320

90 $x = 4.64, y = 2.15$

91 $y - e - 1 = -\dfrac{1}{e + 2}(x - 1)$

92 (a) $\frac{35}{24}$ (b) $2 \ln 2$ (c) 5.2%

94 1.94

95 $x = 10, y = 25$

96 (a) 5   (b) 2.32

98 20.6

99 (a), (b), (c) but NOT (d)

100 $6 \ln 3 - 3$

Examination style paper P2

1 $x = 3, y = 1; x = \frac{1}{3}, y = 9$

2 (a) $2187 - 10\,206x + 20\,412x^2 - 22\,680x^3$

(b) $-32\,886$

3 2.12

4 (a) Meets axes at $(-1, 0), (4, 0)$ and $(0, -3)$: end points $(-3, 14)$ and $(5, 6)$

(b) Range is $-6.25 \leqslant f \leqslant 14$

5 (a) 34.62

(b) over-estimate – explain with a sketch of curve

(c) $9\pi(e^4 - e)$

6 (b) $N = 15$

(c) $(5, 7 - 10 \ln 5)$

7 $\dfrac{\pi}{2}, \dfrac{2\pi}{3}, \dfrac{3\pi}{2}, \dfrac{4\pi}{3}, \dfrac{5\pi}{2}, \dfrac{8\pi}{3}$

8 (a) 25   (b) 0.28   (c) 0.69, 5.02

(d) 55, 5

List of symbols and notation

The following notation will be used in all Edexcel examinations.

$\in$	is an element of
$\notin$	is not an element of
$\{x_1, x_2, \ldots\}$	the set with elements $x_1, x_2, \ldots$
$\{x : \ldots\}$	the set of all x such that $\ldots$
$n(A)$	the number of elements in set A
$\varnothing$	the empty set
$\mathscr{E}$	the universal set
A'	the complement of the set A
$\mathbb{N}$	the set of natural numbers, $\{1, 2, 3, \ldots\}$
$\mathbb{Z}$	the set of integers, $\{0, \pm 1, \pm 2, \pm 3, \ldots\}$
$\mathbb{Z}^+$	the set of positive integers, $\{1, 2, 3, \ldots\}$
$\mathbb{Z}_n$	the set of integers modulo n, $\{0, 1, 2, \ldots, n-1\}$
$\mathbb{Q}$	the set of rational numbers $\left\{\dfrac{p}{q} : p \in \mathbb{Z}, q \in \mathbb{Z}^+\right\}$
$\mathbb{Q}^+$	the set of positive rational numbers, $\{x \in \mathbb{Q} : x > 0\}$
$\mathbb{Q}_0^+$	the set of positive rational numbers and zero, $\{x \in \mathbb{Q} : x \geqslant 0\}$
$\mathbb{R}$	the set of real numbers
$\mathbb{R}^+$	the set of positive real numbers, $\{x \in \mathbb{R} : x > 0\}$
$\mathbb{R}_0^+$	the set of positive real numbers and zero, $\{x \in \mathbb{R} : x \geqslant 0\}$
$\mathbb{C}$	the set of complex numbers
(x, y)	the ordered pair x, y
$A \times B$	the cartesian product of sets A and B, $A \times B = \{(a, b) : a \in A, b \in B\}$
$\subseteq$	is a subset of
$\subset$	is a proper subset of
$\cup$	union
$\cap$	intersection
$[a, b]$	the closed interval, $\{x \in \mathbb{R} : a \leqslant x \leqslant b\}$
$[a, b)$	the interval $\{x \in \mathbb{R} : a \leqslant x < b\}$
$(a, b]$	the interval $\{x \in \mathbb{R} : a < x \leqslant b\}$
(a, b)	the open interval $\{x \in \mathbb{R} : a < x < b\}$
$y\,R\,x$	y is related to x by the relation R
$y \sim x$	y is equivalent to x, in the context of some equivalence relation
$=$	is equal to
$\neq$	is not equal to
$\equiv$	is identical to *or* is congruent to

$\approx$	is approximately equal to
$\cong$	is isomorphic to
$\propto$	is proportional to
$<$	is less than
$\leqslant$, $\not>$	is less than or equal to, is not greater than
$>$	is greater than
$\geqslant$, $\not<$	is greater than or equal to, is not less than
∞	infinity
$p \wedge q$	p and q
$p \vee q$	p or q (or both)
$\sim p$	not p
$p \Rightarrow q$	p implies q (if p then q)
$p \Leftarrow q$	p is implied by q (if q then p)
$p \Leftrightarrow q$	p implies and is implied by q (p is equivalent to q)
$\exists$	there exists
$\forall$	for all
$a + b$	a plus b
$a - b$	a minus b
$a \times b$, ab, $a.b$	a multiplied by b
$a \div b$, $\dfrac{a}{b}$, a/b	a divided by b
$\displaystyle\sum_{i=1}^{n} a_i$	$a_1 + a_2 + \ldots + a_n$
$\displaystyle\prod_{i=1}^{n} a_i$	$a_1 \times a_2 \times \ldots \times a_n$
$\sqrt{a}$	the positive square root of a
$|a|$	the modulus of a
$n!$	n factorial
$\dbinom{n}{r}$	the binomial coefficient $\dfrac{n!}{r!(n-r)!}$ for $n \in \mathbb{Z}^+$ $\dfrac{n(n-1)\ldots(n-r+1)}{r!}$ for $n \in \mathbb{Q}$
$f(x)$	the value of the function f at x
$f : A \to B$	f is a function under which each element of set A has an image in set B
$f : x \mapsto y$	the function f maps the element x to the element y
f^{-1}	the inverse function of the function f
$g \circ f$, gf	the composite function of f and g which is defined by $(g \circ f)(x)$ or $gf(x) = g(f(x))$
$\displaystyle\lim_{x \to a} f(x)$	the limit of $f(x)$ as x tends to a
Δx, δx	an increment of x
$\dfrac{dy}{dx}$	the derivative of y with respect to x
$\dfrac{d^n y}{dx^n}$	the nth derivative of y with respect to x

$f'(x), f''(x), \ldots f^{(n)}(x)$	the first, second, … nth derivatives of $f(x)$ with respect to x
$\displaystyle\int y\,dx$	the indefinite integral of y with respect to x
$\displaystyle\int_a^b y\,dx$	the definite integral of y with respect to x between the limits $x = a$ and $x = b$
$\dfrac{\partial V}{\partial x}$	the partial derivative of V with respect to x
$\dot{x}, \ddot{x}, \ldots$	the first, second, … derivatives of x with respect to t
e	base of natural logarithms
e^x, exp x	exponential function of x
$\log_a x$	logarithm to the base a of x
$\ln x$, $\log_e x$	natural logarithm of x
$\lg x$, $\log_{10} x$	logarithm to the base 10 of x
sin, cos, tan cosec, sec, cot	the circular functions
arcsin, arccos, arctan arccosec, arcsec, arccot	the inverse circular functions
sinh, cosh, tanh cosech, sech, coth	the hyperbolic functions
arsinh, arcosh, artanh, arcosech, arsech, arcoth	the inverse hyperbolic functions
i	square root of -1
z	a complex number, $z = x + iy$
Re z	the real part of z, Re $z = x$
Im z	the imaginary part of z, Im $z = y$
$|z|$	the modulus of z, $|z| = \surd(x^2 + y^2)$
arg z	the argument of z, $\arg z = \arctan\dfrac{y}{x}$
z^*	the complex conjugate of z, $x - iy$
$\mathbf{M}$	a matrix $\mathbf{M}$
$\mathbf{M}^{-1}$	the inverse of the matrix $\mathbf{M}$
$\mathbf{M}^{\mathrm{T}}$	the transpose of the matrix $\mathbf{M}$
det $\mathbf{M}$, $|\mathbf{M}|$	the determinant of the square matrix $\mathbf{M}$
$\mathbf{a}$	the vector $\mathbf{a}$
$\overrightarrow{AB}$	the vector represented in magnitude and direction by the directed line segment AB
$\hat{\mathbf{a}}$	a unit vector in the direction of $\mathbf{a}$
$\mathbf{i}, \mathbf{j}, \mathbf{k}$	unit vectors in the directions of the cartesian coordinate axes
$|\mathbf{a}|$, a	the magnitude of $\mathbf{a}$
$|\overrightarrow{AB}|$, AB	the magnitude of $\overrightarrow{AB}$
$\mathbf{a} \cdot \mathbf{b}$	the scalar product of $\mathbf{a}$ and $\mathbf{b}$
$\mathbf{a} \times \mathbf{b}$	the vector product of $\mathbf{a}$ and $\mathbf{b}$

A, B, C, etc	events
$A \cup B$	union of the events A and B
$A \cap B$	intersection of the events A and B
$P(A)$	probability of the event A
A'	complement of the event A
$P(A|B)$	probability of the event A conditional on the event B
X, Y, R, etc.	random variables
x, y, r, etc.	values of the random variables X, Y, R, etc
x_1, $x_2 \ldots$	observations
f_1, f_2, $\ldots$	frequencies with which the observations x_1, $x_2, \ldots$ occur
$p(x)$	probability function $P(X = x)$ of the discrete random variable X
p_1, p_2, $\ldots$	probabilities of the values x_1, $x_2, \ldots$ of the discrete random variable X
$f(x)$, $g(x), \ldots$	the value of the probability density function of a continuous random variable X
$F(x)$, $G(x), \ldots$	the value of the (cumulative) distribution function $P(X \leqslant x)$ of a continuous random variable X
$E(X)$	expectation of the random variable X
$E[g(X)]$	expectation of $g(X)$
$Var(X)$	variance of the random variable X
$G(t)$	probability generating function for a random variable which takes the values 0, 1, 2, $\ldots$
$B(n, p)$	binomial distribution with parameters n and p
$N(\mu, \sigma^2)$	normal distribution with mean μ and variance σ^2
μ	population mean
σ^2	population variance
σ	population standard deviation
$\bar{x}$, m	sample mean
s^2, $\hat{\sigma}^2$	unbiased estimate of population variance from a sample, $$s^2 = \frac{1}{n-1} \sum (x_i - \bar{x})^2$$
ϕ	probability density function of the standardised normal variable with distribution $N(0, 1)$
Φ	corresponding cumulative distribution function
ρ	product-moment correlation coefficient for a population
r	product-moment correlation coefficient for a sample
$Cov\ (X, Y)$	covariance of X and Y

Index